"Within evangelicalism, two dispositions ___ other's paths. Evangelical churches expr ___ g ___, or they express their faith through cultivating personal spiritual lives. The truth is that both of these impulses are irreplaceable. Spiritual formation is key to missional living, and missional living is key to spiritual formation. Indeed, all of God's people are called to all of God's mission, but we cannot reach others to be fully devoted followers of Christ if we are not living under his lordship and for his glory. *Spirituality for the Sent* frames an important conversation on the interrelatedness of robust spiritual lives and the church fulfilling God's mission."

Ed Stetzer, Billy Graham Professor of Church, Mission, and Evangelism, executive director of the Billy Graham Center for Evangelism, Wheaton College

"Grounded in conciliar Christology, this book represents a significant advance in the understanding of 'missional' in a way that brings together *differentiation*—a deep spirituality and ecclesiology—with *identification*, leading to a wide and well-contextualized transformational mission. I highly recommend it!"

Ross Hastings, Sangwoo Youtong Chee Associate Professor of Theology and Pastoral Theology, Regent College

"Finn and Whitfield's *Spirituality for the Sent* is a welcome broadening and deepening of the missional church discussion. It represents a generous concept of what constitutes evangelical scholarship, bringing a remarkable diversity of voices and approaches into productive interaction. The ongoing challenge of the missional-theological initiative worldwide has been its translation into the practice of the community and the formation of the individual Christian. This substantive volume is a resource that addresses that challenge and leads the conversation forward. It should foster much discussion, encourage ever more provocative research, and embolden more contributions to the conversation."

Darrell L. Guder, Henry Winters Luce Professor Emeritus of Missional and Ecumenical Theology, Princeton Theological Seminary, senior fellow and scholar in residence, St. Andrew's Hall, University of British Columbia, Vancouver

"In *Spirituality for the Sent,* Nathan Finn and Keith Whitfield have presented us with a framework for a spiritually rich and missionally engaged church. By assembling this formidable group of scholars, they have woven together a fresh vision for the church that values spiritual formation, but not at the expense of the church's mission. Indeed, in their vision, spiritual formation is essential for missional effectiveness and sustainability. This book is generous enough in its scope to encourage contemplatives and activists alike."

Michael Frost, author of *The Shaping of Things to Come*

Spirituality
for the Sent

Casting a New Vision *for*
the Missional Church

Edited by Nathan A. Finn
and Keith S. Whitfield

IVP Academic

An imprint of InterVarsity Press
Downers Grove, Illinois

InterVarsity Press
P.O. Box 1400, Downers Grove, IL 60515-1426
ivpress.com
email@ivpress.com

InterVarsity Press® is the book-publishing division of InterVarsity Christian Fellowship/USA®, a
movement of students and faculty active on campus at hundreds of universities, colleges, and schools
of nursing in the United States of America, and a member movement of the International Fellowship
of Evangelical Students. For information about local and regional activities, visit intervarsity.org.

Cover design: Cindy Kiple
Interior design: Dan van Loon
Images: © kaisorn/iStockphoto

ISBN 978-0-8308-5157-7 (print)
ISBN 978-0-8308-9158-0 (digital)

Printed in the United States of America ∞

Library of Congress Cataloging-in-Publication Data
Names: Finn, Nathan A., editor.
Title: Spirituality for the sent : casting a new vision for the missional
    church / edited by Nathan A. Finn and Keith S. Whitfield.
Description: Downers Grove : InterVarsity Press, 2017. | Includes index.
Identifiers: LCCN 2016046955 (print) | LCCN 2016052451 (ebook) | ISBN
    9780830851577 (pbk.: alk. paper) | ISBN 9780830891580 (eBook)
Subjects: LCSH: Christian life. | Spirituality--Christianity. |
    Missions--Theory. | Missional church movement. | Mission of the church.
Classification: LCC BV4501.3 .S66348 2017 (print) | LCC BV4501.3 (ebook) |
    DDC 266.001--dc23
LC record available at https://lccn.loc.gov/2016046955

P 25 24 23 22 21 20 19 18 17 16 15 14 13 12 11 10 9 8 7 6 5 4 3 2 1

Y 34 33 32 31 30 29 28 27 26 25 24 23 22 21 20 19 18 17

Contents

Acknowledgments

Nathan A. Finn *and*
Keith S. Whitfield

THE IDEA FOR THIS BOOK emerged in the fall of 2013, but its roots stretch back more than a decade. The two of us have been interested in spirituality since before we met at Southern Baptist Theological Seminary, where Nathan was beginning his MDiv studies at the same time Keith was beginning his work toward the ThM. As we became friends, we had many conversations about the relationship between theology and ministry; most of them inevitably and understandably intersected with spirituality. Fast forward a few years and Nathan was a rookie professor at Southeastern Baptist Theological Seminary and Keith was a pastor enrolled in Southeastern's PhD program. The school was embracing an increasingly missional vision for theological education and we found that our own interests in theology, spirituality, and, increasingly, mission fit nicely with the ethos at Southeastern. By the time Keith joined the faculty, we were ready to collaborate on a project related to our common interests.

In recent years, we have been blessed with the opportunity to test some of our thoughts on missional spirituality. In 2012, Nathan delivered a lecture to the faculty and students of the School of Christian Ministry at

California Baptist University on the topic "Towards a Missional Spirituality," and in 2014, he designed a new missionally influenced spiritual formation course for Southeastern Seminary. In the 2015–2016 academic year, Nathan gave a chapel address at Union University titled "Spiritual Formation and the Christian University," while at Southeastern Seminary Keith taught a master's elective on "The Doctrine of the Christian Life" and cotaught a doctoral seminar on the same topic. Until recently, when we took on senior academic leadership roles, we each served as elders in our respective churches and were part of pastoral teams that were substantially like-minded with us when it comes to the relationship between spirituality and mission.

We have also been blessed with a lot of great conversation partners, mostly among faculty colleagues at Southeastern Seminary. We are especially grateful for conversations one or both of us have had along the way with Bruce Ashford, Jamie Dew, Stephen Eccher, Drew Ham, Keith Harper, Scott Hildreth, Chuck Lawless, Mark Liederbach, Tracy McKenzie, Greg Mathias, Chuck Quarles, Benjamin Quinn, Alvin Reid, George Robinson, Walter Strickland, Heath Thomas (now at Oklahoma Baptist University), and Steven Wade. For Keith, Eric Johnson of Southern Seminary has inspired and encouraged his interests and thinking on spiritual formation for more than a decade. Our fellow contributors Chris Morgan and Tony Chute, both of California Baptist University, have proven helpful conversation partners for Nathan in particular, as has his Union University colleague George Guthrie. Our other contributors to this volume have become additional fellow travelers in helping us to think about what it means to cultivate spirituality for the sent.

Southeastern Seminary, where we served on faculty together from 2012 to 2015, is a missional seminary that is also committed to advancing scholarship for the sake of the church. We appreciate the considerable encouragement we have received from Southeastern's leadership, and especially Provost Bruce Ashford, as we worked on this project. Keith continues to benefit from the healthy atmosphere at Southeastern. Nathan relocated to Union University in 2015, where he found an institution congenial to pursuing serious scholarship, promoting missional priorities, and emphasizing spiritual formation. He is thankful to his colleagues in Union's School of Theology and Missions for encouraging their new dean to remain committed to research and writing and is particularly grateful to Provost Ben Mitchell for his support.

We have found the team at IVP Academic to be a joy to work with, especially our editor, David Congdon. David has been a strong supporter of this project from the first conversation Keith had with him at a professional meeting in November 2013. We had a lot of ideas about potential chapters and contributors; we are especially grateful to David for helping us think through how to make this book the strongest work it can be. We also appreciate David's patience when this project was delayed by about six months due to Nathan's relocation and the (fortunately!) short-term stalling effect that transition had on this book. Our contributors were similarly patient with us when the delay struck just a couple of months before the chapters were originally due to us. Thanks, everyone—you have done great work and we are honored to include it in this book.

In this project, as in all our projects, our biggest supporters have been our wives and children. Nathan is grateful to Leah and the "Finnlings" for putting up with late nights, early mornings, and the occasional off-the-grid Saturday to work on this project. Keith is grateful to his wife, Amy, and his kids Mary and Drew, as they have been similarly supportive while this book has evolved from idea to finished product. Our families continue to be a key means of sanctifying grace in our lives.

We want to end these acknowledgments where they began: with our student days at Southern Seminary. While we lived in Louisville, both our families were members of Ninth and O Baptist Church. It was a wonderful community of disciples that shaped each of our lives and ministries. To say it another way, the saints of God called by the name Ninth and O were instrumental in our spiritual formation. We are especially grateful for the church's senior pastor, Bill Cook. Bill was a seminary professor who was widely respected as a gifted classroom teacher, but he especially shone as a pastor. Over the years, he has modeled for us and for hundreds of other seminarian church members what it means to be a man of godly integrity, a devoted husband and father, a faithful preacher, and a loving shepherd. We do not remember if Bill has ever quoted these words to us, but we think his life embodies the Pauline principle, "Follow my example, as I follow the example of Christ" (1 Cor 11:1). It is with great joy and deep gratitude that we dedicate this book to Bill. #9thandOForever

Introduction

Nathan A. Finn *and*
Keith S. Whitfield

WE ARE BIG BELIEVERS IN the power of a good conversation. During the fifteen years we have known each other, dating all the way back to our time as seminary students, we have had countless conversations about theology, ministry, spirituality, mission, marriage, politics, denominational life, parenting, food, music, sports—and the list could go on. Though we have been good friends for a long time, part of what makes so many of our conversations particularly fruitful is that we are not just like each other. Nathan is an introvert, while Keith is an extrovert. Nathan hails from a medium-sized church in a small town, while Keith grew up attending a megachurch in a larger metropolitan area. Nathan attended a small Christian liberal arts college and served in local church ministry as an undergrad, while Keith graduated from a large university and then became involved in ministry during seminary. Prior to becoming full-time professors, Nathan worked as a youth minister and seminary archivist while Keith served as a senior pastor and then church planter. Part of what makes our ongoing conversations about life and ministry so fruitful is that we have different personalities, life experiences, and gifts that we each bring to bear on our common interests.

In our experience, the best conversations are often about topics that need to be put in intentional dialogue with one another. In recent decades, evangelicals in North America have shown a growing interest in missional thought and spiritual formation—but not necessarily at the same time. Unfortunately, though the missional church and spiritual formation movements among evangelicals overlap each other chronologically, they have rarely intersected in meaningful ways. If more intentional inter-section was to occur, we believe it would only strengthen both movements as they cross-pollinate one another in ways that would benefit evangelicals and other Christians committed to a missional understanding of the church and the importance of spiritual formation in the Christian life.

We are grateful for a handful of attempts in recent years to put these two movements in dialogue with each other. *Missional Spirituality: Embodying God's Love from the Inside Out* by Roger Helland and Leonard Hjalmarson is a helpful book written from an evangelical perspective, but its intended audience is pastors rather than scholars.[1] The edited volume *Cultivating Sent Communities: Missional Spiritual Formation* is a fine academic contribution that deserves a close reading by scholars engaged in both conversations.[2] However, the contributors represent a more mainline Protestant perspective rather than overtly evangelical commitments. The spring 2013 issue of the *Journal of Spiritual Formation and Soul Care* was dedicated to the relationship between mission and spirituality and included a number of thoughtful essays. That the key evangelical scholarly journal associated with the spiritual formation movement would devote an entire issue to this topic speaks to the importance of these two conversations coming together.

For our part, each of us is heavily invested in one of these movements and keenly interested in the other. Nathan is a historical theologian whose research interests include Christian spirituality, especially as expressed in

---

[1] Roger Helland and Leonard Hjalmarson, *Missional Spirituality: Embodying God's Love from the Inside Out* (Downers Grove, IL: InterVarsity Press, 2011).

[2] Dwight J. Zscheile, *Cultivating Sent Communities: Missional Spiritual Formation* (Grand Rapids: Eerdmans, 2012).

the evangelical and Baptist traditions. Keith is a systematic theologian who specializes in missional thought, especially as it relates to theological method. Aside from our respective specializations, we each try to keep up as much as possible with the major discussions taking place in the other's field. We are also both academic administrators who want to see our professors, students, and staff embody a biblically rich, theologically informed, and contextually appropriate missional spirituality. We find that many of our friends, colleagues, and students feel similarly about the relationship between missional thought and spiritual formation. Thus, we decided in the fall of 2013 that we wanted to invite other evangelical scholars from a variety of theological disciplines and ecclesial traditions to join in our conversation. The book you hold in your hand or are looking at on an electronic screen represents the "first fruits" of what we pray is an ongoing conversation.

This book's purpose is straightforward and, we think, biblical. As our title indicates, we want evangelicals and other Christians to cultivate what we call a "spirituality for the sent" that helps to foster a new vision for the missional church. We believe that scholars with deep interest and expertise in either the missional church or spiritual formation should take the lead in putting these two movements into dialogue with each other. We are convinced that the topics that are talked about in the faculty lounge at evangelical colleges, universities, and seminaries often eventually filter down into evangelical pulpits, small groups, and ministers' conferences. If we are to see evangelical churches embracing a robustly missional spirituality—which is our hope—then evangelical scholars have a strategic role to play in framing the conversation.

Each chapter has been written by a contributor or contributors who we believe offer something important to this conversation. Some are biblical scholars, some are systematic theologians, some are historians, and still others have expertise in the disciplines of practical or pastoral theology. Most are professional academics, many have extensive backgrounds in congregational ministry, and some have more experience in the world of parachurch ministry. They come from different institutions, denominational traditions, and theological perspectives, representing what the late historian Timothy Smith aptly termed the "evangelical kaleidoscope" and what theologian John Stackhouse calls "generic evangelicalism."[3] We wanted a book that all interested evangelicals could appreciate, even if no reader agrees with everything found herein.

Because this book's contributors are drawn from across the evangelical spectrum, we strongly suspect that they would disagree among themselves (and with us!) concerning many of the issues that divide evangelicalism. Nevertheless, other than providing some working definitions of the terms *missional* and *spiritual formation* (see chapter one), as editors we have not attempted to constrain the contributors in any way. We encouraged each to write from his or her own convictions and commend his or her views to the wider evangelical world. Though this approach has led both to some differing emphases (some contributors give more emphasis to personal evangelism, some focus more on social justice) and some overlapping subject matter (St. Patrick of Ireland and Mother Teresa are particularly popular role models for missional spirituality), we think the chapters generally represent the similar-yet-diverse movement that is North American evangelicalism.

In the first chapter, "The Missional Church and Spiritual Formation," the editors briefly narrate the histories of the missional church and spiritual formation movements, respectively. As mentioned above, we also provide some working definitions for both the terms *missional* and *spiritual formation*, since both are contested among evangelicals and others interested in these movements. Our goal in the chapters is to provide some necessary prolegomena for readers who are interested in the subject of this book, but who are less familiar with the development of these movements and the debates among scholars and thoughtful practitioners identified with each movement. In chapter two, Craig Bartholomew addresses "Spirituality, Mission, and the Drama of Scripture." He provides a biblical-theological overview of mission and shows how spirituality is an interconnected theme found across the canon of Scripture. Rightly relating to God and being formed into the image of Christ is an essential

---

[3]Timothy L. Smith, "The Evangelical Kaleidoscope and the Call to Christian Unity," *Christian Scholars Review* 15, no. 2 (1986): 125-40; John G. Stackhouse Jr., "Generic Evangelicalism," in *Four Views on the Spectrum of Evangelicalism*, ed. Andrew David Naselli and Collin Hansen (Grand Rapids: Zondervan Academic, 2011), 116-42.

component of God's mission for the church. According to Bartholomew, "Mission will only be effective and honor God insofar as we are living ever more deeply into God" (53).

In the third chapter, missiologist Susan Booth also draws on biblical theology to examine the place of global missions in a missional spirituality. She argues that "missional advance flows from God's presence in the midst of his people"(54). Authentic spirituality necessarily includes a missional dimension that is global in scope, reflecting God's heart for the nations. Simply put, "A biblical understanding of missional spirituality must include a global focus" (54). Chapter four focuses on the communal nature of missional spirituality, particularly as it is embodied in local congregations. Chris Morgan and Tony Chute, two scholars with expertise in ecclesiology, push back against the overemphasis on individualism present among so many evangelicals, perhaps especially in the area of spirituality. They draw on the Sermon on the Mount and Paul's epistle to the Philippians to make their case that "biblical spirituality is both missional and congregational" (76) and that authentic spirituality, lived out in community with other believers, fuels authentic mission.

Michael Goheen and Tim Sheridan dedicate the fifth chapter to "Missional Spirituality and Cultural Engagement." These two missional theologians argue that cultural engagement is a key facet of mission, especially in an increasingly post-Christian North American context. As such, they offer a spirituality of cultural engagement. After critiquing three different paradigms for cultural engagement advocated by contemporary thinkers, Goheen and Sheridan draw on insights from Lesslie Newbigin and the Dutch Reformed tradition to commend three aspects of a spirituality of cultural engagement: "the communal life of the church, the needed Christian dispositions, and the dynamics of spiritual vitality" (110). In chapter six, Gary Tyra addresses the related theme of how contextualization relates to a missional spirituality. He agrees with the insight of missional theologians that contextualization informed by the *missio Dei* is essential to faithful ministry and argues that contextualization should be as much about spirituality as it is methodology. Following Paul's lead in 1 Corinthians 9:20-22, Tyra contends "we should expect the spirituality (as well as the methodology) of missional communities to necessarily differ from one ministry location to the next" (123).

In the seventh chapter, "Lament as Appropriate Missional Spirituality," Soong-Chan Rah argues that American evangelicals must recover the practice of lament because it is both a biblical emphasis and provides a countercultural witness to American triumphalism and exceptionalism. He contends that lament is important to the personal and especially communal spirituality of missional believers. Even the missional church can suffer from the "hubris that characterizes the theological language and imagination of those who are caught up in American ecclesial triumphalism" (146). Chapter eight, written by Diane Chandler, argues that godly love as expressed in the Great Commandment is the primary Christian virtue on which the Great Commission is based. God's overarching mission is the backdrop to both loving God and one's neighbor and extending God's message of redeeming love through witness and service in the world. Every believer's spirituality, grounded in relationship with God, is not to be isolated from furthering God's mission in the world. The Great Commandment and the Great Commission inseparably intertwine such that every believer's calling is to reflect and enact the divine love of Jesus through the power of the Holy Spirit in contributing to the *missio Dei*.

In chapter nine, Gordon Smith addresses the topic "Missional Spirituality and Worship." He argues that the missional church must be a worshiping community and emphasizes the key role of public corporate worship in forming congregations for mission. Smith believes churches are communities that are by nature liturgical, catechetical, and missional. True worship reflects on and offers praise and adoration for God's work in the world, and authentic worship fuels the church's participating in God's mission. Pentecost provides a biblical paradigm for how mission and worship mutually reinforce each other. As a scholar of worship, Smith calls on the Christian academy to embody missional worship in academic contexts that are forming believers (and others) for a variety of vocations. In chapter ten, Mae Elise Cannon offers a thoughtful, personal reflection on the relationship between missional spirituality and justice. Cannon is a scholar-activist who has dedicated her ministry to advocating for social justice around the globe. She demonstrates that the Great Commission is not only an evangelistic mandate, but it is part of a biblical narrative that speaks regularly to justice, calls on believers to respond to the needs of the poor, and offers examples of prophetic witness, including from Jesus, that commands a merciful response to those in need. As she reminds us, "The final picture of Christ being worshiped at the center of the throne in Revelation includes language from the prophet Isaiah and a reminder of the promises of God to respond to those who are poor and oppressed" (212).

The final chapter is written by George Hunsberger, a distinguished scholar who has helped shape the missional church movement. He argues that missional spirituality is a "journey in the Spirit" and revisits the New Testament terms *spiritual* and *disciple*, offering gentle critiques of how most evangelicals misinterpret these key concepts. Hunsberger dialogues with Newbigin, Jewish scholar Abraham Joshua Heschel, and New Testament scholar Michael Gorman as he demonstrates the various ways we are conformed to God, through Christ, in the power of the Spirit, which includes increasingly owning God's mission for ourselves. He also suggests that "if, as I and others have argued in the book *Missional Church* and elsewhere, the adjective *missional* intends to say that the church is by its very nature 'sent,' then 'spirituality for the sent' is not a subset. It is simply 'Christian spirituality,' a fitting spirituality for the church, the whole church, as God's sent people" (218). We wholeheartedly agree, which is why we believe Hunsberger's chapter offers an excellent conclusion to this book.

We are grateful that you have decided to enter into this conversation. We are firmly convinced that missional churches should embody a spirituality that is shaped by the *missio Dei* as it unfolds in Scripture. Spirituality for the sent really is spirituality for all of God's people. We do not believe this book will answer every question, address every important topic, or even include every insightful conversation partner. Far from it! But we are convinced this book can be a key part of the early stages of a needed conversation. We are hopeful that *Spirituality for the Sent* will inspire—and perhaps even provoke—a whole raft of articles and books that tackle this topic from a wide variety of confessional perspectives.

More importantly, our prayer is that these discussions among scholars and thoughtful ministry practitioners will work their way into a growing number of evangelical congregations that will embody a missional spirituality for the glory of God, the salvation of the nations, and authentic human flourishing among all people until that day when the Lord Jesus Christ returns to finish fixing everything that has been broken and distorted by human sin.

The Missional Church *and* Spiritual Formation

Nathan A. Finn *and*
Keith S. Whitfield

THIS CHAPTER IS AN EXERCISE in prolegomenon. As we mentioned in the introduction, among evangelicals the missional and spiritual formation movements have overlapped chronologically, but rarely intersected in meaningful ways. This book represents an intentional intersection, as evangelical scholars from a variety of disciplines and traditions come together to consider some of the contours of a missional spirituality. Before our contributors highlight some of the facets of a missional spirituality, it is important that we have a cursory understanding of some of the more important individuals and ideas that loom in the background. In this chapter, we briefly narrate the histories of the missional and spiritual formation movements. We also provide some working definitions for both the terms *missional* and *spiritual formation*, since both are contested among evangelicals and others interested in these movements.

The Missional Church

Over the last twenty years or so, the term *missional* has been used widely across denominations and various Christian movements in the English-speaking world. From Vatican II, the ecumenical movement, the rise of the megachurch, and seeker-sensitive churches, to the Gen-X churches of the 1990s, engaging the culture with the gospel has increasingly shaped contemporary ecclesiology. The growing frequency of the adjective *missional* has been rooted in this emphasis. Today, the term can be found among Roman Catholics, mainline Protestants, and evangelicals of nearly every perspective.

The Gospel and Our Culture Network (GOCN) has been most responsible for the popularity of the term in North America.[1] The GOCN began in the late 1980s to promote missionary encounters with North American culture. The network pursued this project by following the work of Lesslie Newbigin (1909–1998) related to the gospel and culture. Newbigin served for many years as a missionary bishop in India before returning to his native England and authoring a number of groundbreaking books on mission.[2] Their work led to the 1998 publication of the book *Missional Church: A Vision for the Sending of the Church in North America*.[3] This network was made up of theological educators, pastors, denominational administrators, and lay leaders from a variety of mainline churches. Yet, their influence extended beyond the boundaries of the mainline church.

Changes in Western culture called for the church in the West to reconsider how it should engage that culture. Many have summed up the changes with the phrase "post-Christian."[4] Newbigin described the current

---

[1] *Missional* has been rarely used until recently. Darrell Guder cites the Oxford English Dictionary records to show that it was first used in 1907. He explains that the GOCN used *missional* because it was "relatively unknown," and they "wanted to stimulate a theological conversation about the church which took seriously the premise that . . . 'the church is missionary by its very nature.'" See Darrell Guder, "The Church as Missional Community," in *The Community of the Word: Toward an Evangelical Ecclesiology*, ed. Mark Husbands and Daniel J. Treier (Downers Grove, IL: InterVarsity Press, 2005), 114.

[2] Several of Newbigin's books are referenced in this chapter. For a full list of his writings, see the bibliography available online at "Lesslie Newbigin Reading Room," Tyndale Seminary, www.tyndale.ca/seminary/inministry/reading-rooms/newbigin.

[3] Darrell L. Guder, ed., *Missional Church: A Vision for the Sending of the Church in North America* (Grand Rapids: Eerdmans, 1998).

[4] See Rodney Clapp, *A Peculiar People: The Church as Culture in a Post-Christian Society* (Downers Grove, IL: InterVarsity Press, 1996); Guder, *Missional Church*, 18-76; and Lesslie Newbigin, *Foolishness to the Greeks: The Gospel and Western Culture* (Grand Rapids: Eerdmans, 1986), 1-41.

context as "churches are in a missionary situation in what once was Christendom."[5] More specifically, for Newbigin, the church existed in a world where religious faith has been relegated to private life. Michael Frost and Alan Hirsch described this shift as the unraveling of Christendom because it was seduced by Western culture. As a result, they write, "the emerging missional church must see itself as being able to interact meaningfully with culture without ever being beguiled by it."[6] Newbigin made a similar observation. He argued, "Missions will no longer work along the stream of expanding Western power. They have to learn to go against the stream."[7] The collapse of colonialism, growth of globalization, increasing population in urban centers, new awareness of social and economic inequality, and technological developments that transform how we are living have produced changes in how mission is pursued.[8]

Within this climate, the missional movement gained momentum. The adjective *missional* was used to describe how the church pursues its missionary task in its culture. The GOCN recognized these changes and started to reenvision ministry in North America as a missionary encounter with Western culture. In doing so, it has helped to recover the missional identity of the church. This development sparked widespread application, so people have referred to missional leadership, preaching, communities, Christians, entrepreneurs, and even—increasingly, we hope—spirituality.

Theologically, the embrace of trinitarian theology as the foundation for mission helped to locate the mission of the church within the *missio Dei*, and the emergence of kingdom of God theology reinforced this development. These theological developments emerged alongside of the growing awareness that the gospel has been held captive by Western culture. In the twentieth century, colonialism, which was propped up by both Catholic and Protestant mission efforts, began to collapse.

---

[5]Lesslie Newbigin, *The Open Secret: An Introduction to the Theology of Mission*, rev. ed. (Grand Rapids: Eerdmans, 1995), 2.

[6]Michael Frost and Alan Hirsch, *The Shaping of Things to Come* (Peabody, MA: Hendickson, 2003), 16.

[7]Newbigin, *The Open Secret*, 5.

[8]Michael Goheen and Timothy Tennent offer similar lists. See Michael W. Goheen, *Introducing Christian Mission Today* (Downers Grove, IL: IVP Academic, 2014), 15-32; and Timothy Tennent, *Invitation to World Missions* (Grand Rapids: Kregel, 2010), 15-51.

Churches in the West began to reconsider missions because their missionary past embarrassed them. Trinitarian studies helped the church to reorient their understanding of missions. Theologian Karl Barth (1886–1968) shared in these concerns, and many have attributed the emphasis on a trinitarian understanding of missions to him. In 1932, Barth delivered a paper at the Brandenburg Missionary Conference, where he became one of the first theologians to articulate missions as God's activity. This shift raised foundational questions about the origin of mission and to whom mission belongs. These questions contributed significantly to missions being seen as a theological discipline. Increasingly, rather than missiologists seeking a *theology of missions*, scholars pursued *mission theology*.

Even before Barth's address, new currents in mission theology were underway at the beginning of the worldwide meetings on mission. In 1910, John Mott (1865–1955) organized the World Missionary Conference in Edinburgh. This meeting marked the peak of mission societies and denominations sending missionaries all over the world to evangelize, plant churches, and establish schools, hospitals, and orphanages. It also marked the start of a series of worldwide meetings on missions that would later give birth to the International Missionary Council (IMC) in 1921. The Edinburgh conference proposed that the church initiate gospel engagement with the non-Christian world. The responsibility for this missionary engagement was placed on individual Christians.[9] While Edinburgh did not establish the missionary identity of the local church, this understanding of the church emerged in 1938 at the IMC meeting in Tambaram.[10] At that meeting, mission theology developed further by connecting the mission of the church to the

---

[9]James A. Scherer, *Gospel, Church, & Kingdom: Comparative Studies in World Mission Theology* (Eugene, OR: Wipf & Stock, 1987), 15. See, "That trust [that is, the responsibility to bring the gospel to others] is not committed in any peculiar way to our missionaries, or to the societies, or to us as members of this Conference. It is committed to all and each within the Christian family; and it is as incumbent on every member of the Church, as are the elementary virtues of the Christian life—faith, hope, and love. *That which makes a man a Christian makes him also a sharer in this trust.*" *World Missionary Conference, 1910,* vol. 9, *The History and Records of the Conference* (New York: Fleming H. Revell Company, n.d.), 109. Emphasis added.

[10]Wolfgang Günther, "The History and Significance of World Mission Conferences in the 20th Century," *International Review of Mission* 92, no. 367 (2003): 526.

eschatological purposes of God. The whole church was called to engage every sphere of life with the gospel.[11]

Viewing the church as central to God's mission raised a whole new set of questions; two of them were particularly important. The first one focused on ecclesiology: What is the proper relationship between a mother church and a daughter church? The second one dealt with missiology: What is the relationship between church and mission? This is the theological milieu that gives birth to mission theology and missional thinking. Much of what happened in the IMC from 1928 onward sought to answer these questions.

By the 1950s, because of concerns over colonialism, the future of foreign missions looked bleak. The 1952 Willingen Conference of the IMC responded to this situation. This watershed meeting resulted in an historic moment for the church, mission, and the word *missional*. The theme chosen for the conference was "The Missionary Obligation of the Church." The role of the church in missions was a matter of considerable debate at the conference. While the conference did not settle the debate, mission theology gained theological cohesion around the concept of *missio Dei*.[12] While the phrase *missio Dei* itself was not used, the idea was present in the adopted reports. Later, Karl Hartenstein used the phrase to report on the results of the conference. It eventually was popularized by Georg F. Vicedom's book *Missio Dei* (translated into English in 1965).[13] The phrase captured the fact that mission belongs to God, and it helped to establish the theological fact that mission is initiated by God and God's mission is broader than the activities of the church.

Missio Dei was widely adopted as a concept that represents new ways to think about missions and become involved in missions. Yet, the concept was burdened with theological ambiguities. The confusion may be introduced with two questions: Does *missio Dei* refer primarily to God's acts or

---

[11]"Tambaram Conference," in *Evangelical Dictionary of World Missions*, ed. A. Scott Moreau (Grand Rapids: Baker Books, 2000), 928.

[12]*Missio Dei* is "mission of God." As David Bosch states it, "The classical doctrine on the *missio Dei* as God the Father sending the Son, and the Son sending the Spirit was expanded to include yet another 'movement': Father, Son, and Holy Spirit sending the Church into the world." See David Bosch, *Transforming Mission* (Maryknoll, NY: Orbis, 1991), 390.

[13]Georg F. Vicedom, *The Mission of God: An Introduction to a Theology of Mission*, trans. Gilbert A. Thiele and Dennis Hilgendorf (St. Louis: Concordia Publishing, 1965).

God's purposes? And, does the concept refer to God's works in creation or redemption? The answers to these questions were debated throughout the 1950s. Ultimately, J. C. Hoekendijk's interpretation prevailed. He argued that God's purposes in the world were to establish *shalom* (peace, integrity, justice, community, and harmony). This emphasis situated the world (or creation) as the primary focus of God's mission. This shift took root in mission theology through subsequent meetings of the IMC and its successor body, the Commission on World Mission and Evangelism (CWME, a body within the World Council of Churches [WCC]), which continued to develop this new understanding of the role of the church in the world.[14] *Missio Dei* was used in a "single sense," as the comprehensive term for God's work in creation. God's redemptive work, therefore, was seen as restoring peace to creation within the historical process.[15] The relationship between the mission of the church and *missio Dei* once followed the model "God-Church-World," but the new order became "God-World-Church."[16] Under this model, the church represented only one form of God's mission.

By the 1970s, the excitement about world mission that was present in the 1950s and the 1960s waned, and many within the WCC began to realize that the church's value in the mission had been undercut to the detriment of the mission and church. This new current gave birth to

---

[14]Ibid., 371. Quote taken from the Assembly's Commission and Division of World Mission and Evangelism report, which Bosch quotes from. Also, the Catholic Church at Vatican II developed an ecclesiology that reflects the missionary nature of the church. In many ways, the emergence of the Catholic documents outpaced the Protestant vision. Ibid., 372.

[15]Johannes Christiaan Hoekendijk, ed., *The Church Inside Out* (London: SCM Press, 1967), 19-20. The Dutch missiologist J. C. Hoekendijk is mostly responsible for the change in how *missio Dei* was conceived in the 1960s. Hoekendijk's view of evangelism is not propagating the gospel message, but rather, it is to accomplish the messianic expectation of Israel, i.e., establishment of *shalom*. This *shalom* is "at once peace, integrity, community, harmony, and justice," and he goes on to say, "This concept in all its comprehensive richness should be our leitmotif in Christian work. God intends the redemption of the whole of creation" (19-20). James A. Scherer in "Church, Kingdom, and *Missio Dei*: Lutheran and Orthodox Correctives to Recent Ecumenical Mission Theology," in *The Good News of the Kingdom: Mission Theology for the Third Millennium*, ed. Charles Van Engen, Dean S. Gilliland, and Paul Pierson (Maryknoll, NY: Orbis, 1993), 82, characterizes this shift in stark terms. He says, "In the decade of the 1960s, *missio Dei* became the plaything of armchair theologians with little more than an academic interest in the practical mission of the church but with a considerable penchant for theological speculation and mischief making" (82). Scherer argues that they traded on a fundamentally different and nontrinitarian understanding of *missio Dei* that was influenced by the contemporary secularization of theology.

[16]Priscilla Pop-Levison, "Evangelism in the WCC: From New Delhi to Canberra," in *New Directions in Mission and Evangelization 2: Theological Foundations*, ed. James A. Scherer and Stephen B. Bevans (Maryknoll, NY: Orbis, 1994), 128.

rethinking the role of the church. The position that was present in the 1938 Tambaram conference was not recovered. However, at Melbourne in 1980, the church's role in mission as a servant and proclaimer of the reign of God was taken more seriously. Much of Melbourne's insights resurface in the 1982 publication of "Mission and Evangelism—An Ecumenical Affirmation." This document sought to regain and reunite the missionary call in the church by drawing on Protestant, evangelical, Orthodox, and Roman Catholic mission theologies. After the tensions experienced during the 1970s with the creation of a new international Protestant mission movement (the Lausanne Committee for World Evangelisation in 1974), the 1982 document was an attempt by CWME at recentering ecumenical mission theology with a clearer commitment to the proclamation of the gospel without losing the prophetic challenge of conferences such as Bangkok or Melbourne. A missiological definition of the church became the official position of the WCC.[17] Yet, this new Protestant ecumenical consensus did not resolve the previous concerns among evangelical theologians and missiologists.

The GOCN attempted to make use of these developments in mission theology to help the church in North America engage its culture as a missionary.[18] The book *Missional Church* addressed this new dilemma for the church. It began by locating the North American church within its changing culture. The contributors argued that because God reigns through the gospel and the church is the people of God, the church should be shaped by God and his kingdom reign. The authors also argued that this shape is expressed in the phrase *contrast community*, which describes a church that is cultivated by the Spirit, equipped by missional leaders, and shaped by missional structures for life and ministry.

---

[17]Darrell Guder, *The Continuing Conversion of the Church* (Grand Rapids: Eerdmans, 2000), 21. At this time, however, a significant ecclesial path was blazed to rethink the traditional structure of local congregations. Guder states, "During the twentieth century, the essentially missionary nature of the church has become the dominant consensus of the worldwide community of Christian leaders and scholars whose common focus is Christian mission." Ibid., 20. For a short treatment of the convergence on the role of mission on the church, see David Bosch, "'Ecumenicals' and 'Evangelicals': A Growing Relationship?," *The Ecumenical Review* 40 (1988): 458-72. A more exhaustive treatment on the issue that extends beyond ecumenical and evangelical concerns is James A. Scherer's *Gospel, Church, and Kingdom*.

[18]Guder, *Missional Church*, 81.

Looking back almost twenty years, their missional vision was well timed, and this has been demonstrated by the popularity of the phrase *missional church* and term *missional*. Ecumenical churches, evangelical churches, and emergent churches have appropriated the term; it has been accepted because believers in a variety of traditions have realized that the culture is changing and the term itself serves as an effective way to communicate a new strategy for engagement.

Yet, the use (and perhaps overuse) of the word did not produce a consensus on what *missional* means or how to use it. Alan Roxburgh notes that *missional* has traveled the road "from obscurity to banality in eight short years and people still don't know what it means."[19] Many people have picked up the term *missional* and have supplied their own theological meaning and missionary emphases to it, which has led us to a place where it is hard to know what one means by *missional* when the word is used. Craig Van Gelder and Dwight J. Zscheile mapped the trends in the missional conversation in their book *The Missional Church in Perspective*. They identified four ways people talk about being missional: (1) discovering how to use *missional* to promote traditional understanding of missions; (2) utilizing *missional* to relate God's sending acts to the role of human agency; (3) engaging missional conversation with congregational practices; (4) and extending the application of mission theology to all areas of life.[20]

While missional thinking will no doubt continue to shape how evangelicals and others think about the church and her missionary task, which understanding of missional carries the day—if any—remains to be seen. In this way, the missional movement parallels a different trend that has also exercised considerable influence on evangelicals. During the same years that evangelicals began engaging with the missional discussion among Catholics and ecumenical Protestants, they became increasingly open to spiritual traditions among these same two groups, as well as Eastern Orthodoxy.

---

[19]Alan Roxburgh, "The Missional Church," *Theology Matters* 10, no. 4 (September/October 2004): 2.
[20]Craig Van Gelder and Dwight J. Zscheile, *The Missional Church in Perspective* (Grand Rapids: Baker, 2011), 67-98.

The Spiritual Formation Movement

Recent movements in Christian spirituality arose within the context of wider trends that transcended Christianity or any other organized religion. The 1960s and 1970s counterculture provided fertile ground for fresh approaches to spirituality. Some of these spiritual trends intersected with evangelicalism, most notably the Jesus People movement among hippies.[21] However, a far larger number of the new spiritualities challenged historic, orthodox Christianity. To cite one famous example, many Americans embraced an eclectic assortment of Eastern spiritual practices that came to be called the New Age Movement. During this period, celebrities such as the Beatles and Shirley MacLaine embraced and promoted beliefs and practices such as Transcendental Meditation, crystal healing, consulting with psychics and mediums, and reincarnation. By the early 1990s, New Age ideas and other alternative spiritualities were becoming more common, even mainstream, through the bestselling writings of Deepak Chopra and James Redfield, the enormous popularity of the *Oprah Winfrey Show*, and a burgeoning alternative medicine industry. By the turn of the twenty-first century, many Americans could be accurately described as "spiritual, but not religious."[22]

At the same time that alternative spiritualities were becoming vogue, Christians in a variety of traditions were reasserting the importance of cultivating a robust spirituality that was informed by Scripture and past Christian spiritual practices. Authors such as the Quaker philosophers Thomas Kelly (1897–1941) and Elton Trueblood (1900–1994), the Lutheran theologian and martyr Dietrich Bonhoeffer (1906–1945), Catholic social activist Dorothy Day (1897–1980), Anglican apologist and novelist

---

[21] See Larry Eskridge, *God's Forever Family: The Jesus People Movement in America* (New York: Oxford University Press, 2013), and Richard A. Bustraan, *The Jesus People Movement: A Story of Spiritual Revolution Among the Hippies* (Eugene, OR: Pickwick, 2014). Portions of this section have been expanded from material originally published in Nathan A. Finn, "Contours of a Healthy Baptist Spirituality," *Criswell Theological Review* 12, no. 1 (Fall 2014): 3-7.

[22] For a history of the New Age Movement and other alternative spiritualities, see Robert C. Fuller, *Spiritual, but Not Religious: Understanding Unchurched America* (New York: Oxford University Press, 2001), and Sarah M. Pike, *New Age and Neopagan Religions in America*, Columbia Contemporary American Religion Series (New York: Columbia University Press, 2004). For broader sociological introductions to American spirituality during this period, see Robert Wuthnow, *After Heaven: Spirituality in America Since the 1950s*, 2nd ed. (Berkeley: University of California Press, 1997), and Wade Clark Roof, *Spiritual Marketplace: Baby Boomers and the Remaking of American Religion* (Princeton, NJ: Princeton University Press, 1999).

C. S. Lewis (1898–1963), Trappist monk Thomas Merton (1915–1968), civil rights activist Martin Luther King Jr. (1929–1968), and Dutch Catholic minister Henri Nouwen (1932–1996) influenced the spirituality of many Catholics and mainline Protestants. Mid-century Christians were introduced (or reintroduced) to classical spiritual disciplines, monasticism, spiritual direction, and contemplative prayer. They read spiritual classics by authors such as Augustine, Thomas à Kempis, Julian of Norwich, Teresa of Avila, Ignatius of Loyola, and George Herbert. Among Catholics, Vatican II emphasized the importance of what came to be called "spiritual formation" in the training of a new generation of clergy.[23] Among Protestants, devotionals such as *The Upper Room*, founded by mainline Methodists, and *Guideposts*, which was more generically Protestant, reminded many of the importance of cultivating one's interior spiritual life. Twelve-step programs, most notably Alcoholics Anonymous, also introduced many mainline Protestants and Catholics to the importance of spirituality. The combination of the ecumenical movement among Protestants and the greater openness of Catholicism to non-Catholic traditions following Vatican II opened the door to far greater spiritual cross-pollination than had normally been the case in previous generations.[24]

Though generally suspicious of both Catholicism and mainline Protestantism, evangelicals also became increasingly interested in spirituality, paralleling the wider trend. Evangelicals read many of the same classic and modern spiritual authors as their mainline and Catholic counterparts; Lewis, Bonhoeffer, and Nouwen proved especially popular among evangelicals. They also read more explicitly evangelical-friendly authors such as the Puritans, William Law, Jonathan Edwards, John Wesley, and the twentieth-century Christian and Missionary Alliance pastor A. W. Tozer

---

[23]The English translations of the relevant Vatican II documents are *Decree on Priestly Training* (1965) and *Decree on the Ministry of Life of Priests* (1968). Both documents are available through the United States Conference of Catholic Bishops. See Church Documents for Priestly Formation, United States Conference of Catholic Bishops, available online at www.usccb.org/beliefs-and-teachings/vocations/priesthood/priestly-formation/church-documents-for-priestly-formation.cfm (accessed September 25, 2015).

[24]See Bradley Holt, *Thirsty for God: A Brief History of Christian Spirituality*, rev. ed. (Minneapolis: Fortress, 2005), 113-19.

(1897–1963). The growing evangelical emphasis on the importance of discipleship, emphasized by authors such as evangelist Robert Coleman and cell group pioneer Ralph W. Neighbour Jr., overlapped with the growing emphasis on spirituality. By the early 1970s, evangelical authors were beginning to write more about the importance of spirituality. For example, in 1973 church historian Richard Lovelace diagnosed a "sanctification gap" among evangelicals in a widely read journal article.[25] Six years later, Lovelace followed up with a book-length account of a healthy evangelical spirituality informed by both the Bible and church history.[26]

Evangelicals increasingly began to echo the language of spiritual formation, which they borrowed from the aforementioned Roman Catholic discussions of spirituality and ministry preparation. Following the lead of the Catholics, in 1972 the Association of Theological Schools highlighted spiritual formation as a needed emphasis in theological education among all of its accredited seminaries and divinity schools, including those sponsored by evangelicals and mainline Protestants.[27] In the ensuing years, evangelical seminaries began to incorporate spiritual formation into their curriculum, notably Dallas Theological Seminary and Southern Baptist Theological Seminary. Many colleges followed suit, including Wheaton College and Biola University. In some schools, spiritual formation was an interdisciplinary emphasis that transcended the curricula, while in others it was seen as a crucial element within the discipline of Christian education, often alongside the related topic of discipleship.[28]

---

[25]Richard Lovelace, "The Sanctification Gap," *Theology Today* 29, no. 4 (January 1973): 363-69.

[26]Richard Lovelace, *Dynamics of Spiritual Life: An Evangelical Theology of Renewal* (Downers Grove, IL: InterVarsity Press, 1979).

[27]Glenn T. Miller, *Piety and Plurality: Theological Education Since 1960* (Eugene, OR: Wipf and Stock, 2014), 58-61. More recently, the Council of Christian Colleges and Universities, a consortium of around one hundred evangelical colleges and universities, has similarly called for an emphasis on spiritual formation. See *CCCU Report on Spiritual Formation* (Washington, DC: Council of Christian Colleges and Universities, 2011), available online at www.cccu.org/~/media/filefolder/CCCU-SpiritualFormation_Booklet .pdf (accessed September 26, 2015). For a recent assessment of the place of spiritual formation in theological education, see Linda M. Cannell, "Theology, Spiritual Formation and Theological Education: Reflections Toward Application," in *Life in the Spirit: Spiritual Formation in Theological Perspective*, ed. Jeffrey P. Greenman and George Kalantzis (Downers Grove, IL: IVP Academic, 2010), 229-49.

[28]For example, see the Bill J. Leonard, ed., *Becoming Christian: Dimensions of Spiritual Formation* (Louisville, KY: Westminster John Knox, 1990), and Kenneth O. Gangel and James C. Wilhoit, eds., *The Christian Educator's Handbook on Spiritual Formation* (Grand Rapids: Baker, 1998). The former is an interdisciplinary study from the faculty of Southern Baptist Theological Seminary, while the latter is a resource for Christian education scholars and practitioners.

While the spiritual formation movement influenced evangelical higher education and ministry preparation, it became far more identified with a handful of authors who shaped popular perceptions of the movement. Most of these evangelical spiritual authors came of age in the 1960s, though instead of finding spiritual sustenance in alternative spiritualities, they looked to classical emphases and disciplines from within the Christian tradition. They were highly educated, in many cases spending portions of their careers in both the evangelical academy and in local churches or parachurch ministries. As historian Chris Armstrong notes, the early leaders of the evangelical spiritual formation movement agreed with Lovelace's diagnosis of a sanctification gap and believed that the "dismal failure of American evangelicals to mature spiritually" was a result of unhealthy tendencies that had carried over from fundamentalism.[29]

Chief among the post-1960s evangelical spiritual authors was Quaker pastor Richard Foster, whose bestselling book *Celebration of Discipline* (1978) could be considered the symbolic beginning of the spiritual formation movement among evangelicals.[30] In 2000, the leading evangelical periodical *Christianity Today* listed *Celebration of Discipline* as one of the ten books that had most shaped Christian thought during the twentieth century. Six years later, the same periodical listed Foster's book as one of the fifty titles that had most influenced evangelicals.[31] Foster's book was an evangelical apologetic for adopting the classical spiritual disciplines as a means of cultivating spiritual maturity. Though an evangelical, Foster was willing to mine church history and learn from the spiritual traditions of diverse movements, including Puritanism, Pietism, the Quakers, Pentecostals, Roman Catholicism, and Eastern Orthodoxy. Foster's other influential books included *Prayer: Finding the Heart's True Home* (1992), *Streams of Living Water: Celebrating the Great Traditions of Christian Faith*

---

[29]Chris Armstrong, "The Rise, Frustration, and Revival of Evangelical Spiritual *Ressourcement*," *Journal of Spiritual Formation and Soul Care* 2, no. 1 (2009): 114.

[30]Foster's book, which has sold more than one million copies, is currently in its third edition. See Richard J. Foster, *Celebration of Discipline: The Path to Spiritual Growth*, 3rd ed. (San Francisco: HarperSanFrancisco, 2002).

[31]See "Books of the Century," *Christianity Today*, April 24, 2000, available online at www.christianitytoday .com/ct/2000/april24/5.92.html (accessed September 26, 2015), and "The Top 50 Books That Have Shaped Evangelicals," *Christianity Today*, October 6, 2006, available online at www.christianitytoday .com/ct/2006/october/23.51.html (accessed September 26, 2015).

(1998), and two coedited volumes on devotional classics (1990) and spiritual classics (2000).[32] In 1988, Foster founded Renovaré as a retreat and training ministry to promote spiritual formation among evangelicals and other interested Christians.[33]

Nearly equal in influence to Foster was the late Dallas Willard, longtime professor of philosophy at University of Southern California. Willard was nurtured in the Southern Baptist tradition, though in the 1970s he attended the Woodlake Avenue Friends Church in Canoga Park, California, where Richard Foster was pastor. During the early part of his career, Willard was known primarily in philosophical circles as a scholar of religious phenomenology, particularly the works of German philosopher Edmund Husserl (1859–1938). By the late 1980s, Willard was becoming more recognizable outside the academy because of his popular books and articles on spiritual formation. Willard's *The Spirit of the Disciplines: Understanding How God Changes Lives* (1988) and *The Divine Conspiracy: Rediscovering Your Hidden Life in God* (1998) are both award-winning books that have shaped the spiritual formation movement, along with Willard's numerous other popular writings.[34] Willard and Foster also helped coedit the *Renovaré Spiritual Formation Bible* (2006), a resource that included both evangelical and mainline contributors. Willard maintained a close relationship with Renovaré until his death in 2013.[35]

Two other key early leaders were tied to Regent College, a school in Vancouver, British Columbia, that was originally founded to train laypersons for Christian service. Scotsman James Houston was an Oxford University geologist who was influenced by C. S. Lewis and who for many years was involved in InterVarsity Christian Fellowship in the United Kingdom. In 1970,

---

[32]For a list of all of Foster's books related to spiritual formation, see his personal website at http://richardjfoster.com/books (accessed September 26, 2015).

[33]See www.renovare.org/.

[34]Willard's former personal website continues to be updated and includes a full list of his books and essays. See www.dwillard.org/defaultNew14.asp (accessed September 26, 2015). For a helpful exposition of the major themes in Willard's spirituality, see Steven L. Porter, "The Willardian Corpus," *Journal of Spiritual Formation & Soul Care* 3, no. 2 (Fall 2010): 239-66. For a more general introduction to Willard's thought, see Gary Black Jr., *The Theology of Dallas Willard: Discovering Protoevangelical Faith* (Eugene, OR: Wipf and Stock, 2013).

[35]InterVarsity Press published a tribute webpage in the days following Willard's death. Numerous leaders in the spiritual formation movement, including Foster, James Bryan Smith, and Gary Moon, wrote moving tributes to Willard's influence.

Houston became the first principal of Regent. After the school became a more traditional divinity school, Houston taught spiritual theology at Regent throughout the 1980s. During that time, though Houston did not write an influential book such as *Celebration of Discipline* or *Spirit of the Disciplines*, he republished updated editions of spiritual classics by historical authors such as Juan de Valdés, John Owen, Blaise Pascal, Jonathan Edwards, and William Wilberforce. Following his retirement, Houston wrote more himself, authoring or coauthoring numerous books related to spirituality.[36]

Eugene Peterson was the longtime pastor of Christ Our King Presbyterian Church in Bel Air, Maryland, before spending twenty-five years on the faculty of Regent College until his retirement in 2006. Though most famous for his biblical paraphrase *The Message: The Bible in Contemporary Language* (2002), Peterson also wrote dozens of books that closely tied spiritual formation to the life of the modern pastor. His better-known works on spirituality include *A Long Obedience in the Same Direction: Discipleship in an Instant Society* (1980), *The Contemplative Pastor: Returning to the Art of Spiritual Direction* (1980), as well as an award-winning five-volume series on spiritual theology published by Eerdmans (2005–2010).[37] In addition to his many books, Peterson was also frequently called on to give a more academic voice to the spiritual formation movement through published essays and public lectures.

Though Renovaré is the most famous parachurch ministry tied to the evangelical spiritual formation movement, over the past thirty years several other ministries and academic programs have been established to promote spiritual maturity among both evangelical laypersons and scholars. For example, two different evangelical organizations exist that are dedicated to spiritual direction, a practice more often associated with Catholic spirituality.[38] Major conferences have been held at evangelical institutions such

---

[36]For a partial list of Houston's published works, see his faculty website at Regent College, available online at www.regent-college.edu/faculty/retired/james-houston (accessed September 26, 2007). See also Aram Haroutunian, "No One Closer: A Conversation with James Houston," *Mars Hill Review* 1, no. 6 (Fall 1996): 51-66, available online at www.leaderu.com/marshill/mhr06/houston1.html.

[37]For a partial list of Peterson's published works, see his faculty website at Regent College, available online at www.regent-college.edu/faculty/retired/eugene-peterson (accessed September 26, 2007).

[38]The Evangelical Spiritual Director's Association's website is available online at http://graftedlife.org /esda/direction/, while the Evangelical Spiritual Director's Network can be found online at https:// evangelicalspiritualdirectorsnetwork.com/ (accessed September 26, 2015).

as Beeson Divinity School (2000) and Wheaton College (2009), along with smaller symposia at numerous schools.[39] Evangelical publishers such as InterVarsity, Baker, Eerdmans, and Zondervan regularly publish books related to spiritual formation, while smaller publishers such as Crossway, NavPress, Moody, and Kregel also frequently publish works in spiritual formation, the spiritual disciplines, and related themes. While not an evangelical initiative, the Society for the Study of Christian Spirituality, an ecumenical scholarly society, includes many evangelical members and publishes a refereed journal titled *Spiritus*.[40]

In addition to individual courses on spiritual formation or the spiritual disciplines, many schools are known for a more extensive emphasis on spiritual formation. As mentioned above, since its founding Regent College has emphasized the discipline of spiritual theology, which in Regent's context represents a more scholarly, intentionally theological approach to spiritual formation.[41] In addition to Houston and Peterson, Regent theologians J. I. Packer, Marva Dawn, and Alister McGrath and church historian Bruce Hindmarsh have also written widely about spirituality.[42] At Westmont College, the Dallas Willard Center for Christian Spiritual Formation hosts conferences and promotes the ministry of Renovaré.[43] Psychologist Gary Moon, the director of the Willard Center, has been an active voice within the spiritual formation movement. At Southern Baptist Theological Seminary, students can earn several master's degrees, a DMin, or a PhD with an emphasis in biblical spirituality, which is more or less the school's preferred

---

[39]The Beeson and Wheaton conferences each resulted in published anthologies of the proceedings. See Timothy George and Alister E. McGrath, eds., *For All the Saints: Evangelical Theology and Christian Spirituality* (Louisville, KY: Westminster John Knox, 2003); and Greenman and Kalantzis, *Life in the Spirit.*

[40]See https://sscs.press.jhu.edu/.

[41]The term *spiritual theology* has different meanings in different contexts. For background on the various uses of the terminology, see Evan B. Howard, *The Brazos Introduction to Christian Spirituality* (Grand Rapids: Brazos, 2007), 19-21.

[42]Though more identified with British institutions, McGrath has been associated in various ways with Regent College off and on since the mid-1990s. He is a leading scholar of spirituality among British evangelicals. See Alister McGrath, *Beyond the Quiet Time: Practical Evangelical Spirituality* (Grand Rapids: Baker, 1995); *Christian Spirituality: An Introduction* (Oxford: Blackwell, 1999); *The Unknown God: Searching for Spiritual Fulfillment* (Grand Rapids: Eerdmans, 1999). For an assessment of McGrath's spiritual theology, see Larry S. McDonald, *The Merging of Theology and Spirituality: An Examination of the Life and Work of Alister E. McGrath* (Lanham, MD: University Press of America, 2006).

[43]See http://dallaswillardcenter.com/.

nomenclature for spiritual theology. The PhD at Southern is the only terminal academic degree in spirituality offered by an evangelical institution.[44] The most influential academic program in spiritual formation is found at Talbot Theological Seminary at Biola University, where the Institute for Spiritual Formation hosts conferences and publishes a refereed journal titled the *Journal of Spiritual Formation and Soul Care*.[45] Students at Talbot can also earn several master's degrees or a certificate in soul care or spiritual formation.

Some evangelicals and fundamentalists have criticized the spiritual formation movement. This is especially true of conservative apologists who associate practices such as contemplative prayer with the Roman Catholic Church, the occult, or the New Age Movement; each of these groups is deemed unacceptable for various reasons. Leaders within the spiritual formation movement have had to balance critiquing spiritual practices that fall short of the biblical witness or the Christian worldview, while also pushing back against right-wing accusations that any spiritual practice with roots among ancient or medieval believers is inherently mystical, and thus sub-Christian.[46] Other evangelicals resonate with the spiritual formation movement in principle, but have framed some of the emphases somewhat differently than early shapers such as Foster, Willard, and Peterson.[47]

Increasingly, the spiritual formation movement has been characterized by two broad trajectories. The older and larger trajectory might be called the "Renovaré" wing of the movement. The Renovaré wing is theologically eclectic, ecumenical, and egalitarian. A Quaker-Wesleyan emphasis on experiencing God permeates the movement, as does a similarly rooted commitment to social justice. Many charismatics and Pentecostals

---

[44]See Jeff Robinson, "SBTS Appoints Renowned Early Church Scholar to Faculty," *Southern News*, May 14, 2007, available online at http://news.sbts.edu/2007/05/14/sbts-appoints-renowned-early-church -scholar-to-faculty/ (accessed September 26, 2007).

[45]See http://www.talbot.edu/isf/.

[46]See Tom Schwanda, "'To Gaze on the Beauty of the Lord': The Evangelical Resistance and Retrieval of Contemplation," *Journal of Spiritual Formation and Soul Care* 7, no. 1 (Spring 2014): 62-84, and John Coe, "The Historical Controversy over Contemplation and Contemplative Prayer: A Historical, Theological, and Biblical Resolution," *Journal of Spiritual Formation and Soul Care* 7, no. 1 (Spring 2014): 140-53.

[47]For example, see Bruce Demarest, *Satisfy Your Soul: Restoring the Heart of Christian Spirituality* (Colorado Springs, CO: NavPress, 1999), and Donald G. Bloesch, *Spirituality Old & New: Recovering Authentic Spiritual Life* (Downers Grove, IL: IVP Academic, 2007).

resonate with the Renovaré approach to spiritual formation. Authors from this perspective tend to be more descriptive in their use of church tradition, drawing on many nonevangelical sources, though always from an evangelical perspective. Not surprisingly, Foster and Willard remain the most influential voices in this trajectory, with Westmont College and especially Biola/Talbot representing academic homes for the Renovaré approach to spiritual formation. The larger evangelical publishing houses have published many of the most influential works from this perspective, as have some more mainstream publishers, especially HarperCollins.

The other trajectory, which is smaller but seems to be growing, might be called the "New Calvinist" wing of the spiritual formation movement.[48] Not everyone in this camp is a consistent Calvinist in the Dortian sense of the term, but this trajectory is decisively less Wesleyan and more overtly committed to biblical inerrancy and a complementarian understanding of gender. A Reformed-Baptist emphasis on the primacy of local churches permeates the movement, and greater emphasis is placed on evangelism than social justice. Authors from this perspective tend to be more judicious in their use of church tradition, focusing more on Reformed and evangelical sources, especially the Puritans, and being less open to insights from medieval Catholic writers. Crossway, Moody, and explicitly Reformed presses such as Reformation Heritage, Evangelical Press, and P&R tend to be the publishers of choice for authors in this camp.

The best-known advocates of the New Calvinist trajectory are theologian J. I. Packer, longtime Navigator's staff member Jerry Bridges, and professor Donald Whitney. Packer's books *A Quest for Godliness: The Puritan Vision of the Christian Life* (1990) and *Rediscovering Holiness* (1992) were shaped by—and commended—the Puritan spiritual tradition. Jerry Bridges's books *The Pursuit of Holiness* (1988) and *The Discipline of Grace: God's Role and Our Role in the Pursuit of Holiness* (1994) focused more on the traditional language of holiness than the newer language of spiritual formation, which is a common practice among New Calvinists. Whitney,

---

[48]The language of "New Calvinism" is taken from Collin Hansen, *Young, Restless, Reformed: A Journalist's Journey with the New Calvinists* (Wheaton, IL: Crossway, 2008).

who teaches at Southern Seminary, is the author of numerous books re-lated to spiritual formation. His *Spiritual Disciplines of the Christian Life* (1991) represented a more Reformed alternative to Foster's *Celebration of Discipline*, while Whitney's *Spiritual Disciplines Within the Church* (1996) highlighted the Reformed-Baptist emphasis on the local church.[49] Southern Seminary and Puritan Reformed Theological Seminary could be considered the academic homes of the New Calvinist approach to spiritual formation.

Moving forward, a major issue facing the spiritual formation movement is whether or not an approach can be found that transcends the aforementioned divide. This will be difficult insofar as the two trajec-tories reflect wider divisions that characterize evangelical theology and identity. While many evangelicals find paradigms such as David Bebbing-ton's justly famous "quadrilateral" of conversionism, biblicism, crucicen-trism, and activism to be generally helpful for descriptive purposes, there is widespread disagreement about how to understand each of those four priorities.[50] By bringing together a diverse group of evangelical scholars in this particular book, we are signaling our own sincere hope for a more unified evangelical identity, which would include a more unified vision for spiritual formation—and mission.

One could argue the spiritual formation movement is dead, not be-cause of failure, but because of its general success in convincing evangel-icals that the sanctification gap is a real problem and that the pursuit of spiritual maturity ought to be an intentional priority.[51] Even the presence of (at least) two different approaches to spiritual formation would suggest the movement has enjoyed a measure of success; different evangelicals care enough about spiritual formation that they argue about the best way to go about it. Perhaps a better analogy than death is evolution. As scholars

---

[49]A full list of Whitney's other books can be found at his personal website, http://biblicalspirituality.org (accessed September 26, 2015).

[50]For the origin of the Bebbington quadrilateral, see David Bebbington, *Evangelicalism in Modern Britain: A History from the 1730s to the 1980s* (London: Routledge, 1989), 2-17. For a recent work that highlights the different trajectories within evangelicalism, see Andrew David Naselli and Collin Hansen, eds., *Four Views on the Spectrum of Evangelicalism* (Grand Rapids: Zondervan, 2011).

[51]Steven L. Porter, "Is the Spiritual Formation Movement Dead?," *Journal of Spiritual Formation and Soul Care* 8, no. 1 (Spring 2015): 2-7.

and practitioners have written about spiritual formation and closely related themes, the spiritual formation movement has become interdisciplinary, transcending the theological and practical disciplines. Much like mission, spiritual formation has become an important aspect of applied theology that attracts attention from various types of scholars, ministry practitioners, and laypersons.

A Word About Definitions

As you can see, both *missional* and *spiritual formation* are contested terms that are understood differently depending on context—including among evangelicals. We want to close out this chapter by offering some working definitions that can frame the discussion in this book and, more generally, that we believe most evangelicals can affirm. These definitions will almost certainly not be the *last* word when it comes to defining these two important terms, but we hope they will represent a *helpful* word as evangelicals hopefully come to a greater consensus in these matters in the years ahead.

When it comes to *missional*, the question is not whether the term should be used, but *how* it should be used. How should we define the word? Chris Wright is right when he suggests, "Missional is simply an adjective denoting something that is related to or characterized by mission, or has the qualities, attributes or dynamics of mission."[52] However, we believe this definition is too thin to give full shape to the missional dimension of Christianity. If *missional* is going to serve the church in forming a people that engages its world with the gospel, then more direction for defining the concept is needed. We use *missional* to describe the posture of a missionary, but we must be able to provide people with a missional orientation, shape, and direction for their lives. Thus, we propose three statements that will help us understand what it means to use the adjective *missional* to modify our church, life, vision, network, and so on.

(1) *Being missional means living directed by the mission of God.* God's purpose is to be known as the Lord over his creation. His people are called to join him by making him known as Lord over all things.

---

[52]Christopher Wright, *The Mission of God: Unlocking the Bible's Grand Narrative* (Downers Grove, IL: IVP Academic, 2006), 24.

(2) *Being missional means living a life shaped by the mission of God.* God's mission establishes a kingdom where he is known as Lord and is praised. The people of God are a kingdom people, who dwell with God through his Spirit, enjoy his blessings, and are known by faith, hope, and love.

(3) *Being missional means living sent on the mission of God.* The church is sent into the world by their Savior with an evangelistic calling: to proclaim that the God of all creation has mercifully made himself known through Jesus Christ and that there is forgiveness of sins and transforming grace available to all who enter his kingdom through repentance and faith.

As with *missional,* when it comes to *spiritual formation* there is no shortage of generally helpful definitions. We will give just two examples. According to Dallas Willard, "spiritual formation for the Christian basically refers to the Spirit-driven process of forming the inner world of the human self in such a way that it becomes like the inner being of Christ himself."[53] While this is a fine basic account of the interior aspects of spiritual formation, it is detached from any sense of Christian community, neglects any mention of God's grace, and fails to explicitly address the outward aspects of Christian maturity. Dallas Theological Seminary offers a more extensive definition that they use in their programs:

> The process by which God forms Christ's character in believers by the ministry of the Spirit, in the context of community, and in accordance with biblical standards. This process involves the transformation of the whole person in thoughts, behaviors, and styles of relating with God and others. Such life change is manifest in a growing love for God and others—a dying to self and living for Christ.[54]

We like this definition because it explicitly addresses the external aspect of spiritual formation. We also appreciate the clear reference to biblical authority and the implicit nod toward the outward fruit of spiritual formation. However, we wish this particular definition said a bit more about the role of God's grace in spiritual formation.

---

[53]Dallas Willard, *Renovation of the Heart: Putting on the Character of Christ* (Colorado Springs, CO: NavPress, 2002), 22.

[54]See "Definition of Spiritual Formation at DTS," available online at www.dts.edu/departments/academic/eml/sf/definition/ (accessed October 2, 2015). The webpage helpfully expounds on each of the clauses in this definition.

In an effort to address all of these important components, we define spiritual formation as "the cultivation of grace-motivated spiritual practices and habits, drawn from the authoritative Scriptures and the best of the Christian tradition, that the Holy Spirit uses to foster spiritual maturity in the life of the believer for the glory of God, the health of the church, and the sake of the world." We hope this definition takes into account the emphases of both the Renovaré and New Calvinist trajectories, including a commitment to biblical authority, the priority of God's grace, the helpfulness of the Christian tradition (and not just a single tradition), a commitment to the importance of the church, as well as both inward (holiness) and outward (mission) foci. We hope this vision of spiritual formation, which is rooted in the great tradition, the Great Commandment, and the Great Commission, is broad enough to make room for Wesleyans and Calvinists, for evangelists and justice advocates, for contemplatives and activists.

2

Spirituality, Mission, *and* *the* Drama *of* Scripture

Craig G. Bartholomew

Introduction

Spirituality has to do with our relationship with the living and true God. As such, it is central to the Bible. *Biblical theology* is that discipline that seeks the unity of Scripture according to Scripture's own categories. It is of vital importance for apprehending Scripture in its totality and for our being taken hold of by God in our totality. Spirituality and biblical theology are thus integrally connected.

There is no one way to do biblical theology. It is helpful to think of Scripture as a grand cathedral with multiple entrances, many unknown to the public but known to the staff. The biblical theological unity of Scripture can thus be approached through many entrances, each of which will give one an angle of vision on the multifaceted unity of Scripture, much as one might admire a diamond from many angles. However, as with a cathedral, it is worth asking if there is a main entrance from which the whole in its proportions becomes most clearly visible. In my opinion "covenant" in the Old Testament and "the kingdom of God" in the New Testament stand out as the leading contenders in this respect, and they are reverse sides of the same coin, as Gordon Spykman notes:

> The dual idea of covenant/kingdom is not an occasional theme scattered randomly across the pages of Scripture. It pulsates with the very heartbeat of all biblical revelation. It is the very matrix and enduring context of our life in God's world. . . . The biblical idea of covenant-and-kingdom is a bi-unitary index to the meaning of creation. . . . Covenant suggests the idea of an abiding charter, while kingdom suggests the idea of an ongoing program. Covenant is more foundation oriented; kingdom is more goal oriented. Covenant may thus be conceived of as kingdom looking backward to its origins, but with abiding significance. Kingdom may then be conceived of as covenant looking forward with gathering momentum toward its final fulfillment. Thus nuanced, covenant and kingdom are interchangeable realities.[1]

The minute one starts to explore covenant and kingdom, one is pushed into the grand story of the Bible, so that a narrative biblical theology becomes exceptionally fertile. Following Tom Wright's creative proposal, Mike Goheen and I develop such a biblical theology in our *The Drama of Scripture*, in which we argue that the grand story of the Bible is best understood as a drama in six acts:[2]

Act 1	God Establishes His Kingdom: Creation
Act 2	Rebellion in the Kingdom: Fall
Act 3	The King Chooses Israel: Redemption Initiated
Interlude	A Kingdom Story Waiting for an Ending: The Intertestamental Period
Act 4	The Coming of the King: Redemption Accomplished
Act 5	**Spreading the News of the King: The Mission of the Church**
Act 6	The Return of the King: Redemption Completed

Act 5 is in bold because this is the act of the biblical drama in which we find ourselves. Although it is perfectly acceptable to see acts 2–6 as all

---

[1] Gordon J. Spykman, *Reformational Theology: A New Paradigm for Doing Dogmatics* (Grand Rapids: Eerdmans, 1992), 257-58.

[2] Craig G. Bartholomew and Michael W. Goheen, *The Drama of Scripture: Finding Our Place in the Biblical Story*, 2nd ed. (Grand Rapids: Baker Academic, 2014); *The True Story of the Whole World: Finding Your Place in the Biblical Drama* (Grand Rapids: Faith Alive, 2004).

about mission, it is act 5 in particular that is the great time of and for mission. Act 4 ends with the Great Commission and Jesus' ascension to the highest place of authority at the right hand of God, from which he pours out the Holy Spirit on the day of Pentecost, inaugurating the global era of mission.

Since the mid-twentieth century, a penetrating insight that has become increasingly common is that mission is rightly understood as the *missio Dei*. The triune God is the great missionary, and his people are called to accompany him in his work of redemption. This penetrating insight ties in closely to the view of the Bible as telling the true story of the whole world. The Bible not only does this, but it also invites us to become a participant in this great story. The Jewish theologian and philosopher Will Herberg puts it evocatively thus:

> It is (to borrow from Kierkegaard) as though we sat witnessing some tremendous epic drama being performed on a vast stage, when suddenly the chief character of the drama, who is also its director, steps forward to the front of the stage, fixes his eye upon us, points his finger at us, and calls out "You, you're wanted. Come up here. Take your part!" . . . Unless we receive this call and respond to it, the redemptive history that we apprehend is not redemptive. It does not really tell us who we are, where we stand, and what we may hope for; it does not really give meaning to existence.[3]

The New Testament uses a range of vocabulary to describe the process of becoming part of God's story, of taking our part in his redemptive history: entering the kingdom, repenting and believing, being born again, being adopted into God's family, being justified before God, being saved, receiving eternal life, and so forth. For our purposes it is worth noting how many of such expressions bespeak a deeply personal relationship with God. In John's Gospel, which uses the language of the kingdom of God sparingly, an equivalent expression is "eternal life," which is the life of the age to come that has now already broken into history in Jesus. It is a rich expression encapsulating the eschatology of the New Testament. In

---

[3]Will Herberg, and Bernard W. Anderson, *Faith Enacted as History: Essays in Biblical Theology* (Philadelphia: Westminster, 1976), 41.

Jesus' high priestly prayer in John 17:3, Jesus defines eternal life: "Now this is eternal life: that they know you, the only true God, and Jesus Christ, whom you have sent."

Knowing God is at the heart of eternal life and utterly central to the kingdom of God, and thus of mission. Undoubtedly such knowledge includes knowing many things about God, but it is far more than cognitive, propositional knowledge, important as that is. God is at least personal, if not more so, and we are called to enter into deep, interpersonal relationship with him. Spirituality is the name for this deep relationality.

We are well aware that a good marriage does not just happen. The reality of becoming "one flesh" begins with wedding vows, but it takes a lifetime of work and attentiveness in order for two different people genuinely and deeply to become one. Churches have recognized this in their teaching, marriage seminars, and counseling. The same is true of our relationship with God. Conversion is the beginning and, as with marriage, habitual practices need to be developed to facilitate an ever-deeper growth into relationship with God.

Vita Contemplativa—Vita Activa

In the history of Christian spirituality much has been written about the relative merits of the contemplative life (*vita contemplativa*) in relation to the active life (*vita activa*). The former concentrates on prayer and developing a deep relationship with God, whereas the latter concentrates on service of God in his world, what we might call mission. While some are undoubtedly called to one or the other as their main form of service, things always get messy when a wedge is driven between the two.[4]

In South Africa, where I grew up, there is a large monastic settlement in Marianhill, in KwaZulu Natal. When you drive in to the settlement, across the entrance in large letters is the great Benedictine motto: "Ora et Labora" (Prayer and Work). As the monastic tradition at its best recognizes with this motto, even if one's primary calling is to a life of prayer, it needs to be accompanied by work. Similarly, the active life, and thus mission, is full of

---

[4]Cf. Miroslav Volf, *Work in the Spirit: Toward a Theology of Work* (Eugene, OR: Wipf and Stock, 1991), 70.

dangers once it becomes separated from a deep spirituality. Within evangelical circles, it is, alas, not uncommon to find types of hyperactivism done in the name of God and mission, yet unaccompanied by lives lived ever more deeply into God.

In my view Elizabeth O'Connor gets the balance right in her important book, *Journey Inward, Journey Outward*.[5] If we think of the journey outward as responding to God's call to serve him by word and deed in his world, then this journey should always emerge out of and return into a deep journey into God, in community. Mission needs to start from, and continually return to, spirituality.

Creation, Fall, and Spirituality

Act 1 of the drama of Scripture is fundamental to all that follows. As is widely recognized, the creation account in Genesis 1 and 2 is polemical, even as it sets out its own view. In the Enuma Elish, for example, Marduk says to Ea,

Blood I will mass and cause bones to be.
I will establish a savage, "man" shall be his name.
Verily, savage-man I will create.
He shall be charged with the service of the gods
That they might be at ease![6]

Similarly, in the Atrahasis Epic humans are created in response to the gods complaining about the burden of work. A god is slaughtered, and his flesh and blood is mixed with clay to make humans. Mami proclaims to the gods,

You commanded me a task—
I have completed it.
You slaughtered a god together with his rationality.
I have removed your heavy labor,
have placed your labor-basket on man.
You raised a cry for mankind;
I have loosened your yoke, have [established] freedom.[7]

---

[5] Elizabeth O'Connor, *Journey Inward, Journey Outward* (New York: HarperCollins, 1975).
[6] Joan O'Brien and Wilfred Major, *In the Beginning: Creation Myths from Ancient Mesopotamia, Israel and Greece* (Atlanta: Scholars Press, 1982), 25.
[7] Ibid., 82-83.

Genesis 1 and 2 form a stark contrast with such views. The world is created as the perfect home for humans in Genesis 1:1–2:3 so that, to a major extent, God's labor is *for* humans and their well-being. In Genesis 2, the first couple are placed in a park named "Eden," a play on the Hebrew word for delight. Much has been written about the *imago Dei*; suffice it here to note that there is a functional dimension to the image—royal stewardship over the creation—as well as an ontological one. Humans are creatures of language, gendered, rational, and relational, and capable of intimate relationship with God. The tree of life is a sign of God as the coinhabitant of humankind in the creation. The unusual juxtaposition of the name Yahweh with Elohim in Genesis 2 serves as a reminder that the transcendent Creator God (Elohim of Gen 1) is also Yahweh, the redeemer God of Israel. The image of Yahweh Elohim walking in the garden in the cool of the day is thus a beautiful evocation of the intimacy God desires with humans (Gen 2:8).

For spirituality, the doctrine of creation serves as a reminder that humans are embodied creatures and that this is good. As such, Genesis 2–3 brings into sharp relief the various relationships that constitute a human being. A helpful way to illustrate this is in figure 1.

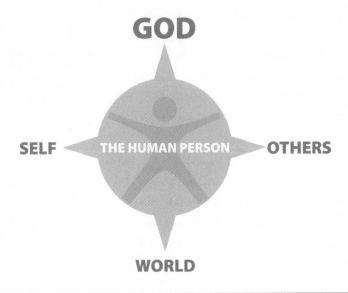

Figure 1. Human relationships

The relationship with God is primary, hence the larger font. Although an individual, the human person is never a human being in isolation, hence the relation to "others," which includes neighbors, the marriage one-flesh relationship, communities, and so forth. Humans are unique in their capacity for self-reflection, and thus the human person can be thought of as being in relationship with his or her self. Functionally humans are called to steward God's world and thus are always in relation to the world as embodied creatures. It is noteworthy that although the whole world is created as a perfect home for humans, the first couple is placed in a particular place, namely Eden. Humans are always in a particular place, and thus place is an integral part of being human and thus of spirituality.[8]

God's intention was that humans would grow ever more fully into relationship with him and thus also grow in the other relational dimensions of their being. The fall changed all that. What is vital to note for spirituality is that the shattering of humankind's relationship with God also shatters the other relationships that constitute human beings. This is clearly evident in Genesis 3 and the chapters that follow. Sin manifests itself in all dimensions of human life. But so too does redemption, and the doctrine of creation and the model of anthropology depicted above remind us that restoration of our relationship with God should lead to a normative reshaping of all dimensions of our lives: our relationships with others, our relationship with ourselves, and our relationship to the world. Genuine spirituality is formative of the whole person in community.

Formatio

The Christian tradition has a word for *formatio*, and it is one that we need to recover, namely "sanctification." Too often in the evangelical tradition, conversion moves straight to mission, bypassing sanctification, with disastrous results. Formation is indispensable to the practice of mission, and mission should emerge out of formation and always be accompanied by it.

---

[8]See Craig G. Bartholomew, *Where Mortals Dwell: A Christian View of Place for Today* (Grand Rapids: Baker Academic, 2011), 319-23.

In this respect, act 3 of the drama of Scripture contains invaluable re-sources. In Genesis 12; 15; 17, we learn of the Abrahamic covenant with its goal of blessing the nations, code for a recovery of God's purpose of blessing for the whole creation. Why then, one might well wonder, do we need Genesis 12–50 with the often bizarre stories of the patriarchs? The answer is that having received the promise, the patriarchs need to be formed to become like the promise. Responding to God's call (Gen 11:27–12:9) is only the beginning of a long journey with God. The patriarchs need to become like the one who has graced them with the gift of the covenant. Genesis—indeed, the whole Bible—is ruthless in re-vealing to us the flawed character of God's chosen people and God's in-volvement with them in shaping them through events and circumstances to become more like him. According to Martin Buber, the Bible "is the history of God's disappointments."[9] For Buber "the biblical point of view . . . proclaims that the way . . . from the Creation to the Kingdom is trod not on the surface of success, but in the deep of failure."[10]

The Akedah in Genesis 22 is certainly the most radical example of such "testing," as Abraham, having waited so long for an heir, has to be willing to forego the covenant—the implication of the sacrifice of Isaac—in order to become worthy of the covenant.[11] The extensive story of Joseph (Gen 37–50) is likewise a story of formation. Jacob's spoilt son endures being sold into slavery and thrust into prison before rising to prominence in Israel and being the means of saving the Israelites from extinction, as well as becoming reconciled to his family.

In a fascinating book, Aaron Wildavsky attends to Moses as a political leader, exploring how Moses' experience "reveals the dilemmas of lead-ership under the major types of rule, from slavery in Egypt, to anarchy before the Golden Calf episode, to equity (association without authority) in the desert, until his final effort to institutionalize hierarchy."[12] Moses was certainly a political leader, but his leadership emerges out of his en-counter with Yahweh and his developing relationship with him. As is the

---

[9]Martin Buber, *Israel and the World* (New York: Schocken, 1948), 127.
[10]Ibid., 133.
[11]Cf. Leon R. Kass, *The Beginning of Wisdom: Reading Genesis* (New York: Free Press, 2003).
[12]Aaron Wildavsky, *Moses as Political Leader* (New York: Shalem, 2005), 3.

double bind of leadership, Moses is *being formed* even while he is, under God, *helping form* the people of God. After his world-class education in Pharaoh's household, Moses is forced to flee into the desert after killing an Egyptian who was beating an Israelite. Moses has discovered who his people are and has become sensitive to their suffering, but he must still meet their God, and this he does in the wilderness while shepherding sheep (Ex 3), a far cry from Pharaoh's household. The desert as a meeting place with God is a major biblical motif and also a central one in Christian spirituality, notably with the desert fathers and mothers.[13] In the desert, the normal trappings of life are stripped away and thus the path cleared for encounter with God.

When the Israelites are liberated from slavery, they are led by Moses through the desert to Sinai. Liberation is one thing, formation another,[14] and it soon becomes apparent that the Israelites will need to undergo a long period of formation to become the people of God. They are desperate to be free from Pharaoh's oppression, but becoming holy and trusting Yahweh is another thing altogether. Their time in the wilderness exposes their superficial commitment to Yahweh and their reluctance to face the hardships involved in becoming his people.

In Exodus 19:3-6, Yahweh sets out a glorious picture of his intentions for the Israelites; they are to be a kingdom of priests and a holy nation, God's treasured possession. In Exodus 19–24 we have the Sinai covenant code in which the terms of the covenant between Yahweh and the Israelites are set out. As in Eden, instruction from Yahweh (*torah*) is by no means antithetical to spirituality and full humanity. On the contrary, it is the vehicle for living according to the grain of creation and thus the key to human flourishing. In its succinct form, the Decalogue covers relationship to God, to one another, and to animals. Spirituality is woven into the Decalogue. The preamble alerts us to the fact that spirituality and life flow

---

[13] Cf. Douglas Burton-Christie, *The Word in the Desert: Scripture and the Quest for Holiness in Early Christian Monasticism* (New York: Oxford University Press, 1993).

[14] Once the Israelites leave Egypt, formation is already under way. Formation is holistic. Cf. Ellen Davis, *Scripture, Culture, and Agriculture: An Agrarian Reading of the Bible* (Cambridge: Cambridge University Press, 2008), for an example of how the Israelites are to develop a radically different approach to food compared with Egypt's agribusiness.

from gratitude to God for his redemption. In her cultus, Israel is to have no other God than Yahweh; her devotion is to be complete, in stark contrast to other ancient Near Eastern nations. The second and third commandments deal with resisting any attempt to (mis)represent God or to seek magical control over him through his name. In this way, the Decalogue calls for a spirituality that is genuinely centered on God rather than a form of religion that seeks to use God for our own purposes. As René Girard has observed, the tenth commandment is remarkable in its attempt to curb misdirected desire, the gateway to breaking commandments six through nine.[15]

If one compares the Decalogue with the anthropology represented above, it becomes clear that the Decalogue is aimed, in its ancient Near Eastern context, at redirecting the life of God's people to normative, created, human life, so that they can flourish and be a royal priesthood, a window to the world, as it were, which the nations can peer through to see what human life is intended to be. The Decalogue points the way to a right relationship with God, and commandments five through ten regulate a right relationship with neighbor and world. Patrick Miller thus rightly observes that in the Decalogue we find the ethos of the good neighborhood.[16]

It should also be noted that the covenant code and the law collections in the Old Testament alert us unequivocally to the fact that a true spirituality will lead to all of our life coming under God's reign. A similar emphasis is found in Psalms 1; 2, the introduction to the Psalter. Psalm 1 focuses on the individual believer, only moving to the plural when it deals with the wicked. In Psalm 2, we find ourselves amidst the tumult of the nations. A key point of this juxtaposition of these two psalms as the introduction to the Psalter is that Torah (God's instruction) is as relevant to politics and the life of nations as it is to the individual believer.

The tremendous possibilities set before the Israelites are, however, conditional on them obeying God and keeping his covenant, conditions at which they continually fail. The golden calf incident is the great example

---

[15]René Girard, *I See Satan Fall Like Lightning* (Maryknoll, NY: Orbis, 2001).
[16]Patrick Miller, *The Way of the Lord: Essays in Old Testament Theology* (Grand Rapids: Eerdmans, 2007).

of a collapse back into idolatry, and an indication of the need the Israelites will have for mediation between them and the Holy One. As Israel becomes institutionalized, the Levitical priesthood will become the diplomatic corps, as it were, to mediate between God and his people and to provide a way for forgiveness and cleansing so that they can remain in a healthy relationship with God. The ongoing possibility and experience of forgiveness is an indispensable part of spirituality.

The Old Testament provides important insights into the holistic dimensions of spirituality because of its focus on Israel as an ancient Near Eastern nation in the land. She has a temple, a capital in Jerusalem, law courts in the city gates, marketplaces, agriculture, families, and homes. The Shema in Deuteronomy 6 alerts us not only to the fact that God's Torah is to inform every aspect of her life but also of the vital importance of the home as a center of spirituality.[17] Parents play a vital role in passing on a genuine commitment to God to their children (Deut 6:7), and the home is to be suffused with a sense of God's presence and Torah. Generally, and this is particularly true of less urbanized societies like Israel, we spend more time in the home than anywhere else. Thus, the home is a kind of gateway in and out of society, and the Shema (Deut 6:4) envisions that gateway awash with Yahweh's Torah. The home as a place for encounter with Yahweh is thus a crucial and easily ignored dimension of spirituality.

Through the tabernacle and then the temple, God is genuinely present amidst his people. As he was the coinhabitant in Eden, so he is the coinhabitant and king in Israel. As one author has perceptively noted, once the temple is established, God has an address on earth! The palace of the king is also in Jerusalem, but it is subservient to the God who dwells in the temple.

Zion, and thus spirituality, is designed to be central to the life of the people of God. In the law collections, for example, we find a liturgical

---

[17]N. T. Wright speaks of "the breathtakingly renewed *Shema* of 1 Corinthians 8.6. . . . The christologically revised prayer of the Jewish people forms the theological heart of highly practical teaching: One God, the father; one lord, Jesus the Messiah, and all things coming *from* the father and *through* the lord. . . . That revised monotheism—in the form, appropriately, of a prayer—stood at the heart of Paul's socio-cultural vision." N. T. Wright, *Paul and the Faithfulness of God* (Minneapolis: Fortress, 2013), 1516.

calendar for the year with compulsory pilgrimages to be made to Jerusalem three times per year.[18] The Psalms of Ascent are likely a hymnbook for such journeys. The significance of such a pilgrimage should not be underestimated. Work had to be put aside for the time being, and with one's family, one would make the slow journey to Jerusalem, celebrate the feast, and then make the slow journey back. This provided lots of time out for reflection, and the aim of the feasts was to recenter God's people in the grand story of which they were a part, so that they could return to their towns and villages, now to live that story more fully.

In the New Testament, pilgrimage is no longer mandatory, just as worship is no longer centralized in Jerusalem. However, as Eugene Peterson has noted, pilgrimage remains an important tool for spirituality,[19] not least in our speed-driven age in which technology and fast means of travel make it harder and harder for us to live slowly and deeply. Even as church attendance declines in the West, numbers of pilgrims to "holy" sites continue to increase. Thousands, for example, make the pilgrimage to Santiago de Compostela each year. What we must learn from pilgrimage in the Old Testament is that it is not an escape from life, but a temporary time-out, creating the space for reflection so that when we return to our "normal" lives, we can now live them more fully for God.

If one has any doubt about the reality and depth of spirituality in the Old Testament, the Psalms remove it. In his classic book on prayer, Hans Urs von Balthasar rightly notes that in the Bible God speaks to us and then instructs us how to respond to him.[20] We see the latter above all else in the Psalter, with its 150 psalms that address the smorgasbord of human experience, from joy and celebration to despair and lament.[21] It is likely that the division of the Psalter into five books deliberately mirrors the five books of the Pentateuch, confirming von Balthasar's point. The

---

[18]See Craig G. Bartholomew and Fred Hughes, eds., *Explorations in a Christian Theology of Pilgrimage* (Aldershot, UK: Ashgate, 2004).

[19]Eugene Peterson, *The Contemplative Pastor: Returning to the Art of Spiritual Direction* (Grand Rapids: Eerdmans, 1989).

[20]Hans Urs von Balthasar, *Prayer* (San Francisco: Igantius, 1986).

[21]See Craig G. Bartholomew and Andrew West, eds., *Praying by the Book: Reading the Psalms* (Carlisle, UK: Paternoster, 2002); Bruce K. Waltke and James Houston, *The Psalms as Christian Worship: A Historical Commentary* (Grand Rapids: Eerdmans, 2010).

Pentateuch tells us the story of the world and instructs us how to live; the Psalter provides us with words for our relating to God as we seek to live rightly amidst all the circumstances of life.

Old Testament wisdom is likewise a major source for spirituality.[22] The relationship between wisdom and the other major genres in the Old Testament is contested.[23] Old Testament wisdom is rooted in a theology of creation and is concerned with finding God's ways amidst the myriad challenges of daily life. The well-known Canadian literary scholar Northrop Frye argues rightly, in my view, that "the conception of wisdom in the Bible, as we see most clearly in some of the psalms, starts with the individualizing of the law, with allowing the law, in its human and moral aspect, to permeate and inform all one's personal life."[24] Spirituality is at the heart of this permeation.

The fundamental principle of Old Testament wisdom is that the fear of Yahweh is the beginning of wisdom. "Beginning" should be understood as both starting point and foundation. If the quest for wisdom—how to navigate the challenges and opportunities of life—does not begin with a holy reverence for Yahweh, it will soon lose its way. But this starting point is also the perduring foundation for wisdom; true wisdom never relinquishes the fear of Yahweh but grows into it ever more deeply.

Job and Ecclesiastes are classic Old Testament texts for spirituality,[25] serving as reminders that wisdom is no technique easily mastered. Wisdom involves deep formation of the heart, positioning the person as a creature before the Creator, Redeemer God. In Job, we have a remarkable spirituality of suffering, a classic text dealing with the dark night of the soul. In Ecclesiastes, we find more of an intellectual, but still excruciating, struggle over the meaning of life.[26] Intriguingly, in both cases, resolution comes,

---

[22]See Craig G. Bartholomew and Ryan P. O'Dowd, *Old Testament Wisdom: A Theological Introduction* (Downers Grove, IL: IVP Academic, 2011).

[23]See Craig G. Bartholomew, "Old Testament Wisdom Today," in David G. Firth and Lindsay Wilson, eds., *Interpreting Old Testament Wisdom Literature* (Downers Grove, IL: InterVarsity Press, 2017), 3-33.

[24]Northrop Frye, *The Great Code: The Bible and Literature* (Toronto: Penguin, 1982), 121.

[25]See Craig G. Bartholomew, "Hearing the Old Testament Wisdom Literature: The Wit of Many and the Wisdom of One," in *Hearing the Old Testament: Listening for God's Address*, ed. Craig G. Bartholomew and David J. H. Beldman (Grand Rapids: Eerdmans, 2012), 302-31; Craig G. Bartholomew, *Ecclesiastes*, BCOTWPC (Grand Rapids: Baker Academic, 2009).

[26]See Bartholomew, *Ecclesiastes*.

not through rational answers to their problems, but through an encounter with God as Creator. Job's long, circular struggle culminates in the speeches of God that take Job on a tour of the creation, leading him to confess that before he had, as it were, only heard of God, but now he has seen (Job 42:5). Many scholars struggle to see how the book of Job resolves Job's crisis. Spirituality is the key. Readers are privy to the opening scenes in the book—in which the Satan negotiates with God about his servant Job—but Job is not. Job's suffering is excruciating but profoundly formative.

Qohelet finds himself in a major crisis about whether or not life is meaningful. No matter what area of life he explores, his epistemology of observation, experience, and reason leads him to the conclusion that all is enigmatic. Resolution comes, signalled first by the delightful proverb in Eccl 12:1-7, through a return to the starting point of wisdom, indicated by the exhortation, "Remember your Creator . . . before . . . before . . . before. . . ."

The prophets continually call Israel back to a true spirituality grounded in the covenant. Some of the prophets also give us a glimpse into the inner life of one who is called to proclaim God's word to God's people. After his triumph on Mount Carmel, Elijah collapses before Jezebel's threat and journeys into the wilderness, where he has the space to recover and be re-energized. Jeremiah stands out among the prophets with his so-called confessions, in which he agonizes before God with the task entrusted to him. Hosea, comparably, is called to embody in his family life God's struggle with his people. Habakkuk also has to come to grips with the coming judgment on Israel and find his way to a point where he can trust God, even though there is no fruit on the vine. Jonah is a narrative about formation, and as the story develops, we come to see that it is not really about Jonah but about Israel. Will she be formed to become compassionate like Yahweh, or will she resist the formation process?

Because God is the center of the Old Testament, so too is spirituality. In modernity much Old Testament study focuses on just about every aspect of the texts rather than the relationship with God that is at their heart. This is tragic, and we need to retrieve the Old Testament as a major part of the Christian Bible, with all its resources for formation.

Act 4: The Christ Event

Act 4 is the center of the Bible. The Christ event is an explosion of good news with light radiating in all directions. Jesus is sent by the Father and empowered by the Spirit to embody the kingdom of God in first-century Judea, to found the missional, new people of God, who will be called to bear witness to the good news of the kingdom in all nations. Not surprisingly, the New Testament is chock-full of data about spirituality.

First of all, note should be taken of Jesus' own spiritual practices.[27] Already as a boy, Jesus is aware of the temple as his Father's house. At the outset of his public ministry, he is led by the Spirit into the wilderness, where he fasts, is tempted by and resists Satan using his knowledge of Scripture, and in the process confirms his calling as that of the cross. Clearly, Jesus participated in the synagogue services and the regular feasts, the public worship of his day, but what is remarkable is his private devotion. Nowhere is this more to the fore than in Luke's Gospel, in which Jesus is referred to as praying seven times, seven being a symbol of the fullness and exemplary nature of his prayer life.[28] Luke shares with the other Gospels[29] an emphasis on Jesus' practice of withdrawing to lonely places in order to commune with his Father. What is unique to Luke is his emphasis on Jesus praying at crucial moments in the narrative of his public ministry (Lk 3:21; 5:16; 6:12; 9:18; 9:28; 11:1; 22:41). It is as Jesus is praying when he is baptized that the heavens are opened, the Spirit descends on him, and the Father makes his declaration from heaven. It is as Jesus is praying that the transfiguration occurs, and so on. The message could hardly be clearer: Jesus' mission moves forward at every step immersed in prayer. Prayer leads to the revelation of his purpose and mission. Little wonder that his disciples, Jews who had to pray from childhood, when they witnessed Jesus praying, came and asked him to

---

[27]Cf. Stephen C. Barton, *The Spirituality of the Gospels* (Eugene, OR: Wipf and Stock, 1992).

[28]See Craig G. Bartholomew and Robby Holt, "Prayer in/and the Drama of Redemption in Luke: Prayer and Exegetical Performance," in *Reading Luke: Interpretation, Reflection, Formation*, ed. Craig G. Bartholomew, et al., SAHS 6 (Grand Rapids: Zondervan, 2005), 350-75; L. Daniel Chrupcala, *Everyone Will See the Salvation of God: Studies in Lukan Theology*, Analecta 83, Studium Biblicum Franciscum (Milano: Edizioni Terra Santa, 2015), 201-36; Craig G. Bartholomew, *Jesus and Prayer in Luke* (Bellingham, WA: Lexham, 2016).

[29]In the Synoptics there are three parables about prayer and all occur in Luke: Lk 11:5-13; 18:1-8, 9-14. The latter two are mentioned only in Luke.

teach them to pray. As Chrupcala notes, "Luke . . . offers to the Christian community a precious aid to the *imitatio Christi*. Indeed, for him, Jesus' style of prayer is not a simple reflection of the historical Jesus tradition, even if it was very important for his Christological framework. It serves to outline also the paradigm of Christian prayer. . . . In the Lukan work, the Christian community is invited to contemplate the praying image of Jesus . . . in order to assimilate . . . his example in life (Acts)."[30]

As others have noted, the Lord's Prayer is eschatologically charged;[31] it is the prayer of and for the kingdom. At its heart is Jesus' induction of his disciples into a relationship with "Our Father in heaven," a relationship of great intimacy with the transcendent God. It evokes the goal of biblical spirituality as God's glory manifest in the world: "hallowed be your name." True spirituality is first of all about God and his glory, not first about our well-being. And the missional vision is utterly comprehensive: "your will be done, on earth as in heaven." There is no room here for a sacred/secular dichotomy between proclamation (evangelism) of the Word and obedience to the Word. This is an issue that has bedeviled evangelical discussions in mission and that came to the fore in and after the Lausanne Congress in 1974. Lausanne rightly affirmed both evangelism and sociopolitical involvement as constitutive of the church's mission, although Billy Graham contested this in a follow-up meeting and John Stott had to stand his ground against Graham on this issue.[32] The Manilla Manifesto more helpfully defines the mission of the church as the whole church taking the whole gospel to the whole world.[33] I say "more helpfully" because obedience to the Word is an indispensable part of evangelism, which becomes implausible if it does not take place in the context of the plausibility structure of lived Christianity.

The twelve disciples, modeled on the twelve tribes of Israel, form the foundation of the New Testament church. Jesus' strategy in this respect is

---

[30]Chrupcala, *Everyone Will See*, 201-2.

[31]See N. T. Wright, "The Lord's Prayer as a Paradigm for Christian Prayer," in *Into God's Presence: Prayer in the New Testament*, ed. Richard N. Longenecker (Grand Rapids: Eerdmans, 2001), 132-54; Brant Pietre, "The Lord's Prayer and the New Exodus," *Letter and Spirit* 2 (2006): 69-96.

[32]Timothy Dudley-Smith, *John Stott: A Global Ministry* (Leicester, UK: Inter-Varsity Press, 2001), 220-24.

[33]See "The Manila Manifesto," www.lausanne.org/content/manifesto/the-manila-manifesto.

noteworthy. He calls twelve to follow him and then disciples them inten-
sively for three years in order to prepare them for their ministries. It is
rightly recognized that the eyewitness testimony of the twelve underlies
the New Testament; what must not be forgotten is the formative experience for the twelve of living and ministering with Jesus during his public
ministry. Jesus instructs the public, but he also disciples the twelve. Leon
Morris, for example, suggests that much of the material unique to John's
Gospel comes from Jesus' personal teaching of the disciples.[34] If James's
brother John is the beloved disciple in John's Gospel, his formation is remarkable. He moves from being "Boanerges"—"son of thunder"—which
I take to mean that he had a short fuse and much unresolved anger, to the
disciple who reclines on Jesus' breast, a picture of remarkable, male intimacy. Following Jesus brought healing to John's unresolved issues in
relationships with others and himself.

In his remarkable work *Mimesis*, Erich Auerbach deals with the narrative in Mark of Peter's betrayal of Jesus to show how, under the influence of the incarnation, the Gospels bring something to life in literature
that Greco-Roman literature was unable to do. Auerbach asks why this
narrative generates in us the most serious sympathy.

> Because it portrays something which neither the poets nor the historians
> of antiquity ever set out to portray: the birth of a spiritual movement in the
> depths of the common people, from within the everyday occurrences of
> contemporary life, which thus assumes an importance it could never have
> assumed in antique literature. What we witness is the awakening of "a new
> heart and a new spirit." All this applies not only to Peter's denial but also to
> every other occurrence which is related in the New Testament. . . . Peter
> and the other characters in the New Testament are caught in a universal
> movement of the depths which at first remains almost entirely below the
> surface and only very gradually . . . emerges into the foreground of
> history. . . . What we see here is a world which on the one hand is entirely
> real, average, identifiable as to place, time and circumstances, but which on
> the other hand is shaken in its very foundations, is transforming and
> renewing itself before our eyes. For the New Testament authors who are

---

[34]Leon Morris, *The Gospel According to John*, rev. ed., NICNT (Grand Rapids: Eerdmans, 1995), 43-45.

their contemporaries, these occurrences on the plane of everyday life assume the importance of world-revolutionary events, as later on they will for everyone.[35]

In the context of the kingdom, a spirituality of the ordinary emerges in which life is charged with the grandeur of God.

The Gospels[36] conclude with the resurrection of Jesus and the Great Commission. In Matthew's version, making disciples of the nations is at the heart of the command, and we have seen just how central spirituality is to discipleship. The mission articulated in the Great Commission cannot be restricted to evangelism and the making of converts; the disciples are instructed to make more disciples and to teach those disciples to obey all Jesus commanded them. Jesus also assures the disciples of his ongoing presence with them (Mt 28:20). In Luke 24:45-49, Jesus rehearses his story—"the Messiah will suffer and rise from the dead"—on the basis of which repentance and forgiveness of sins will be preached to all nations starting at Jerusalem. Biblically, "repentance" involves a turning back to God for forgiveness of sins so that one can be reconciled to God. Relationship with God is once again central.

John's Gospel articulates the Great Commission specifically in terms of sending: "As the Father has sent me, I am sending you" (Jn 20:21). This evokes the continuity of the ministry of the disciples with that of Jesus, so that Acts is rightly described as the acts of Jesus by the Spirit through his apostles. We have seen how Jesus' being sent included prayer as a central dimension of his mission. And so it is with Jesus' followers. Mission is *missio Dei*, and it is vacuous without an ever-deepening relationship with God.

Act 5: The Great Time of World Mission

Acts is volume 2 of Luke's work. It is the connecting link between the Gospels and the Epistles; indeed, the latter would make no sense without Acts. The Epistles result from the mission of the church emerging from the

---

[35]Erich Auerbach, *Mimesis: The Representation of Reality in Western Literature*, Princeton Classics (1953; reprint, Princeton, NJ: Princeton University Press, 2003), 43.

[36]This may not be true of Mark since the earliest manuscripts do not have Mark 16:9-20.

outpouring of the Spirit at Pentecost; they are in fact missional documents. C. K. Barrett observes of Acts 16–28 that they "may without exaggeration be regarded as a missionary biography of Paul."[37] And, just as prayer is central to Luke's Gospel, so too it is central to Acts.[38] The Spirit directs the mission of the early church, and just as Acts is awash with the Spirit, so too it is awash with prayer, as we would expect. Luke's Gospel begins in the temple with prayer (Lk 1:10, 13) and it ends in the temple with all the disciples there, praising God continually. Similarly, Acts opens with the disciples in the upper room praying constantly (Acts 1:14), and a disciple to replace Judas as an apostle is elected following prayer (Acts 1:24-25).

At Pentecost, Peter preaches the sermon that will found the early church, with about three thousand being converted. The response of this group is notable: "They devoted themselves to the apostles' teaching and to fellowship, to the breaking of bread and to prayer.... They broke bread in their homes and ate together with glad and sincere hearts, praising God and enjoying the favor of all the people" (Acts 2:42, 46-47).

Key elements of Christian spirituality are immediately manifest. The communal dimension is front and center, as is the Eucharist, if we understand "the breaking of bread" to refer to communion. Their spirituality is also one of the Word (the apostles' teaching) and prayer. One might expect to read that they devoted themselves to the Old Testament, and doubtless they could not attend to the teaching of the apostles without doing so. However, the Old Testament was now fulfilled in Jesus, and thus they rightly devoted themselves to the teaching of the apostles because it was there they found trustworthy witness to Jesus. And all of this returned them again and again to prayer,[39] to living communion with the triune God.

---

[37]C. K. Barrett, *The Acts of the Apostles: A Shorter Commentary* (New York: Continuum, 2002), xxxi.

[38]Cf. Acts 1:14, 24; 2:42; 3:1; 4:24; 6:4, 6; 7:59; 8:15, 22, 24; 9:11, 40; 10:2, 4, 30, 31; 11:5; 12:5, 12, 13, 16; 13:3; 14:23; 16:13, 16; 20:36; 21:5; 22:17; 26:29; 27:29; 28:8. Joel Green, "Persevering Together in Prayer: The Significance of Prayer in the Acts of the Apostles," in Longenecker, *Into God's Presence*, 184, notes that "over thirty times in the Acts of the Apostles, Luke characterizes Jesus' followers as being at prayer or narrates episodes of prayer. These scenes are most prevalent in the first half of the book, as though, having established a pattern of pervasive prayer, Luke has no need to repeat himself again and again."

[39]In Acts 2:42 the Greek reads "the prayers" and as Joel Green, "Persevering Together," loc 2481-82, notes, "Since these first believers are depicted by Luke as Jewish, we may justifiably assume that 'the prayers' refers to the patterns of prayer associated with Jews during this period."

Such devotion to prayer manifests the early church as a continuation of Jesus' ministry. Green notes in relation to Acts 1:14,

> Although taught to pray (cf. Lk 11:1-13) and instructed to pray (cf. Lk 22:40, 46), heretofore in the narrative of Luke-Acts the disciples have not been depicted as persons who engaged in prayer. On the other hand, one of the characteristic activities of Jesus was prayer, and throughout the Third Gospel prayer had been the means by which Jesus' identity was manifested, God's plans were revealed, and people aligned themselves with God's plans. Prayer on the part of Jesus' followers—"especially the habitual prayer reported in this text as characterizing the disciples"—is, therefore, clearly of consequence.[40]

One could say that this early group manifested life as God intended it to be. A major difference that Pentecost makes is that the disciples start to develop prayer lives like that of Jesus. There is deep commitment to one another to ensure that everyone has what they need (Acts 2:45). The community is christocentric in its devotion to the apostles' teaching and its living faith manifest in prayer and praise. Such life is inherently plausible and missional. We read that they enjoyed "the favor of all the people. And the Lord added to their number daily those who were being saved" (Acts 2:47). Here we see what David Bosch has described as one of the great needs in contemporary mission, namely, plausibility structure.[41] Christians need to live in such a way that their words are inherently plausible. As St. Francis is supposed to have said, Preach the gospel at all times, and if necessary, speak! Similarly, in 1 Corinthians 14, Paul encourages a form of worship such that when the unbeliever comes along he or she is convicted of sin and brought to worship God, proclaiming, "God is really among you!" (1 Cor 14:24-25). Genuine worship and spirituality are inherently plausible and attractive, without necessarily being intentionally missional. Eugene Peterson perceptively asserts,

> I want to simplify your lives. When others are telling you to read more, I want to tell you to read less; when others are telling you to do more, I want

---

[40]Green, "Persevering in Prayer," loc. 2470-75.

[41]David Bosch, *Believing in the Future: Towards a Missiology of Western Culture* (Harrisonburg, PA: Trinity Press, 1995).

to tell you to do less. The world does not need more of you; it needs more of God. Your friends do not need more of you; they need more of God. And you don't need more of you; you need more of God.[42]

Luke's Gospel emphasizes the role of the temple as a house of prayer (cf. Lk 1:8-23; 23; 2:27-32, 36-38; 18:10-14; 19:46; 24:53), and in Acts the temple also functions in this way (cf. Acts 2:47; 3:1; 21:20-26; 22:17-21). However, there is continuity and discontinuity with Judaism. Paul's testimony about God speaking to him while he was praying in the temple in Jerusalem is decisive in this respect (cf. Acts 22:17-21). As Green observes,

> Here is a fail-proof apologetic for Paul's mission. It was in the Jerusalem temple, while praying, that Paul received the divine mandate to take the gospel to the Gentile world. What is equally clear, though, is that this experience of prayer in the temple served to undermine for Paul the centrality of the temple for faith and life. Thus a form of continuity with Judaism—that is, prayer to God in the temple in Jerusalem—has resulted in a divine mandate that subverts the central role of the temple for Jewish life.[43]

A major indication of this discontinuity is the pattern of praying to Jesus.

Prayer plays a central role in Acts as the mission of the early church unfolds. Leaders are appointed after prayer, persecution and hardship are endured through prayer, prayer accompanies innovations in mission, and salvation is achieved through prayer. Green rightly notes of the early Christians, "As people of prayer, they serve an agenda that is not their own but God's, act as instruments of God who exercise God-given authority, and minister with the confidence of those who have learned from their leader the boundless graciousness and faithfulness of God."[44] In Acts, prayer is thus a means by which God's purposes are revealed and grasped, and the means by which his people align themselves with the *missio Dei*.

---

[42]Eugene H. Peterson, *Subversive Spirituality* (Grand Rapids: Eerdmans, 1997), 30.
[43]Green, "Persevering Together," 187.
[44]Ibid., loc. 2594-95.

Prayer and Missional Communities

If Acts provides us with an insight into the integrality of spirituality and mission, so do the New Testament Epistles. Once churches were established, letters became a major way of communicating with them and providing them with ongoing pastoral care. Not surprisingly, the New Testament epistles are awash with prayer. Richard Longenecker, for example, points out that "terms having to do with prayer appear more frequently in Paul's letters than in the writings of any other New Testament author."[45] Tom Wright evocatively and rightly notes that,

> if we are to paraphrase Paul's very soul, to study his heart in its pilgrimage to the promised inheritance, to catch his deepest aims and intentions at the moment when, by his own account, the divine breath was groaning in him and the Heart-Searcher himself was listening to the resultant inarticulate desires, we must recognize in him a kind of tune which all things hear and fear, the deep and constant gospel-inspired activity which, in form as well as in substance, might have seemed folly to the Greeks and a scandal to the Jews. We have at several points noticed Paul's prayers, not simply as pious attachments to the outside of his theological or practical teaching but as their very heart. This is the place to end, and perhaps to begin.[46]

Longenecker explores the Jewish background to Paul's prayers and identifies three major components in them: adoration, thanksgiving, and prayers for the readers. In a real sense, the Pauline epistles are enclosed in prayer. They invariably begin with a salutation along the lines of, "Grace and peace to you . . ." and end with some form of benediction. Paul is intensely aware that God is the great missionary and that the life and development of the churches depends on God.

Intriguingly, as Longenecker observes, it is often hard to determine the precise boundaries of prayers within Paul's letters. Ephesians 1:3-23 is a good example of this, in which praise flows into reflection on what God has done for us in Christ, which moves on to Paul's description of his

---

[45]Richard N. Longenecker, "Prayer in the Pauline Epistles," in Longenecker, *Into God's Presence*, loc. 2723-24.
[46]Wright, *Paul and the Faithfulness of God*, 1516.

prayer for the "Ephesians."[47] In Ephesians 1:17-18, the word *know* occurs twice, and clearly it involves far more than knowing "about." Paul is concerned that his readers might "know him [the God of our Lord Jesus Christ, the glorious Father] better."

There is an immense amount of material relating to prayer and thus spirituality in the New Testament,[48] and we cannot begin to excavate it all here. Intriguingly, the Bible ends with a prayer in Revelation 22:20: "Amen, Come Lord Jesus." Richard Bauckham notes that

> the prayer for the parousia in 22:20b, therefore, encompasses and completes all other prayers. It is, as it were, the most that can be prayed. It asks for everything—for all that God purposes for and promises to his whole creation in the end. In the understanding that this everything is to be expected of Jesus, who declares himself "the Alpha and the Omega, the first and the last, the beginning and the end" (22:13), it takes the form of the simple entreaty to the Lord Jesus to come.[49]

Conclusion

We live amidst a welcome renaissance of interest in and practice of spirituality among evangelicals. Alas, I have heard it said that spirituality has given back prayer to evangelicals and taken away the Bible. It is indeed possible for spirituality to become separated from Scripture, but this is deeply ironic when we consider just how central spirituality is to the Bible and to mission. Biblical studies has not always helped, in light of its tendency to do just about everything with the Bible other than use all its resources to direct us to the central character of the Bible, namely God, and relationship with him.

Spirituality and the Word are inseparable in biblical spirituality. The first group of believers in Acts is exemplary in this respect, devoting themselves to the teaching of the apostles and to prayer. Of course, for this relationship to function effectively, we need a biblical hermeneutic aimed at

---

[47]It is possible that Ephesians was a circular letter to several churches in different cities. On Ephesians 1 see Wright, *Paul and the Faithfulness of God*, 1517-18.

[48]See Longenecker, "Prayer in the Pauline Epistles."

[49]Richard Bauckham, "Prayer in the Book of Revelation," in Longenecker, *Into God's Presence*, 270.

listening for God's address through his Word.[50] And we need a type of spirituality that is rooted and grounded in Scripture.[51]

At the heart of Scripture, the Christian life, spirituality, and mission is the glory of God. Romans 11:36 aptly expresses this:

> For from him and through him and for him are all things.
> To him be the glory forever! Amen.

Mission will only be effective and honor God insofar as we are living ever more deeply into God. In a Catholic document on the consecrated life, we read that

> John Paul II reminds consecrated persons that living spiritually means first of all starting afresh from the person of Christ, true God and true man, present in his Word, "the first source of all spirituality." . . . "It is especially necessary that listening to the Word of God should become a life-giving encounter . . . which draws from the biblical text the living Word which questions, directs and shapes our lives."[52]

Later in the same document, it is rightly noted,

> An authentic spiritual life requires that everyone, in all the diverse vocations, regularly dedicate, every day, appropriate times to enter deeply into silent conversation with him by whom they know they are loved, to share their very lives with him and to receive enlightenment to continue on their daily journey. It is an exercise which requires fidelity, because we are constantly being bombarded by the estrangements and excesses which come from today's society, especially from the means of communication. At times fidelity to personal and liturgical prayer will require a true effort not to allow oneself to be swallowed up in frenetic activism.[53]

It is as we are living ever more deeply into God that we will hear his call to mission, as we accompany him in his work in our world.

---

[50] Cf. Craig G. Bartholomew, *Introducing Biblical Hermeneutics: A Comprehensive Framework for Hearing God in Scripture* (Grand Rapids: Baker Academic, 2015).

[51] Cf. J. Magrassi, *Praying the Bible: An Introduction to Lectio Divina*, trans. E. Hagman (Collegeville, MN: Liturgical Press, 1998).

[52] *Starting Afresh from Christ: A Renewed Commitment to Consecrated Life in the Third Millennium* (Sherbrook, Canada: Médiaspaul, 2002), 45-46.

[53] Ibid., 49.

3

Missional Spirituality *and* Global Missions

Susan Booth

"COVER THE EARTH." The logo of an international paint company combines this motto with the image of an upturned can pouring red paint over all the globe. The prophet Habakkuk captures God's mission with similar imagery: "For the earth will be filled with the knowledge of the glory of the LORD as the waters cover the sea" (Hab 2:14). Missional advance flows from God's presence in the midst of his people. Authentic spirituality should therefore include a missional dimension that is global in scope. A biblical understanding of missional spirituality must include a global focus.

Missional Spirituality and the Tabernacling Presence of God

The tabernacling presence of God in the midst of his people is the *goal* and *means* of mission; it is also the essence of Christian spirituality.[1] Because the relational

---

[1] This chapter defines the tabernacling presence of God as the special relational presence of God at the nexus of God, people, and place. For a more in-depth survey, see

presence of God is the linchpin that holds both of these concepts together, authentic spirituality and missional thought are integrally related to one another. A cursory survey of God's tabernacling presence at key junctures across the canon reveals both missional and spiritual dimensions that are global in scope.

God's presence in Eden. From the beginning, the tabernacling presence of God has been central to God's creative work and his expansive plan for the whole of creation. God places Adam and Eve in Eden, a garden sanctuary where the first humans enjoy spiritual communion with God who "was walking in the garden" in their midst (Gen 3:8).[2] God intends to fill the earth with people who properly acknowledge his glory. The world is not simply a habitation suitable for humans. It is "designed to be filled, flooded, [and] drenched" with the presence of God himself.[3] God's first recorded words to humanity are a global commission: fill the earth with worshipers who govern creation in his name (Gen 1:28).[4] Because of Adam and Eve's sin, however, God expels the couple from his unmediated presence in Eden. God's original purpose then shifts into a rescue mission: to redeem his people and to restore the world as a sanctuary where he might dwell in their midst.

God's presence with the patriarchs. Genesis 12:1-3 introduces God's redemptive plan to dwell with his people throughout earth. God promises to bless Abraham with a great nation of descendants and to bless all the peoples of the earth through his offspring. Since this global promise is ultimately fulfilled in Abraham's descendant, Jesus Christ, the apostle Paul labels it "the gospel in advance" (Gal 3:8). In a similar vein, Christopher Wright calls God's command to Abraham—"Go . . . and be a blessing"—the "Great Commission" in advance.[5] Abraham believes God, and the Lord

---

Susan Maxwell Booth, *The Tabernacling Presence of God: Mission and Gospel Witness* (Eugene, OR: Wipf and Stock, 2015).

[2]G. K. Beale, *The Temple and the Church's Mission: A Biblical Theology of the Dwelling Place of God*, New Studies in Biblical Theology 17 (Downers Grove, IL: InterVarsity Press, 2004), 66-67, explains that this same Hebrew verbal form of *hithallek* also describes God's presence in the midst of his people in the tabernacle in Lev 26:12 and 2 Sam 7:6-7.

[3]N. T. Wright, *Surprised by Hope: Rethinking Heaven, the Resurrection, and the Mission of the Church* (New York: HarperOne, 2008), 102.

[4]Beale, *The Temple and the Church's Mission*, 117.

[5]Christopher J. H. Wright, *The Mission of God: Unlocking the Bible's Grand Narrative* (Downers Grove, IL: IVP Academic, 2006), 214. This global scope is underscored repeatedly (Gen 18:18; 22:18; 26:4).

appears to him at Shechem, where the patriarch builds an altar and worships. As the patriarchs travel throughout the land, they continue this spiritual pattern of building altars and calling on the name of the Lord. Yet, in this encounter, we see again the fundamental biblical relationship between authentic spirituality and a global commission. Because Abraham's worship stands in contrast to that of the surrounding pagan religions, Allen Ross calls him a "witnessing worshiper."[6]

God's presence in the tabernacle. After God calls Moses to deliver his people from slavery in Egypt, he leads them to Sinai, where the Lord gives Moses instructions for building the tabernacle. These instructions include commandments for how they are to live with God's presence in their midst and how they are to fulfill God's mission by being a distinct, spiritual community who will display his glory before the nations. But while Moses is receiving the law from God, the Israelites jeopardize the blessing of having God's tabernacling presence when they bow down before a golden calf (Ex 33:5). Moses responds to this situation by praying that the Lord would not remove his presence. Moses' prayer reveals the connection between divine presence and the spiritual and missional vitality of God's people (Ex 33:15-16). The Lord shows mercy to Moses and Israel. He restores his presence and pursues the divine mission to create a people who manifest God's presence and display his glory before the nations. Once the tabernacle is complete, the Lord's presence takes up residence in the center of his people (Ex 40:34).

God's presence in the contrast community. As a contrast community living on display before the nations, the Israelites are to showcase the Lord's presence and his glory by obeying the commands of his law. His presence among them calls for a holistic holiness that extends from their food and clothing to their sexual and business practices. It affects how they treat the marginalized and even how they treat the land. Their obedience, worship, and praise are meant to magnify the mighty works of God before a watching world, causing them to marvel

---

[6]Allen Ross, *Recalling the Hope of Glory: Biblical Worship from the Garden to the New Creation* (Grand Rapids: Kregel, 2006), 145.

at God's presence tabernacling among them. The focus of God's commands is not on a legal system but rather on "the prophetic attunement to a living power which surrounds and penetrates the wholeness of human existence."[7] God's unique presence among his people is the source of authentic spirituality for them and source of their capacity to be a witness to the nations. In Deuteronomy 4, Moses explains the link between obeying God's commands and Israel's mediatorial role to the nations. He says,

> Observe them carefully, for this will show your wisdom and understanding to the nations, who will hear about all these decrees and say, "Surely this great nation is a wise and understanding people." What other nation is so great as to have their gods near them the way the LORD our God is near us whenever we pray to him? . . . Acknowledge and take to heart this day that the LORD is God in heaven above and on the earth below. *There is no other.* (Deut 4:6-7, 39; emphasis added)

Those who dwell in the presence of the one true God have an obligation to make him known to others. Israel's spirituality through obedience thus contains an embedded missional impulse.[8]

This same missional impulse reverberates throughout David's song of thanksgiving with which he welcomed the ark into Jerusalem:

> Sing to the LORD, all the earth;
> proclaim his salvation from day to day.
> Declare his glory among the nations,
> his marvelous deeds among all peoples.
> For great is the LORD, and most worthy of praise. . . .
> For all the gods of the nations are idols,
> but the LORD made the heavens. (1 Chron 16:23-26)

The remainder of David's hymn is a gloriously global summons to worship, commanding all creation to join in worship of the one true God—every people and every place.

---

[7]Samuel Terrien, *The Elusive Presence: Toward a New Biblical Theology*, Religious Perspectives 26 (San Francisco: Harper & Row, 1978), 129-30.

[8]When the Israelites later failed to display God's glory, the Lord delivered the ark into the hands of the Philistines, and he himself displayed his glory in their sight.

God's presence in the temple. Sometime after David's celebration over the ark's arrival into Jerusalem, David becomes uncomfortable with the fact that while he dwells in a house of cedar, the ark of God dwells in a humble tent (2 Sam 7:2). He proposes to address the problem by building a dwelling place for the Lord. Reminding David that the mission belongs to him, God refuses David's offer, pointing out that in all his "moving about" in a tent,[9] never once had he asked for a house of cedar for himself. God promises instead to build a "house" for David through his offspring—a dynasty, a throne, and a kingdom that will endure forever (2 Sam 7:12-13). While the Lord concedes that David's son would eventually build a physical house for his name, the focus is on the dynastic covenant with David rather than the future temple.

The eventual construction of the temple highlights the intertwined themes of God's presence, spirituality, and mission. When Solomon consecrates the temple, he declares that it is a place for God's presence: "I have indeed built a magnificent temple for you, a place for you to dwell forever" (1 Kings 8:13). At the same time, he recognizes that God does not need a structure built by human hands: "But will God really dwell on earth? The heavens, even the highest heaven, cannot contain you. How much less this temple I have built!" (1 Kings 8:27). Kneeling in prayer, Solomon asks God to hear the prayers of his people, to forgive their sins, and to amend the consequences of their sins. He pleads with the people to be completely devoted to the Lord. As always, God's presence in their midst requires cleansing from sin and total spiritual consecration. Solomon's prayer also acknowledges that there are significant missional implications for the sanctuary. He requests that the Lord answer foreigners' prayers directed toward the temple "so that all the peoples of the earth may know your name and fear you, as do your own people Israel" (1 Kings 8:41-43). Then, after the priests set the ark in its place, the presence of the Lord descends on the temple, filling it with his glory. God's tabernacling presence among his people is the source of authentic spirituality and the means of fulfilling his mission.

---

[9] Literally, "walking back and forth"—an echo of God's presence in Eden (2 Sam 7:6; cf. Gen 3:8).

Isaiah also links the themes of spirituality and mission when he recounts his vision of the Lord in the heavenly temple, surrounded by seraphim who proclaim, "Holy, holy, holy is the LORD Almighty; the whole earth is full of his glory" (Is 6:3; cf. 11:9). Their anthem praises God's character and echoes his mission that every person on the planet should know his glory. These themes also are present in Isaiah's own spiritual experience and calling. For instance, Isaiah's sin reduces him to despair before God's holy presence, but the Lord graciously cleanses him with a coal from the altar. Isaiah then immediately responds to God's missional heart cry: "'Whom shall I send? And who will go for us?' . . . 'Here am I. Send me!'" (Is 6:8). Isaiah's final chapter concludes with an image of survivors from all nations, assembled in spiritual worship before the Lord, whose glorious presence fills the new heavens and earth.

Ezekiel also receives a series of visions regarding the temple. The first vision pictures God's glory enthroned above wheels within wheels, underscoring the truth that the God of Israel is not bound to the temple in Jerusalem; rather he is sovereign over the entire earth. Ezekiel's second vision depicts the rampant idolatry occurring within the temple precincts back in Jerusalem. In a reversal of the tabernacle/temple dedication accounts, the glory of God's tabernacling presence departs from the temple, making a way for the army of Nebuchadnezzar and the judgment of God. Daniel Block observes, "Nothing, not even the temple, is more sacred to God than a sanctified people."[10] In spite of God's repeated warnings, the nation remains entrenched in their sin; the Lord therefore refuses to dwell in their midst. Since the Israelites fail to live as a people who display his glory, then God displays it himself by judging his own people in the sight of the nations, so that "then all people will know that I [am] the LORD" (Ezek 21:5). The inconceivable occurs; news comes that Jerusalem and the temple were destroyed (Ezek 33:21). However, God had not abandoned his people forever. The book of Ezekiel closes with a third vision of a massive temple complex so large that it resembles a city where the Lord takes up residence: "Son of man, this is the place of my throne and the

---

[10]Daniel I. Block, *The Book of Ezekiel: Chapters 1-24*, New International Commentary on the Old Testament (Grand Rapids: Eerdmans, 1997), 83.

place for the soles of my feet. This is where I will live among the Israelites forever" (Ezek 43:7).

The rebuilt temple does not begin to approximate Ezekiel's vision—or for that matter, Zechariah's vision of an expanded Jerusalem, overflowing with a multitude of "many nations" who have joined themselves to the Lord who dwells in their midst (Zech 2:11). Zechariah 8:21-23 describes how this multicultural assembly might come together:

> The inhabitants of one city will go to another and say, "Let us go at once to entreat the LORD and seek the LORD Almighty. I myself am going." And many peoples and powerful nations will come to Jerusalem to seek the LORD Almighty and to entreat him. This is what the LORD Almighty says: "In those days ten people from all languages and nations will take firm hold of one Jew by the hem of his robe and say, 'Let us go with you, because we have heard that God is with you.'"

Firmly grasping the corner tassels of a Jew's garment conveys a sense of urgency and passion, as well as submission. The passage, which reveals "an ever-broadening circle of people" included in God's redemptive scheme, "makes Zechariah one of the most universalistic of all the prophets."[11] The number ten signifies completeness and highlights the universality of this pilgrimage of people who speak every language on earth. Individual worshipers attract those from other nations to join the worshiping community. There is a strong sense of both centripetal and centrifugal movement. The good news will cover the earth, and the presence of God displayed in the lives of his people will attract others, who are compelled to go to distant cities, imploring still others to join them. This passage directly links the missional expansion of the community of faith with an authentic spirituality that offers proof of the God who is vibrantly present in the midst of his people.

God's presence in Jesus. The Gospels record a startling development in the biblical theme of God's tabernacling presence. No longer is the meeting place of God and man found in a place or man-made structure.

---

[11]Carol L. Meyers and Eric M. Meyers, *Haggai, Zechariah 1-8*, Old Testament Library (Philadelphia: Westminster, 1984), 441.

Instead, it is found in the God-man, Jesus Christ—the pioneer of God's mission and the source of Christian spirituality. The Gospel of John reveals that Jesus fulfills the temple, as the place for God to be with his people. God the Son literally takes up residence in the midst of his people in a tent of human flesh: "The Word became flesh and made his dwelling [tabernacled] among us. We have seen his glory, the glory of the one and only Son, who came from the Father, full of grace and truth" (Jn 1:14). When Nathanael hails Jesus as the Son of God and King of Israel, Jesus commends him and says, "You will see 'heaven open, and the angels of God ascending and descending on' the Son of Man"—a clear echo of Jacob's dream at Bethel, "the House of God" (Jn 1:51). Jesus defends his right to clear the temple with his cryptic statement, "Destroy this temple, and I will raise it again in three days" (Jn 2:19). After his death and resurrection, Jesus' disciples finally realize that "the temple he had spoken of was his body" (Jn 2:21). Jesus not only fulfills the meaning of the tabernacle and the temple, but he is the very reason those man-made structures were ever built.[12]

The tabernacling presence of God in Christ provides for a rich spirituality for his disciples and prompts them to missional activity. In John 13–17, Jesus explains what will happen when he is no longer physically present with them. The Father will send the Holy Spirit as a Helper who will dwell in them. Furthermore, the Father and the Son will make their spiritual home with those who love and obey Jesus. In other words, Jesus' followers will experience a mutual indwelling that involves all three persons of the Trinity: "On that day you will realize that I am in my Father, and you are in me, and I am in you" (Jn 14:20; cf. Jn 14:16-17, 23). Jesus also explains that his departure is to their advantage because the Spirit will enable the disciples in their own mission. The Holy Spirit teaches believers and helps them recall Jesus' own teaching; thus, he is linked to their witness (Jn 14:26; 15:26-27). The God who takes on human flesh dwells with God's people through the Spirit, making them agents of gospel mission.

---

[12] Edmund P. Clowney, "The Final Temple," *Westminster Theological Journal* 35 (1973): 177.

This privilege of divine indwelling comes with the responsibility of cultivating an authentic spirituality, a state that results in a missional lifestyle. Jesus explains that his followers must spiritually abide in him just as a branch abides in the vine—a metaphor that illustrates the necessity of their absolute dependence on the indwelling Spirit. Because the Spirit of God is present in the lives of believers, obedience should flow from the wellspring of their love for Jesus. The one who steadfastly abides in Jesus cannot help but bear much fruit, because fruit-bearing is the spiritual mark of a true disciple (Jn 15:5, 16). D. A. Carson explains that "this fruit is nothing less than the outcome of persevering dependence on the vine, driven by faith, embracing all of the believer's life and the product of his witness."[13] Carson maintains that no matter how comprehensive the nature of the fruit, "the focus on evangelism and mission is truly central."[14] Just as the life of the vine courses through the branches, Jesus' mission will spiritually flow into the hearts and lives of his disciples as well.

God's presence in the church. Jesus' ongoing presence with his people for the purpose of mission is also the theme of his final postresurrection command—a worldwide commission with an explicit dimension of spirituality: "But you will receive power when the Holy Spirit comes on you; and you will be my witnesses in Jerusalem, and in all Judea and Samaria, and to the ends of the earth" (Acts 1:8). A few days later the Holy Spirit falls on Jesus' followers, recalling the descent of God's glory on Sinai, the tabernacle, and the temple. G. K. Beale contends that this event marks the descent of the eschatological temple from heaven: "God's tabernacling presence descended in the form of the Spirit, making those identified with Christ into part of that temple."[15] This outpouring of the Spirit occurs at Pentecost when large numbers of Diaspora Jews had gathered in Jerusalem from the corners of the earth, and each person hears the gospel proclaimed in his or her heart language. Not only is this miracle a sign of the Spirit's presence and power; it also serves the purpose of spreading the gospel on a global scale from the moment of the church's inception.

---

[13]D. A. Carson, *The Gospel According to John* (Grand Rapids: Eerdmans, 1991), 519.

[14]Ibid., 523.

[15]G. K. Beale, "The Descent of the Eschatological Temple in the Form of the Spirit at Pentecost," *Tyndale Bulletin* 56, no. 2 (2005): 83.

Throughout the book of Acts, the presence and power of the indwelling Spirit directs the mission of God as the church expands across the globe.

The New Testament epistles also bring together the themes of spirituality and mission by describing the church as a God-filled temple, both corporately (1 Cor 3:16-17) and individually (1 Cor 6:19-20).[16] Just as the glory of God filled the former earthly shrines, so also the Spirit-filled followers of Christ are to display God's glory. The indwelling presence of the Spirit calls believers to live holy lives as a contrast community (2 Cor 6:14-15). Believers can have a profound effect on the watching world. Paul tells the Corinthians that if an unbeliever enters the orderly worship of the gathered church, he will hear the prophetic word of God and come under conviction (1 Cor 14:24-25). God's tabernacling presence on display in the midst of his Spirit-filled people will have a missional effect.

Paul explains in Ephesians that God's tabernacling presence sets the church apart as a Spirit-filled community that exists in a missional context. Christ has abolished the enmity that existed for so long between Gentiles and Jews. He gives both access to God by the Spirit and makes both "members of [God's] household" (Eph 2:18-19). God's worldwide mission to people from every ethnic background and social standing results in all the saints being built together into a sanctuary for God's Spirit to dwell in. Paul commands the Ephesian believers to be filled continually with the Spirit, evidenced in their speaking, singing, giving thanks, and mutual submission (Eph 5:18-21) and obvious in their households and workplaces (Eph 5:22–6:9). The proper result of God's Spirit dwelling with them should lead to joyful, ordered, and holy lives that contrast sharply with the world around them.

God's presence in the new creation. The hope of God's tabernacling presence with his people culminates in the final chapters of Revelation (Rev 21:2, 9; cf. Rev 19:6-9). No longer is God's dwelling place high above his people. His dwelling place is now with his peoples (Rev 21:3).

---

[16]See also 1 Pet 2:5-12, where Peter describes the church as "living stones" being built into "a spiritual house." Peter applies several former descriptors of Israel to these Gentile believers, reminding them that the spiritual transformation in their own lives would compel them to proclaim God's marvelous deeds with others.

Beale points out that whereas the Old Testament prophecies refer in the singular to the "people" among whom God dwells, John's use of "peoples" highlights the inclusion of many nations among the redeemed people of God.[17] Indeed, God has redeemed people from every corner of the globe (Rev 5:9). This multicultural multitude will fall on their faces in worship, and the One sitting on the throne will "spread His tabernacle over them" (Rev 7:15 NASB). This vision of God's tabernacling presence dwelling in the midst of his sanctuary people gathered from all corners of the earth is the ultimate fulfillment of God's mission in the world.

God's presence, spirituality, and mission. This brief survey of the Bible shows that God's relational presence in the midst of his people is both the goal and the means of the mission of God.[18] From creation to new creation, God's mission includes the nations of the world. God's first spoken words call humanity to fill the whole earth with worshipers. Jesus' last spoken words call his disciples on a global mission to make disciples of all the nations. The Bible closes with a universal invitation to all who are thirsty to come drink the water of life (Rev 22:17). The Spirit extends the invitation through the testimony of God's people. Jesus' return is imminent. Until then, the mission of the church is to expand the knowledge of God's glory globally. God has equipped the church to accomplish this task by filling them with his presence through the Spirit.

The presence of God in the midst of his people is the essence of authentic spirituality. Richard Foster claims that God's intention for human life is the "Immanuel Principle," that is, for his dwelling place to be with humanity. Foster observes, "This dynamic, pulsating, *with-God* life is on nearly every page of the Bible." God's oft-repeated promise, "I am with you," naturally begs the personal, existential question: "Will you be with me?"[19] Foster calls God's people to know this truth experientially. He explains, "[In meditation] we create the emotional and spiritual space which

---

[17]G. K. Beale, *The Book of Revelation: A Commentary on the Greek Text*, New International Greek Testament Commentary (Grand Rapids: Eerdmans, 1999), 1047.

[18]See John Ryan Lister, "'The Lord Your God Is in Your Midst': The Presence of God and the Means and End of Redemptive History" (PhD diss., Southern Baptist Theological Seminary, 2010).

[19]Richard J. Foster, *Life with God: Reading the Bible for Spiritual Transformation* (New York: HarperOne, 2008), 7-8.

allows Christ to construct an inner sanctuary in the heart. . . . We who have turned our lives over to Christ need to know how very much he longs to eat with us, to commune with us. He desires a perpetual Eucharistic feast in the inner sanctuary of the heart."[20]

In a similar fashion, Dallas Willard argues that a primary purpose of God dwelling with his people is for their spiritual vitality as a community of believers. He says, "The purpose of God with human history is nothing less than to bring out of it . . . an eternal community of those who were once thought to be just 'ordinary human beings.'"[21] God's intention since the beginning of time is to make his home in this community where he will be its "prime sustainer and most glorious inhabitant."[22] But the reality of life lived under God's rule is not reserved for eternity alone. God intends for us to experience spiritual life overflowing toward mission. Willard says, "The kingdom of the heavens, *from the practical point of view in which we all must live,* is simply our experience of Jesus' continual interaction with us in history and throughout the days, hours, and moments of our earthly existence."[23] Willard contends that discipleship—"real-life apprenticeship to Jesus"[24]—and the practice of spiritual disciplines enable believers to live out the reality of Christ's dwelling—their missional calling—in the midst of his people. He says, "This community will, in its way, pervade the entire created realm and share in the government of it."[25]

Integrating Authentic Spirituality and Mission

Since the presence of God is the cornerstone for both authentic spirituality and a missional perspective, these two concepts dovetail closely. That, however, is not readily apparent. Those involved in the missional and spirituality conversation cite Matthew 28:18-20 as central to their thought, but

---

[20]Richard J. Foster, *Celebration of Discipline: The Path to Spiritual Growth,* rev. ed. (San Francisco: Harper-Collins, 1978, 1988), 20.

[21]Dallas Willard, *The Divine Conspiracy: Rediscovering Our Hidden Life in God* (San Francisco: Harper-Collins, 1997), 385-86.

[22]Ibid.

[23]Ibid., 280.

[24]Ibid., 281.

[25]Ibid., 385-86.

they read this passage through different lenses. Missional thinkers like Wilbert Shenk see and highlight mission: "The Great Commission institutionalizes mission as the *raison d'être*, the controlling norm of the church."[26] Spiritual formation advocates like Foster underscore a different phrase in the Great Commission: "Here it is absolutely clear what 'spiritual formation' is all about: disciples are 'to obey everything that I have commanded you,' and to teach others to do the same."[27] James Wilhoit concludes, "Spiritual formation is *the* task of the church. Period."[28] Lamenting the pervasive nominalism found in today's churches, Willard describes this same phrase as "the Great *Omission* from the Great Commission."[29] Instead of making disciples, he argues, the church has made converts and has subsequently failed "to teach them how to live as Christ lived and taught."[30] Although these authors' corrective for inadequate discipleship is commendable and sorely needed, the corresponding emphasis on mission must not be neglected. Authentic spirituality must be integrated with missional expansion.

It is helpful to picture this integration as a spatial relationship where spirituality is a vertical axis that transects the horizontal plane of mission in this visible world. There is always the temptation to emphasize one over the other. Perhaps the default perspective is to be so consumed with life in this world—much less mission—that one simply fails to glance "up" at God. Advocates for spiritual formation have convincingly demonstrated the value of spiritual disciplines for developing authentic spirituality. In some sense, the disciplines provide a spiritual lens that helps disciples perceive the presence of God in all aspects of life. Yet, because the transcendent is not readily perceptible, one temptation might be to eliminate as much of the horizontal as possible in order to focus on the vertical. (As an extreme example, think of a recluse attempting to live a "spiritual" existence atop a pole.)

---

[26]Wilbert R. Shenk, *Write the Vision: The Church Renewed* (Valley Forge, PA: Trinity Press, 1995), 90.

[27]Foster, *Life with God*, 96.

[28]James C. Wilhoit, *Spiritual Formation as If the Church Mattered: Growing in Christ Through Community* (Grand Rapids: Baker Academic, 2008), 15.

[29]Dallas Willard, *The Spirit of the Disciplines: Understanding How God Changes Lives* (San Francisco: Harper-Collins, 1988), 15. Italics original.

[30]Ibid., 260. Italics original.

Disciples, therefore, also need a missional lens that enables them to look at all of life as a mission field. Developing an intentional missional perspective is a bit like clicking on the "street-level view" of an online map in order to see and engage the needs of the surrounding community. The perception of a neighborhood immediately jumps from 2D to 3D as "real-life people" come into view. This altered perspective creates overwhelming opportunities for the missional church. In fact, a second temptation might be to head off in all directions at once, attempting to establish God's kingdom on earth through one's own efforts. The challenge is to maintain a Godward focus in the midst of living a missional life. It is at this juncture that the two streams of spiritual formation and missional thought have several insights to offer each other.

Insights from spiritual formation for mission. To begin with, spiritual formation has valuable insights for mission. The missional church must be connected to the presence of the living God in their midst. Because the mission belongs to him, the Spirit directs and empowers the mission of the church. The practice of spiritual disciplines can help position a church to hear from the Lord. For example, when the church at Antioch set aside Barnabas and Saul, they heard the Spirit speak in the context of corporate prayer and fasting. In order to lead the church to hear from God, those in leadership must be first and foremost disciples of Jesus. Fueled by their passion for the task at hand, driven missionaries and church planters may find it all too easy to neglect adequate time with the Lord or to leap before looking to him—especially where the needs and work to be done clamor loudest. In cultural settings where there are very few other Christians, it is vitally important that believers develop a deep, authentic spirituality that helps them consistently live out the reality of God's tabernacling presence.

Another area where spiritual formation can help the missional church is in understanding what a disciple is and how to make one—after all, the assignment is to make disciples! Willard decries the trend to make converts rather than disciples and outlines the process of becoming disciple makers.[31] The desire for results and rapid reproduction can

---

[31]See Willard, *Divine Conspiracy*, chapter 8.

sometimes lead to a streamlined movement that dries up quickly because it is dangerously shallow. Foster wisely cautions, "Without the tempering of the sacramental life, evangelism and discipleship can be reduced to formulas for admittance to heaven instead of a call to a rich, God-soaked life."[32] Eschewing truncated "gospels of sin management," Willard contends that an intentional corrective must start with "*discipleship evangelism*"—sharing the gospel in a way that calls for "whole life" apprenticeship to Jesus: "a straightforward presentation, in word and life, of the new reality of life under God's rule, through reliance upon the word and person of Jesus."[33] These authors' concern for evangelism that leads to life transformation is a welcome corrective to the problem of inadequate discipleship—or worse, false conversions.

Still, surprisingly few books on spiritual formation include the importance of gospel witness and even fewer address mission. Although neither Willard nor Foster include evangelism on their lists of spiritual disciplines, some do. Adele Calhoun numbers witness as one among sixty-two disciplines: "Every disciple has the very life of God pulsing through his or her body. . . . Testifying to this good news requires no strategy or program. It depends on responding to the Spirit's nudge to open your mouth and heart for the sake of others."[34] Evangelism also makes Donald Whitney's list of ten disciplines, where he calls for intentionality: "We must discipline ourselves to get into the context of evangelism; that is we must not just wait for witnessing opportunities to happen."[35] Even so, Whitney's missional perspective is more local than global. When Whitney does address foreign missions, he appeals to following the example set by Jesus and reflects on the formative impact of missional engagement.[36] Wilhoit mentions mission only once, noting that a "mission trip" can provide an excellent introduction to the "joy of service."[37] Overall, the surprising brevity of attention given to evangelism

---

[32]Foster, *Life with God*, 123.

[33]Willard, *Divine Conspiracy*, 41, 58.

[34]Adele Ahlberg Calhoun, *Spiritual Disciplines Handbook: Practices That Transform Us* (Downers Grove, IL: InterVarsity Press, 2005), 160.

[35]Donald S. Whitney, *Spiritual Disciplines for the Christian Life* (Colorado Springs, CO: NavPress, 1991), 100.

[36]Ibid., 105.

[37]Wilhoit, *Spiritual Formation as If the Church Matters*, 171.

and mission creates the impression that *making* disciples of all nations is not as important as *being* a disciple.

Insights from missional thought for spiritual formation. At this point, missional thought has valuable insights for those in spiritual formation. The task of the church cannot be limited to spiritual formation alone. Neither can the sole focus be on individuals becoming like Christ. According to Jesus' teachings, to love Christ supremely finds expression in obeying all his commands, including the missional aspects of the Great Commission: going and sharing the gospel with all who have not heard. As Shenk clarifies, "When the people of God live in covenantal relationship with God, they will find this fire [of God's passion for the world's salvation] burning within them too."[38] If Foster is right and meditation is "to think God's thoughts after him, to delight in his presence," then meditation should inevitably lead to mission. Foster's "Immanuel Principle" is the thread that runs through Scripture,[39] and Matthew 1:21-23; 28:19-20 both demonstrate that God's presence with his people is missional. The Immanuel Principle should include the affirmation that "God will be with us on mission." Lesslie Newbigin understands the missional implication of God calling a people for himself. He says, "[The church] is not meant to call men and women out of the world into a safe religious enclave but to call them out in order to send them back as agents of God's kingship."[40]

Foster shows the connection when he deals with the fact that Jesus continues to work in the world through his Spirit-empowered people. He observes, "[The Spirit] lead[s] Philip to new unreached cultures (Acts 8), revealing his Messiahship to Paul (Acts 9), teaching Peter about his Jewish nationalism (Acts 10), guiding the Church out of its cultural captivity (Acts 15)."[41]

---

[38]Shenk, *Write the Vision*, 87.

[39]Foster, *Life with God*, 7-8.

[40]Lesslie Newbigin, *Foolishness to the Greeks: The Gospel and Western Culture* (Grand Rapids: Eerdmans, 1986), 124.

[41]Foster, *Celebration of Discipline*, 18. Other such examples easily spring to mind as well: the Spirit's setting aside Paul and Barnabas for mission (Acts 13); leading Paul into Europe (Acts 16); and directing him to remain in Corinth for fruitful ministry (Acts 18).

A missional lens also adds a missional dimension to the various spiritual disciplines. For example, those who read, study, and meditate on God's Word find fresh insights through the use of a missional hermeneutic.[42] Prayer and fasting include confession for neglecting God's mission, as well as petitions for spiritual renewal, boldness in witness, the missionary task, and laborers for the harvest. Simplicity, frugality, and sacrifice find purpose in giving toward mission, and worship and celebration highlight the character and activity of a missionary God. Witness and mission, however, are not simply one of a dozen spiritual disciplines; instead, they belong to the overarching definition of what a disciple is. After all, as Jesus called his disciples, he commanded, "Come, follow me . . . and I will send you out to fish for people" (Mt 4:19). Shenk underscores, "To be a disciple of Jesus Christ and a member of his body is to live a missionary existence in the world."[43] Being a disciple is not enough. Ultimately, Jesus commanded his disciples to be disciple-makers.

Shenk goes on to identify two modes of mission in Acts. The first is an "organic mode" that was the heartbeat of the early church. When persecution forced believers to flee to Antioch, they continued to live out the spiritual reality of Christ's abiding presence wherever they went, resulting in spontaneous witness and a magnetic attraction that the Lord used to draw others to himself and to plant a church (Acts 11:19-26). The second is a "sending mode" where—under the Spirit's direction—the same church in Antioch set apart missionaries and sent them to specific places with the purpose of giving a gospel witness in key cities and regions (Acts 13:1-3).[44] Significantly, both of these missional modes play a vital role in fulfilling the Great Commission and depend on authentic spirituality.

The necessity of a global perspective. A reminder of the global nature of Jesus' commission may be helpful not only for spiritual formation but also for missional thought as well. Michael Goheen explains the distinction between the comprehensive term *mission*—"the whole task of the church to witness to the whole gospel in the whole world"—and the

---

[42]See Wright's *Mission of God.*
[43]Shenk, *Write the Vision,* 90.
[44]Ibid., 92-93.

narrower term *missions* with an *s*, which seeks "to establish a witness to the gospel in places or among peoples where there is none or where it is very weak."[45] While there are definite advantages to viewing every place as a mission field and every believer a missionary, there can be an un-intended result. Goheen cautions, "In the burgeoning missional church movement little is said about taking the gospel to places where it is un-known. Mission has swallowed up missions."[46] At this critical juncture, the missional church must zoom out from a street-level view to a God's-eye view of the earth in order to see it from his perspective. God's concern for the nations threads throughout both Testaments, and every iteration of Jesus' commission is global (Mt 28:18-20; Mk 16:15; Lk 24:45-48; Jn 20:21 [cf. 17:18]; Acts 1:8). Furthermore, Paul expresses the priority of proclaiming the gospel where the name of Christ is not yet known (Rom 15:20-21). Goheen observes, "Mission looks to the ends of the earth and the redemption of all nations. This universal vision will be the ultimate horizon of the mission of the church."[47] In order to fulfill the Great Commission, we must focus not only on the spiritual and missional dimensions, but also on this global dimension as well. As Newbigin points out, "We can only confess Christ truly where we go with him to the ends of the earth."[48]

The church faces an unfinished task. According to current global re-search, 59 percent of the world's 11,500 people groups have less than a 2 percent evangelical Christian presence. Fifty-seven percent of the world's population is considered unreached with the gospel. This number includes the Last Frontier, those least-reached people groups (12.6 percent of the world's population) who have little or no access to evangelical resources.[49] The immensity of the task looms even larger under the projection that the current world population of 7.2 billion is

---

[45]Michael W. Goheen, *Introducing Christian Mission Today: Scripture, History and Issues* (Downers Grove, IL: IVP Academic, 2014), 402.

[46]Ibid., 403.

[47]Ibid., 405.

[48]Lesslie Newbigin, *A Word in Season: Perspectives on Christian World Missions* (Grand Rapids: Eerdmans, 1994), 2.

[49]"Global Status of Evangelical Christianity," International Mission Board Global Research, August 2015, 1-2. Online: http://public.imb.org/globalresearch/Documents/GSECOverviews/2015-08_GSEC _Overview.pdf.

on track to balloon to 9 billion by 2050. Only a minimal fraction of Christian giving actually targets these who are least evangelized.[50] In my own denomination, recent budget constraints prompted the offer of a voluntary retirement incentive, resulting in a 20 percent reduction of the missionary force.[51]

A renewed vision for mission. A renewed vision for mission recovers the understanding that the Great Commission is the responsibility of the local church. Every church should cast vision, equip, and mobilize believers to be on mission with God in the workplace and neighborhood. The entire population of the world must be reached in every generation, because places that are considered reached today are just one generation from paganism. As Newbigin observed on his return to England after years as a missionary in India, the mission field is now on our very doorstep.[52] Church attendance in the West has plummeted in reverse proportion to the soaring numbers of those who claim no religious affiliation. Globalization has brought the nations of the world to our shores, and they now live among us. We can no longer sustain the dichotomy that evangelism is local and mission is "across the sea." International mission agencies need to work with local churches, equipping them with missiological methods such as cultural exegesis, worldview analysis, and contextualization. At the same time, in light of an increasing pluralism, churches must remain anchored to the sufficiency of Christ alone for salvation, even as they begin to reflect the multicultural makeup of their communities.

But the mission must not stop with the local church attuned to its surrounding missional opportunities. As Newbigin explains, "The Church wherever it is, is not only Christ's witness to its own people and nation, but also the home-base for a mission to the ends of the earth."[53] The church in every place must maintain God's perspective of the earth,

---

[50]Goheen, *Introducing Christian Mission Today*, 420-21.

[51]"IMB: 1,132 Missionaries, Staff Accept VRI, HRO," *Baptist Press*, February 24, 2016. Online: www.bpnews .net/46374/imb-1132-missionaries-staff-accept-vri-hro.

[52]Lesslie Newbigin, *England as a Foreign Mission Field: An Address Given to the Assembly of the Council of Christian Churches* (UK: Birmingham Council of Churches, 1986).

[53]Newbigin, *A Word in Season*, 2.

targeting in particular those seemingly impenetrable people groups and massive cities that as yet have little or no gospel witness. David Platt argues that the urgency of the global task calls for "limitless pathways" for sending not just thousands of missionaries, but hundreds of thousands.[54] He sees globalization as a divine opportunity that calls for the filling of nontraditional missionary roles from the ranks of students, retirees, and professionals. The magnitude of the task also calls for an understanding that the commission does not rest with the Western church alone. The growing numbers of non-Western missionaries will only increase as the geographical center of Christianity continues to shift to the southern hemisphere. Goheen points out, "If mission is in, from, and to all six continents, then [interdependent] partnership is a necessity."[55] The church must do whatever it takes to make disciples of *all* nations.

A vision for spiritual renewal. At the same time that there is a need for a renewed vision for mission, there is an even greater need for spiritual renewal. Christians must awaken to the *current* reality of the presence of God dwelling in their midst. Following Christ entails transformation: a reorientation of the heart's desire and a radical shift in allegiance to the One who has been given all authority. As a contrast community, believers' holistic holiness should stand out brightly against the surrounding darkness. As God's display people, their worship and transformed lives bear witness to an authentic spirituality that answers the unmet craving of those whom the Spirit is drawing. The overwhelming nature of the global commission calls for an absolute reliance on the Holy Spirit's presence and power. The Spirit's presence will also embolden, empower, and compel disciples to share the great salvation God has wrought through his tabernacled-in-flesh Son. Spiritual disciplines practiced individually and corporately will enable believers both to experience the reality of God's presence and to hear his directions for mission. The church must teach every disciple to observe all that Jesus commanded—including the command to make disciples of all nations.

---

[54]David Platt, International Mission Board Annual Report delivered to the Southern Baptist Convention, Columbus, Ohio, June 17, 2015. Online: www.imb.org/updates/storyview-3325.aspx#. Platt is the president of the Southern Baptist International Mission Board.

[55]Goheen, *Introducing Christian Mission Today*, 428.

Conclusion

Missional spirituality calls for the simultaneous integration of two perspectives—through the use of bifocal lenses, if you will. The lower portion of the lens helps disciples focus up close on their spiritual relationship with the indwelling Christ, while the upper section brings missional opportunities of the surrounding community into sharp focus. Perhaps an even better analogy, however, is that the Great Commission calls for trifocal lenses—the top portion enabling disciples to focus clearly on the global horizon. Undoubtedly, personality, giftedness, calling, and even seasons of life influence whether one tends to gravitate toward spiritual solitude in a prayer closet, missional conversations in a coffee house, or church plants in Jakarta. Genuine missional spirituality, however, calls for progressive lenses that hold all three dimensions in proper focus: spiritual, missional, and global.

As Jesus' disciples, we need to become like Moses, who without God's presence refused to take another step on mission, and like Isaiah, whose experience of God's presence led him to see mission in every single step he took. We, too, must answer the Lord's heart cry: "Will you be with me—on mission?" The Great Commission calls for an authentic spirituality that prompts both organic and sending modes of mission. We may desire to withdraw from the world to sit and stay at Jesus' feet, but until he returns, we must also get up and go. We are the Sent. God's command to engulf every point of latitude and longitude with the knowledge of his glory still resounds: "Cover the earth!"

4

Missional Spirituality *as* Congregational

Anthony L. Chute *and*
Christopher W. Morgan

ONE OF OUR COLLEAGUES DESPISES the words *spiritual* and *spirituality* (and despises is probably an understatement). He finds the terms superficial, fuzzy, and loaded with assumptions of how ordinary matters must be unspiritual. The terms are confusing, as there are a myriad of views on spirituality; the Islamic mystic Sufi tradition, Bhavana in Buddhism, yoga in Hinduism, and channeling in New Age all come to mind. Even in the Christian tradition, influencers as wide-ranging as Gregory of Nyssa, Augustine of Hippo, Francis of Assisi, Martin Luther, John Wesley, Francis Schaeffer, and Richard Foster have all addressed it and each with significant differences. Because of this, spirituality often connotes different things to different people.

In contemporary evangelicalism we primarily view spirituality in individualistic ways. Spirituality is often understood to be about my personal experience with God, my Bible study, my devotional life, or my spiritual disciples, such as fasting, giving, and praying. While such an approach is certainly valid, it does neglect the communal nature of biblical spirituality and calls for a renewed vision on how biblical spirituality is both missional and congregational. This vision derives from the Sermon on the Mount, where Jesus calls a kingdom community, clarifies spirituality for his new community, and shows that its spirituality fuels its mission. This vision also springs from the Great Commission, in which Jesus teaches that the mission of his kingdom community reproduces spirituality. In order to demonstrate how this vision is lived out in the context of local churches, we have chosen to examine this concept in Paul's epistle to the Philippians. The Philippian church serves ably as a model of missional spirituality, as it was commended for its faithful witness to the gospel while positively interweaving spirituality and mission. In other words, the book of Philippians shows how biblical spirituality is both missional and congregational.

Jesus Calls a Kingdom Community

Depicting the genealogy, birth, early childhood, baptism, and temptation of Jesus, Matthew shows that Jesus is Israel's Messiah, the Son of Abraham, the new Moses, the new David, even the Son of God (Mt 1:1–4:16).[1] Matthew then recounts Jesus' launching of his public ministry: "From that time on Jesus began to preach, 'Repent, for the kingdom of heaven has come near'" (Mt 4:17). Continuing the legacy of the Old Testament prophets and John the Baptist (Mt 3:2), Jesus calls people to repent, to turn from their sin to God, because the "kingdom of heaven has come near." But what is this kingdom?

The "kingdom" refers to God's rule and reign over his people, which will finally and ultimately "come at the end of the age in a mighty irruption into history inaugurating the perfect order of the age to come." And yet this kingdom "has already come into history in the person and mission of Jesus," and thus the "presence of the future"[2] is already evident. So God's reign is present and future, already and not yet, his active invasion of history now

---

[1] See Charles L. Quarles, *A Theology of Matthew*, Explorations in Biblical Theology (Phillipsburg, NJ: P&R, 2013), 13-17.

[2] George Eldon Ladd, *The Presence of the Future*, rev. ed. (Grand Rapids: Eerdmans, 1974), 144-49.

and his final establishment of the age to come. It is a sovereign rule, a dynamic power and a divine activity. As the bearer of this kingdom, Jesus naturally demands repentance to enter his Messianic community, since the present way of the world must be rejected, while the new age of God's rule and its corresponding way of life must be embraced. As such, repentance is not only the way *into* the kingdom, but is also the way *of* the kingdom.

The community of Jesus is made up of followers of Jesus, "the present-in-history king,"[3] whose disciples come under him, walk alongside him, believe his teachings, embrace his way of life, and participate in his mission (Mt 4:17-19). These disciples later become part of "the twelve," which, as Eckhard Schnabel observes, sheds light on the nature of Jesus' kingdom community: "Seen in the context of Jesus' proclamation of the dawn of God's kingdom, the number 'twelve' speaks of the eschatological gathering of Israel."[4] The twelve disciples were not physical descendants of the twelve Israelite tribes but correspond to them by representing symbolically the "restoration of the people of God in the last days."[5] They are therefore the "nucleus of the eschatological community," both as first-fruits of it and as participants in Jesus' mission of final restoration.[6]

Matthew summarizes Jesus' initial ministry as teaching, preaching, and healing (Mt 4:23-25). Although details about his teaching and healing are not here spelled out, he teaches in the synagogues, presumably to call out his Messianic community, and heals all kinds of diseases, showing that the kingdom of God has begun in him. The content of Jesus' preaching is particularly crystallized in the phrase "the good news [gospel] of the kingdom" (Mt 4:23; cf. Mt 9:35; 24:14). Robert Yarbrough explains,

> Here we see that there is a "gospel" associated with the kingdom. What is the relationship between "gospel" and "kingdom"? First, it is "good news," a "favorable announcement," which is the basic meaning of the original

---

[3] Robert W. Yarbrough, "The Kingdom of God in the New Testament: Matthew and Revelation," in *The Kingdom of God*, Theology in Community 4 (Wheaton, IL: Crossway, 2012), 110.

[4] Eckhard J. Schnabel, *Early Christian Mission: Jesus and the Twelve*, vol. 1 (Downers Grove, IL: IVP Academic, 2004), 224.

[5] Ibid., 270.

[6] Ibid., 271.

(*euangelion*). . . . In the context of Matthew, this can be no other "gospel," no greater good news, than that of the kingdom.

Second, it transmits kingdom tidings. It announces that the reign of the God of Abraham, Isaac, and Jacob, a reign never totally rejected among the Jews over the pre-Christian centuries but often obscured, is now present in a new way, to a new extent, and for a new purpose. Synagogue teaching is being updated and upgraded. Sick and sorrowing are being restored. Third, it is inextricably bound to Jesus the king, as Matthew has already established.[7]

Jesus' kingdom community is thus characterized by repentance unto God's rule, discipleship under Jesus' teachings and way of life, and participation in Jesus' mission. Jesus' kingdom community forms the "nucleus" of the eschatological community—people already changed by Jesus' kingdom invasion and serving his mission, proclaiming the gospel of the kingdom, and awaiting his final establishment of the new age.

Jesus Clarifies True Spirituality for His Kingdom Community

It is in this context of calling his kingdom community that Jesus gathered his disciples, went up on a mountain, sat down, and taught them what has been called the "Sermon on the Mount" (Mt 5–7). As Stanley Hauerwas observes, "The sermon . . . is not a list of requirements, but rather a description of the life of a people gathered by and around Jesus."[8] Indeed, the Sermon on the Mount functions much like the Ten Commandments did for Israel, as a divinely established community ethic addressing what it meant to live as the covenant people of God, his treasured possession, a kingdom of priests, and a holy nation (Ex 19:5-6). Similarly, in the sermon Jesus sets forth his vision of his new holy, covenant, kingdom community, reordering its values and clarifying true spirituality.

In the sermon's Beatitudes, Jesus sets forth the values of his kingdom community, and thus spirituality itself. His people are not driven by

---

[7]Yarbrough, "The Kingdom of God in the New Testament," 110-11.
[8]Stanley Hauerwas, *Matthew*, Brazos Theological Commentary on the Bible (Grand Rapids: Baker, 2007), 61.

wealth, power, honor, or comfort, but by faith, hope, and love. True spirituality is linked to kingdom character.

Jesus begins by pronouncing God's blessings on his kingdom community (Mt 5:3-12). Jesus expresses these blessings in a pattern, first by pronouncing "blessed" those who are marked by particular characteristics: the poor in spirit, those who mourn, the meek, those who hunger and thirst for righteousness, the merciful, the pure in heart, the peacemakers, and those persecuted for righteousness sake.

Jesus here links God's blessing, his kingdom community, and true spirituality. As such, disciples of Jesus live out a spirituality marked by dependence on God, repentance, humility, true righteousness, integrity, reconciliation with others, and persecution for following Christ faithfully.

Jesus then relates the blessings themselves: theirs is the kingdom of heaven; they shall be comforted; they shall inherit the earth; they shall be satisfied; they shall receive mercy; they shall see God; they shall be called the sons of God; and theirs is the kingdom of heaven. Note that these are described in the plural, suggesting the communal context.

The first and last Beatitudes also end with the same overarching blessing: "Theirs is the kingdom of heaven" (Mt 5:3, 10). The middle six Beatitudes relate future blessings (note the recurring "will be" in Mt 5:4-9). God blesses Jesus' people, who are a community of the kingdom now ("theirs is the kingdom") and await a fuller, final display of the kingdom ("will be"). John Stott puts it well: "The blessing promised . . . is the gloriously comprehensive blessing of God's rule, tasted now and consummated later, including the inheritance of both earth and heaven, comfort, satisfaction and mercy, the vision and sonship of God."[9]

The rest of the Sermon on the Mount expands on the kingdom character of spirituality. In Matthew 5:17-48, Jesus calls for holistic holiness, highlighting that true righteousness is Word saturated and is both internal and external, a matter of a loving heart and obedient behavior (see also Lev 19:1-18). In Matthew 6:1-18, Jesus calls for genuine worship, stressing that God (not others or ourselves) is the sole audience

---

[9]John R. W. Stott, *The Message of the Sermon on the Mount*, Bible Speaks Today (Downers Grove, IL: InterVarsity Press, 1985), 38.

of worship (using the examples of three spiritual disciplines: giving, praying, and fasting) and that living all of life in light of God's kingdom is the central focus of prayer. In Matthew 6:19-34, Jesus sets forth kingdom values, contrasting earthly wealth with kingdom significance. In Matthew 7, Jesus demonstrates the centrality of generous love, overturning judgmentalism and advancing the Golden Rule. Along the way, Jesus clarifies what it means to be his disciple. Jesus' disciples possess true righteousness as they live out true spirituality, marked by kingdom character, holistic holiness, genuine worship, kingdom values, and generous love.

The Spirituality of Jesus' Kingdom Community Fuels Its Mission

A community so enthusiastic about the Messiah's arrival and committed to live out such a spirituality might be expected to be self-focused, cloistered and separated from the rest of society. Jesus, however, interweaves his community's spirituality with its mission. Indeed, the spirituality of the community fuels its mission.

> Jesus' call, "Come, follow me . . . and I will send you out to fish for people" (Matt 4:19), reveals that part of being Jesus' disciple is following him. And inherent in following Jesus is becoming "fishers" of people, and thus participants in Jesus' own mission. From the beginning of Jesus' ministry, "discipleship and mission are inseparably linked," as his disciples are called and sent: called to follow the way of the kingdom and sent to call others to do the same.[10]

Jesus also stresses the inherently missional nature of his kingdom community as he calls them to be the "salt of the earth" and "light of the world" (Mt 5:13, 14). Jesus already stunned his listeners with the Beatitudes, in which he associated God's kingdom not with human strength and honor but with spiritual poverty, crying, meekness, hunger, mercy, peace, and persecution. Stott rightly asks, "What possible influence could the people described in the beatitudes exert in this hard, tough world? . . . Incredible as it sounds, Jesus referred to that handful of Palestinian peasants as the

---

[10]Schnabel, *Early Christian Mission*, 1:272-79.

salt of *the earth* and the light of *the world,* so far-reaching was their influence to be."[11]

Fundamental to these images is the distinctiveness of the kingdom community (Mt 5:3-12). The world is in decay, and the holy kingdom community is the salt. The world is in darkness, and the holy kingdom community is the light. Both images not only assume the community's distinctiveness; they also clarify the community's mission. As the salt of the earth, Jesus' disciples "purify the world by living holy lives and proclaiming the gospel of the kingdom."[12] Further, "Jesus insisted that the disciples' mission of shining in the world, extending salvation to the ends of the earth by proclaiming the gospel of the kingdom, and living transformed lives, is intrinsic to genuine discipleship."[13]

The Mission of Jesus' Kingdom Community Reproduces Spirituality

Thus Jesus interweaves his community's spirituality with its mission. Not only does the spirituality of the community fuel its mission, but the mission of Jesus' kingdom community also reproduces spirituality.

This is suggested in Matthew 4:17-19, as Jesus calls for followers who fish for others, who likewise become followers of Jesus and presumably fish for others, too. It is also suggested in Matthew 5:3-16, as Jesus' people who are salt and light point others to God through their distinctive goodness, which points to God as their Father. Some persecute them as a result of their strong identification with God (Mt 5:10-12), but others glorify God and thus also become followers of Jesus, characterized by righteousness.

What Jesus suggests in Matthew 4:17; 5:3-16 he spells out plainly in Matthew 28:18-20: the mission of his kingdom community is reproductive spirituality. In Matthew 28:18-20, Jesus gives the Great Commission to his disciples. He begins by asserting that he is the exalted Son who is Lord over all, both in heaven and on earth, including over all nations (Mt 28:18; see also Dan 7:14). The universality of the commission

---

[11]Stott, *The Message of the Sermon on the Mount,* 57, italics his.

[12]Charles Quarles, *Sermon on the Mount: Restoring Christ's Message to the Modern Church* (Nashville: B&H, 2011), 80.

[13]Ibid., 86. See also 194-205.

is striking: Jesus has all authority, directs the disciples to make disciples of all nations, instructs them to teach all that he has commanded them, and charges them to do so until the end of the age. The particularity of the commission is also striking: Jesus uniquely is Lord, he alone is worthy of worship by all nations, his teachings have binding authority, and his presence is with his people as they participate in his mission.[14]

The essence of Jesus' Great Commission is found in its command: make disciples of all nations. Jesus calls his disciples to make other disciples, who are also expected to follow Jesus, listen to his teaching, and reflect his ways. Such disciples live in community, in fellowship with the teacher and with each other as fellow followers of Jesus, the Teacher. Schnabel comments, "The directive to 'make disciples' demonstrates the ecclesiological dimension of the mission of the Twelve: missionary work and church must not be separated, since the very goal and purpose of missionary work is the creation of a community of disciples."[15] Making disciples of all nations expands the mission beyond Israel to all Gentile peoples.[16]

The central command of making disciples is elucidated by three participles: going, baptizing, and teaching. Matthew apparently uses "go" as an introductory circumstantial participle that is rightly translated as coordinate to the main verb—here "Go and make" (cf. Mt 2:8; 9:13; 11:4; 17:27; 28:7).[17] The participle establishes the motion necessary for the accomplishment of the command. So "go" here is the action necessary to accomplish the command of making disciples. This makes good sense of the context, since the disciples can make other disciples of all nations only if they go to people who do not yet know Jesus.

Jesus calls the disciples to make disciples of all nations also by "baptizing them in the name of the Father and of the Son and of the Holy Spirit" (Mt 28:19). Those who follow Christ depict their new allegiance

---

[14]Schnabel, *Early Christian Mission*, 1:353-55.

[15]Ibid., 356.

[16]"Nations" does not refer to a geopolitical nation-state but connotes Gentiles and something akin to peoples, families, clans, and tribes. See Gen 12:3; Dan 7:13-14; Mt. 24:14; Rev 5:9-10.

[17]David W. Chapman, "The Great Commission as the Conclusion of Matthew's Gospel," in *All for Jesus: A Celebration of the Fiftieth Anniversary of Covenant Theological Seminary*, ed. Robert A. Peterson and Sean Michael Lucas (Fearn, Ross-shire, UK: Mentor, 2001), 91.

to Jesus through baptism. Through baptism, the new disciple publicly identifies with Christ as Lord, with one another in Jesus' kingdom community, and with the entire Trinity.

Making disciples of all nations also includes "teaching them to obey everything I have commanded you" (Mt 28:20). The disciples do not make their own disciples but point people to becoming followers of Jesus, the Teacher. As such, the disciples do not put forward their own teachings but faithfully pass on the teachings of the Teacher. Both believing and practicing Jesus' teachings are required, by the disciplers and by new disciples.

Thus Jesus declares that the mission of his kingdom community is disciple making, and as such is reproductive spirituality. His people are to be focused on the intentional "multiplication of other faithful followers of the King among the nations."[18]

Synthesis

Thus far, we have noted several tenets of missional spirituality. First, Jesus calls a kingdom community composed of his disciples who are changed by his kingdom invasion, embracing his teachings, following his way of life, and participating in his mission.

Second, Jesus clarifies true spirituality for his kingdom community. His disciples' lives are marked by dependence on God, repentance from sin, humility, mercy, integrity, peace, faithfulness, and true righteousness. They worship genuinely as a way of life, giving, praying, and fasting for the kingdom to come. Not preoccupied with wealth, significance, or the approval of others, Jesus' disciples prize God and his kingdom above all else.

Third, the spirituality of Jesus' kingdom community fuels its mission. As Jesus' disciples follow him, they fish for others. And as the disciples' lives reflect the beatitudes, they serve society as salt and light to the nations.

Fourth, the mission of Jesus' kingdom community reproduces spirituality. The followers of Jesus fish for others, who become followers of Jesus and fish for still others. As the disciples embody true spirituality in their

---

[18]Jeff Lewis, "God's Great Commissions for the Nations," in *Discovering the Mission of God: Best Missional Practices for the Twenty-first Century*, ed. Mike Barnett and Robin Martin (Downers Grove, IL: IVP Academic, 2012), 104.

lives, they are salt and light, and this leads others to know and follow God, too. These disciples have a mission: to make other disciples of all nations. Thus, in and through the community of Jesus, spirituality and mission interweave, each spiraling into the other, each fueling each other, and each increasingly reproducing missional spirituality. We see from the Sermon on the Mount that spirituality is neither a superficial add-on to Christian living nor an individual quest for Christian greatness; it is a missional community engaged in gospel labors.

The Example of Philippians

Since the community of Jesus fosters missional spirituality, it follows that local churches are central to this process. Missiologist Jeff Lewis aptly maintains that the "local church is a community of the disciples of the King, who are liberated from the slavery of living for self, called to be fully engaged in his redemptive mission among the nations (both locally and globally), and charged with the nurturing and training of God's children to be disciplers of the nations."[19] The question remains, how does such missional spirituality get lived out in and through the local church?

As we have considered this question, we have found Paul's letter to the Philippians to be an example of missional spirituality in the church, the kingdom community called out of the world and yet responsible for being a light in it (Phil 2:15). While many other good examples also exist, we find Philippians particularly helpful, as it incorporates and applies many of Jesus' own principles toward a congregational missional spirituality.

Note, for instance, the theme of gospel partnership that frames the letter. D. A. Carson and Douglas Moo refer to Philippians as "that comparative rarity: a letter to a church of Paul's own foundation with which he is, on the whole, well pleased."[20] The source of Paul's pleasant tone is not a complete absence of controversy but the shared partnership in the gospel he has experienced with the Philippian

---

[19]Jeff Lewis, "The Church: A Community of Disciplers of the Nations," sermon on May 6, 2015, www.youtube.com/watch?v=6nzeiTFGzvM.

[20]D. A. Carson and Douglas J. Moo, *An Introduction to the New Testament*, 2nd ed. (Grand Rapids: Zondervan), 512.

church. Indeed, Paul begins and ends the letter by highlighting this gospel partnership:

- "I thank my God every time I remember you. In all my prayers for all of you, I always pray with joy because of your partnership in the gospel from the first day until now." (Phil 1:3-5)

- "Whether I am in chains or defending and confirming the gospel, all of you share in God's grace with me." (Phil 1:7)

- "Yes, and I ask you, my true companion, help these women since they have contended at my side in the cause of the gospel." (Phil 4:3)

- "When I set out from Macedonia, not one church shared with me in the matter of giving and receiving, except you only." (Phil 4:15)

This partnership was reciprocal—Paul first brought the gospel to the Philippians, and they in turn continued to support his missionary endeavors through their prayers and financial resources.[21] Moreover, the Philippian church remained steadfast in their faith and continued this missional partnership, despite the presence of internal and external threats to the gospel. Paul expressed his confidence that "he who began a good work in you will carry it on to completion until the day of Christ Jesus" (Phil 1:6). In short, Paul founded a church that remained grounded in the gospel, he praised them for their participation in spreading the gospel, and he expressed his confidence that they would continue to be transformed by the gospel. This apostolic bill of good health came at a time when the gospel had just begun making its way through Europe, and as such provides a positive model of congregational missional spirituality.

Missional Spirituality as Congregational

From a church-planting perspective, Paul's decision to preach the gospel in Philippi was fitting in many ways. Founded and named after the father of Alexander the Great, the city of Philippi proved attractive to inhabitants and travelers alike with its rich heritage, prime location, and privileged

---

[21]Ralph Martin quotes J. J. Müller to make the following observation: "The Philippians indicated the reality of their partnership in the gospel not 'a quiet enjoyment of it, but (by) a keen activity in the interest of it.'" Ralph P. Martin, *Philippians*, TNTC (Grand Rapids: Eerdmans, 1959), 47.

status. It was the site of Brutus's and Cassius's defeat of Mark Antony and Octavian in battle; it was the passageway to Rome's eastern provinces via the Egnatian Way; and it was governed according to Roman law, thus providing its people with full rights as Roman citizens. As Gerald Hawthorne notes, Paul's purpose in planting a church in Philippi was strategic indeed: "Choosing Philippi, thus, as the place to launch the gospel on European soil fitted in with Paul's mission strategy of selecting important cities of repute and strategic location as ideal centers from which the good news of the gospel might radiate out."[22]

Interestingly, however, Paul never attributes the successful spread of the gospel to such external factors. He points instead to the power of the gospel itself as the underlying requisite for fruitful missional labors. Indeed, Paul even draws attention to his status as a prisoner to illustrate this point: "Now I want you to know, brothers and sisters, that what has happened to me has actually served to advance the gospel. As a result, it has become clear throughout the whole palace guard and to everyone else that I am in chains for Christ" (Phil 1:12-13). Moisés Silva captures an important nuance here: "The apostle . . . did not merely say that the gospel had continued to make progress *in spite of* adversity; rather, the adversity itself had turned out for the advancement of the gospel."[23]

Moreover, the substance of Paul's letter stresses congregational spirituality as key to reaching the world with the life-changing power of the gospel. Paul, therefore, urges the Philippian Christians to "conduct yourselves in a manner worthy of the gospel of Christ. Then, whether I come and see you or only hear about you in my absence, I will know that you stand firm in the one Spirit, striving together as one for the faith of the gospel" (Phil 1:27).[24] A significant element of Paul's instruction is obscured in most English Bibles, which translate the term *politeuesthe* without reference to the underlying political language inherent within its

---

[22]Gerald F. Hawthorne, "Philippians, Letter to the," in *Dictionary of Paul and His Letters*, ed. Gerald F. Hawthorne, Ralph P. Martin, and Daniel G. Reid (Downers Grove, IL: InterVarsity Press, 1993), 708.
[23]Moisés Silva, *Philippians*, 2nd ed., BECNT (Grand Rapids: Baker Academic, 2005), 62. Italics in original.
[24]Many consider Phil 1:27-30 to be the central passage/thesis of Philippians. See, for example, Peter T. O'Brien, *The Epistle to the Philippians*, NIGTC (Grand Rapids: Eerdmans, 1991), 143-44.

cognate term, *polis*.[25] By utilizing citizen imagery in the context of gospel living, Paul seems to be playing on the Philippians' pride in their status as Roman citizens while informing them that they are now citizens of a higher kingdom. Peter O'Brien recovers this nuance well in his translation of Phil 1:27: "Now, the important thing is this: as citizens of heaven live in a manner that is worthy of Christ."[26] Understood this way, Paul is both stating a fact and encouraging the Philippians to act accordingly: merely living moral lives according to Roman law is not missional living. They are citizens of heaven; therefore, their behavior, if it is to attract others to Christ, must reflect the values of heaven.

Note also how this heavenly citizenship language mirrors Jesus' language concerning the kingdom of heaven. Paul's instructions, if robed in kingdom language, would essentially read like this: as citizens of heaven's kingdom, the church must live according to the values of the kingdom and thus point others to follow the King. And what does conduct worthy of this heavenly citizenship/kingdom look like? It resembles the teachings provided in the Sermon on the Mount. This is not to say that Paul consciously or intentionally draws from Jesus' sermon in order to instruct the Philippians, but rather that the apostles did what Jesus commanded: they embraced his kingdom teachings and set out to make disciples of all nations, going, baptizing, and teaching other disciples to obey what Jesus taught. Thus, we should not be surprised to find congregations in the New Testament practicing missional spirituality.

Thus, in a way that resembles Jesus' teachings in the Sermon on the Mount, Paul calls the Philippian church to a missional spirituality. In particular, he exhorts the church to pursue holiness that will foster mission advancement; to give generously for gospel partnership; to pray for missional purposes; to endure suffering faithfully as a gospel witness; and to live in missional unity. In sum, Paul's teaching to the Philippian church about missional spirituality is fleshed out in his teachings on the following themes:

---

[25] The term *polis* means "city," and the passive verb *politeuesthe* means "to live as a citizen." The ESV helpfully provides a footnote with an alternate translation: "Only behave as citizens worthy."

[26] O'Brien, *Epistle to the Philippians*, 144-47.

- missional holiness
- missional giving
- missional praying
- missional suffering
- missional unity

Missional holiness. Paul's reference to the Philippians as saints (Phil 1:1), his commendation for their partnership in the gospel (Phil 1:5), his recognition of their heavenly citizenship (Phil 3:20), and his effusive language in describing them as "my brothers and sisters, you whom I love and long for, my joy and crown" (Phil 4:1), all provide clear indication that he acknowledged them as Christian family members, citizens of the heavenly kingdom.[27] Their standing in the Lord, however, did not excuse them from pursuing holiness through obedience to God. Paul's exhortation to "conduct yourselves in a manner worthy of the gospel of Christ" (Phil 1:27) is thus followed by no fewer than eighteen commands relating to the Philippians' progress in the faith.[28] This expectation of believers' pursuing holiness through obedience underscores the call for congregational spirituality.

Even Paul's own spiritual progress was not merely a personal endeavor but rather the fulfilling of his duty as a disciple of the Lord in the service of the church. Alec Motyer rightly notes that Paul

> has previously shown himself as a zealous individualist [in Phil 3:4-6] all out for his own spiritual growth. The prize-winner dare not pause to help others over the hurdles. But see here another side of the apostle, when he weeps with care for people, and when he takes pains to lead the Philippians in the way of Christ. Individual care for one's own spiritual progress must keep in touch with pastoral responsibility for the souls and welfare of others.[29]

---

[27]By contrast, note the language Paul uses for those who have not yet embraced the gospel. He refers to those who reject, in part or in whole, the claims of Christ as "evildoers" (Phil 3:2) and "enemies of the cross of Christ" (Phil 3:18).

[28]See Phil. 2:2, 5, 12, 14, 29; 3:1, 2, 15, 16, 17; 4:1, 3, 4, 5, 6, 8, 9, 21. Frank Thielman, *Philippians*, NIV Application Commentary (Grand Rapids: Zondervan, 1995), 90-91.

[29]J. Alec Motyer, *The Message of Philippians*, Bible Speaks Today (Downers Grove, IL: InterVarsity Press, 1984), 184.

Paul is thus able to encourage the Philippians to undertake the same duty as disciples by using his life as a model: "Join together in following my example, brothers and sisters" (Phil 3:17). Paul also encourages the Philippians to follow others in the congregation who exemplify the same spiritual traits: "Keep your eyes on those who live as we do" (Phil 3:17).

Such congregational spirituality also includes a missional emphasis, as developed in Philippians 2:14-16. In this passage Paul commands the church to stop complaining, because such negativity "affected the moral life of the church and its witness to the world."[30] He instead calls the church to live with character, to purity and blamelessness, which he prays for at the outset of the epistle (Phil 1:9-11). Paul then stresses the church's "moral distinctiveness" as key to its ability to serve as lights shining in a dark world (Phil 2:15).[31] Richard Melick points out, "By their lives, the Philippians were actually holding fast to the gospel. By so doing, their lives also became the measuring rod and illumination of the world around them."[32]

Missional giving. One of the key gauges of spirituality throughout all Scripture is the relation between people and their possessions. In the Sermon on the Mount, Jesus instructs his disciples to "store up for yourselves treasures in heaven," noting that "where your treasure is, there your heart will be also" (Mt 6:20, 21). Disciples are told not to worry about the most basic needs in life lest it divert their attention from their primary focus, the kingdom of God (Mt 6:25-33). Thomas Schreiner notes how excessive concern for personal security reflects a deficit of personal and corporate spirituality: "Worrying about wealth uncovers a lack of trust in God's fatherly care, and even more fundamentally a desire to live for oneself rather than for the kingdom of God."[33]

Paul seems to have embodied the teachings of Jesus well in this matter, as stated in Philippians 4:11-12: "I have learned to be content whatever

---

[30]Richard R. Melick Jr., *Philippians, Colossians, Philemon*, NAC 32 (Nashville: Broadman & Holman, 1991), 112.

[31]Ibid., 113.

[32]Ibid.

[33]Thomas R. Schreiner, *New Testament Theology: Magnifying God in Christ* (Grand Rapids: Baker Academic, 2008), 761.

the circumstances. I know what it is to be in need, and I know what it is to have plenty. I have learned the secret of being content in any and every situation, whether well fed or hungry, whether living in plenty or in want." Such sacrifices notwithstanding, Paul was blessed by the financial contributions of the Philippian church, using this instance to instruct them about missional giving. The church had supported Paul's missionary labors with financial gifts on at least three occasions (Phil 4:15-17). Their initial gift made quite an impression on Paul, as they were apparently the only congregation contributing to his missional labors: "I set out from Macedonia, not one church shared with me in the matter of giving and receiving, except you only" (Phil 4:15).

Paul notes that their giving is not merely a matter of parting with their own finances but also of becoming conformed to the image of Christ. In Phil 4:10 he describes their giving as a demonstration of their "concern" (*phronein*) for him, a word Paul uses throughout the epistle to "point out proper Christian attitudes in following the mind of Christ."[34] Moreover, he notes their giving was a spiritual blessing far beyond material gifts. O'Brien notes, "Paul did not covet the Philippians' gifts; instead, he had his heart set on the compound interest that kept accruing to their account (v. 17), that is, their ongoing spiritual progress and God's blessing in their lives by which they would continually grow in the graces of Christ until the parousia."[35]

In all this, Paul is confident the Philippians will experience more than just his appreciation for their generosity: "And my God will meet all your needs according to the riches of his glory in Christ Jesus" (Phil 4:19). This statement underscores the uniquely Christian relationship Paul shared with the Philippians, as social conventions of the day would otherwise have placed Paul in their financial debt. In this case, however, Paul is not in debt because God is the one who repays, thus highlighting the fact that "Paul and the Philippians share a friendship founded, directed and sustained by Christ. Their giving and Paul's receiving happens in and through Christ. . . . Indeed, from this Christ-focused perspective

---

[34]Melick, *Philippians, Colossians, Philemon,* 153.
[35]O'Brien, *Epistle to the Philippians,* 515.

it is not always clear who is giver and who is receiver."[36] Christians who are in the habit of giving to the mission of God can therefore enjoy Christian partnership with the people of God and will, in due time, be rewarded by him.

Missional praying. Missional spirituality is seen also in the congregational prayers of Paul and the Philippian church. Paul's prayers are filled with gratitude for the Philippian church in light of their partnership in the gospel. He prays for them neither in passing nor out of mere duty, but "in all my prayers for all of you, I always pray with joy" (Phil 1:3-5). Moreover, he prays specifically for their spirituality, namely that their "love may abound more and more in knowledge and depth of insight, so that you may be able to discern what is best" (Phil 1:9-10). Paul thus reminds the Philippians that they are being prayed for and are encouraged to grow as disciples in answer to his prayers; yet he also recognizes that he is in need of their prayers as well.

The Philippian Christians most certainly prayed that Paul would be delivered from prison, and he seems to address this matter when he states his confidence that "through your prayers and God's provision of the Spirit of Jesus Christ what has happened to me will turn out for my deliverance" (Phil 1:19). However, the scholarly consensus is that Paul took heart in the Philippians' praying for something much more significant than his physical deliverance, namely, his ability to persevere in the faith during such a trying time.[37] This judgment is based on understanding the term *sōtēria* in its full eschatological context, not simply as a reference to deliverance from present trouble. Thus Paul not only asks for their prayers, but also trusts that his divinely appointed future somehow rests in their prayerful hands. Frank Thielman provides a helpful observation in this regard: "Although it grates against Western notions of the autonomy of the individual, Paul did not conceive of sanctification and ultimate salvation as solely private

---

[36]Stephen E. Fowl, *Philippians*, Two Horizons New Testament Commentary (Grand Rapids: Eerdmans, 2005), 197.

[37]See Silva, *Philippians*, 69-72; O'Brien, *Epistle to the Philippians*, 107-12; and Gordon Fee, *Paul's Letter to the Philippians*, NICNT (Grand Rapids: Eerdmans, 1995), 130-32. For a different perspective see Gerald F. Hawthorne, *Philippians*, WBC (Waco: Word, 1983), 39-42.

enterprises. Individual Christians need the prayerful intercession of their brothers and sisters for their spiritual well-being so that they 'may be pure and blameless until the day of Christ' (1:10)."[38] Thus, such congregational and missional prayer is critical to Paul's own spirituality and to gospel advancement.

Missional suffering. The book of Philippians also points to the sober reality of missional suffering. Paul refers to the theme often, even mentioning his own imprisonment four times in the first chapter (Phil 1:7, 13, 14, 17). Paul himself is in prison because of his commitment to the mission, and he is grateful that the Philippians have stood by him (Phil 1:7). Many did not, as Paul relates how he suffered persecution from fellow evangelists: "The former preach Christ out of selfish ambition, not sincerely, supposing that they can stir up trouble for me while I am in chains" (Phil 1:17). While the exact nature of their attempt to rub salt in Paul's prison wounds is contextually vague, the very fact that gospel evangelists would leverage Paul's situation to their own advantage is disturbing. Kent Hughes states the feeling of indignation well: "The sheer cussedness of this is astonishing."[39] Paul's reaction, however, sidesteps the personal affront altogether and instead focuses attention on the ground gained through the spread of the gospel: "But what does it matter? The important thing is that in every way, whether from false motives or true, Christ is preached. And because of this I rejoice" (Phil 1:18).

This is not a noble attempt at positive thinking, nor making the best of a bad situation. Paul's use of the term *rejoice* resembles that of Jesus in the Sermon on the Mount (Mt 5:11-12) and thus demonstrates that Paul "can and does submit his own personal interests to those of the wider horizon of the gospel."[40] Likewise, Paul's frequent usage of the terms *rejoice* and *joy* in the letter shows that joy is not only a dominant theme in his life, but also an attitude that should characterize Christians—in all situations,

---

[38] Thielman, *Philippians*, 81.

[39] R. Kent Hughes, *Philippians, Colossians, and Philemon: The Fellowship of the Gospel and the Supremacy of Christ*, Preaching the Word (Wheaton, IL: Crossway, 2013), 51.

[40] O'Brien, *Philippians*, 107.

even missional suffering.[41] Thus Paul can hedge between the choice of living or dying. Knowing as he does that Christ will be honored either way, and admitting that being in the presence of Christ is far better (Phil 1:20-21), he ultimately prefers to live "for your progress and joy in the faith, so that through my being with you again your boasting in Christ Jesus will abound on account of me" (Phil 1:25-26). Paul endures suffering for the sake of the gospel and the sake of God's people, thereby adding to their joy in the Lord.

By putting the interests of the Philippians above his own, Paul can easily transition to asking members of the Philippian church to do the same. Indeed, his clarion call for the church to live worthy of the gospel urges them to stand firm in unity, strive together side by side, and not be frightened by their opponents (Phil 1:27-28). The conflict was real and nerve-racking, but Paul reminds the church that "it has been granted to you on behalf of Christ not only to believe in him, but also to suffer for him" (Phil 1:29). Paul embodied missional suffering, and it was necessary for the Philippian church to embody it as well.

Missional unity. An often forgotten but major aspect of missional spirituality is church unity. Church unity is important for many reasons, but one key reason is that unity affects the church's mission.[42] Paul integrates the missional nature of church unity into the whole of the letter, often linking it to other missional matters. For example, missional unity is linked to missional giving, which displays and extends missional unity and partnership (Phil 1:3-8; 4:10-20). Missional unity is similarly linked to missional praying, which also displays and extends the unity and partnership (Phil 1:3-11, 19-26). Missional unity is likewise linked to missional holiness, as the unity and holiness foster both the shining as lights in the world and the commitment to the word of life (Phil 2:1-16).[43]

---

[41]See Phil 1:4, 18, 25; 2:2, 17, 18, 28, 29; 3:1; 4:1, 4, 10.

[42]For a more extended treatment of church unity, see Christopher W. Morgan, "Toward a Theology of the Unity of the Church," in *Why We Belong: Evangelical Unity and Denominational Diversity*, ed. Anthony L. Chute, Christopher W. Morgan, and Robert A. Peterson (Wheaton, IL: Crossway, 2013), 19-36.

[43]For more on how God uses church unity in accomplishing of his mission, see Christopher W. Morgan, "The Church and God's Glory," in *The Community of Jesus: A Theology of the Church*, ed. Kendell H. Easley and Christopher W. Morgan (Nashville: B&H Academic, 2013), 213-36.

Missional unity is particularly stressed in Paul's charge to live worthy of the gospel (Phil 1:27-30). He urges the Philippians to stand firm "in the one Spirit, striving together as one for the faith of the gospel" (Phil 1:27). His concern for unity is highlighted against the backdrop of potential divisions, including a conflict between Euodia and Syntyche (Phil 4:2). Paul's solution is to call the Philippians to look not "to your own interests but each of you to the interests of the others" (Phil 2:4). The call to displace one's sense of being in the right for the sake of unity is counterintuitive to the ways of the world, but kingdom disciples have an example in the King himself, who

> being in very nature God . . .
> humbled himself
> by becoming obedient to death—
>   even death on a cross! (Phil 2:6, 8)

Thielman correctly avers that Jesus' "equality with God led him to view his status not as a matter of privilege but as a matter of unselfish giving."[44] This act of selfless service was the ultimate act of humility and became Paul's model of humility in the service of congregational unity as he called the Philippians to "do nothing out of selfish ambition or vain conceit. Rather, in humility value others above yourselves" (Phil 2:3). Although humility is not often on display in heated church disputes, kingdom citizens are called at every stage of life to embrace the beatitudes and corresponding reversal of human values that Jesus expressed in the Sermon on the Mount. Disciples thus avoid disunity in the church when they depend on God, live meek lives, and seek to be peacemakers; consequently, the church does not negate its witness to the world by internal divisions becoming public scandals. Paul therefore reminds the church of the importance of unity in its mission: "Do everything without grumbling or arguing, so that you may become blameless and pure, 'children of God without fault in a warped and crooked generation.' Then you will shine among them like stars in the sky" (Phil 2:14-15).

---

[44] Thielman, *Philippians*, 116.

Conclusion

How might we respond to our beloved colleague in the event that one of us inadvertently uses the word *spiritual* in his presence? Perhaps by noting that, misunderstandings aside, Jesus began a kingdom community of disciples whose lives are marked by true spirituality. This spirituality involves every part of life, including attitudes and expectations, as well as integrity before God and others, combining obedience with love. Far from being individualistic or detached from the world, such spirituality fuels the mission of the kingdom community as its distinctiveness is requisite for its roles as salt and light. Indeed, the church's holistic holiness, generous giving, fervent praying, faithful suffering, and priority of unity are inevitably linked to its mission. Further, the mission of the kingdom community is profoundly spiritual in nature, as the church strives to make disciples of all nations, disciples who live according to Jesus' teachings and who teach others to do the same. As such, biblical spirituality is missional and congregational.

5

Missional Spirituality *and* Cultural Engagement

Timothy M. Sheridan *and*
Michael W. Goheen

EVERY GENERATION IS CALLED TO engage culture with the gospel. Christianity's current situation looks more like a battlefield strewn with casualties on all sides. Engagement with North American culture feels like walking through a field with undetonated land mines. Each step may ignite an explosion of cultural backlash, inciting the next round of culture wars. Just mention the words *same-sex marriage* and you will start to feel the shrapnel fly. This generation's *Obergefell v. Hodges* may trump a previous generation's *Roe v. Wade* with the number of volleys made between those entrenched on opposing sides of this cultural divide. The pattern of polarized positions and the dizzying confusion of how Christians engage North American culture is likely to continue for many years.

A robust missional engagement with North American culture is an urgent task facing the North American church today. As Lesslie Newbigin believed, "there is no higher priority for the research work of missiologists than the question of what would be involved in a genuinely missionary encounter between the gospel and this modern Western culture."[1] An essential undergirding component of this missionary encounter must be the development and practice of *a spirituality for cultural engagement.* In this chapter we will address that issue. But before we do, we will address three other preliminary issues that will properly set the stage. First, we note important theological foundations for cultural engagement. Second, we examine our cultural context by providing a missiological analysis of North American culture. Third, we describe the form of cultural engagement appropriate for the North American context, in conversation with two theological traditions. And in that context, we are ready, finally, to sketch a missional spirituality appropriate for cultural engagement in North America.

Foundations for Cultural Engagement

Cultural engagement is not an option but will be part of the mission of a faithful church. That demand arises from four theological considerations. The first is an understanding of the gospel as the good news of the kingdom. That is, in the person and work of Jesus Christ, God is restoring his gracious and loving rule over the whole of creation and every aspect of human life. Culture lies within the scope of God's reign. The second is an understanding of the comprehensive and restorative nature of salvation. The scope of God's saving work through Christ is truly comprehensive, restoring the whole of human life. The nature of this salvation is restorative, seeking the restoration of *this* creation and not escape to another realm. The scope of salvation includes, of course, human culture. The third is the lordship of Jesus Christ. Followers of Christ are called in the whole of life to bear witness to Christ's lordship. He is more than a personal savior; he is Lord of all. Fourth, the church is the new humanity that shares in the future life of the kingdom now, as sign, foretaste, and instrument. As Herman Ridderbos observes, because of this reality, the life of the church comes to expression in the totality of her existence, and not only as she

---

[1]Lesslie Newbigin, *Foolishness to the Greeks: The Gospel and Western Culture* (Grand Rapids: Eerdmans, 1986), 3.

gathers for worship.[2] Therefore, in *both* the gathered community for worship *and* the scattered community in the world, the people of God represent the church as the new humanity that shares in and makes known the life of the kingdom of God.

But to engage our culture it is essential to understand the nature of culture. The rich work of mission studies offers incomparable insight to study culture for the sake of missional engagement—a body of work that unfortunately "has largely ignored the culture that is the most widespread, powerful and persuasive among all contemporary cultures—namely . . . modern Western culture."[3]

A starting point is to ask the most basic question: How do we understand "culture"? Paul Hiebert describes culture as "the integrated system of learned patterns of behavior, ideas and products characteristic of a society."[4] This integrated system is comprised of both cultural forms and the various functions, meaning, and usage given to those forms, as embodied in the behavior, ideas, and cultural products. Moreover, each culture has a framework that integrates each of these elements, an "integrating force," as Harvie Conn puts it.[5] As Conn suggests, "Every cultural form serves particular functions, conveys meaning to the participants of a culture and, since relatively passive in and of itself, is dependent for its meaning and function on how active human agents use it in their cultural framework."[6]

Unfortunately, most contemporary sociologists and anthropologists who study culture have been blind to the role of religion, describing religion as just another human activity within the cultural framework, an activity that has to do with supernatural beings, the afterlife, moral issues, and related religious practices within culture. They miss the centrality of the religious dimension of culture, but missionaries have not! Conn speaks of the religious direction as providing the most important

[2]Herman Ridderbos, *Paul: An Outline of His Theology* (Grand Rapids: Eerdmans, 1975), 328-30.
[3]Newbigin, *Foolishness to the Greeks*, 2-3.
[4]Paul Hiebert, *Cultural Anthropology* (Philadelphia: Lippincott, 1976), 45.
[5]Harvie Conn, "Conversion and Culture: A Theological Perspective with Reference to Korea," in *Down to Earth: Studies in Christianity and Culture*, ed. John Stott and Robert Coote (Grand Rapids: Eerdmans, 1980), 148.
[6]Ibid.

clue to the heart of the culture's integrity. Religion is not simply one aspect of culture but a core power that animates, unifies, and directs the whole of human cultural activity. As J. H. Bavinck put it, "Culture is religion made visible."[7]

To argue that culture is religion made visible is to speak of "religious belief" in a way that is not common in North America. It is common to relegate "religious beliefs" to the so-called private realm of life, which is held in sharp distinction to the public realm. Rather than see religious beliefs as one narrow aspect of life, it is in line with Scripture to see religious beliefs as the foundational beliefs that give shape and direction to the entirety of a particular culture. The religious beliefs that shape culture are the fundamental and comprehensive beliefs held in common that provide direction and meaning for the entire culture. "Religion is not an area of life, one among many, but primarily a direction of life.... Religion, then becomes the heart of a culture's integrity, its central dynamic as an organism, the totalistic radical response of man-in-covenant to the revelation of God."[8]

Here we can locate the important place of a worldview. As Conn suggests, a culture's worldview provides insight into the "deep structures" of a culture, "a deep-rooted 'map' of reality ordinarily unquestioned by the culture."[9] Even though it is ordinarily unquestioned, it is imporant to articulate this deep-rooted map of reality if we are to understand the religious core of a culture. Indeed, a worldview is "an articulation of the basic beliefs embedded in a shared grand story that are rooted in a faith commitment and that give shape and direction to the whole of our individual and corporate lives."[10]

What is the function of a worldview in culture?[11] First, a worldview originates in a grand story about the world, or what in our postmodern culture has become known as a *metanarrative*. This grand story is what

---

[7]J. H. Bavinck, *The Impact of Christianity on the Non-Christian World* (Grand Rapids: Eerdmans, 1949), 57.
[8]Conn, "Conversion and Culture," 149-50.
[9]Ibid., 154.
[10]Michael Goheen and Craig Bartholomew, *Living at the Crossroads: An Introduction to Christian Worldview* (Grand Rapids: Eerdmans, 2008), 23.
[11]Ibid., 23-25.

gives purpose and direction to our lives, and explains the world and our place in it. Second, these grand stories are shared and embodied in a communal way of life. The communal nature of these stories means that we have all been formed tacitly yet deeply by this story, since it has shaped the community into which we have been born and in which we live. Third, these grand stories are an expression of the ultimate religious faith commitments of our hearts, as they ultimately direct human life either toward the Creator God or toward some created thing. Fourth, these grand stories have within them the answers to the most ultimate questions facing humans, including the following: "What is life all about?," "Who are we?," "What kind of world do we live in?," "What's wrong with the world?," and "How can it be fixed?" The answers to these questions form our most basic beliefs about life and the world. Fifth, these grand stories, with these basic beliefs, give shape and normative direction to the entirety of our lives. They not only describe the world for us, but they provide us with a vision of how the world ought to be as well. This vision is not simply for our personal lives; it shapes and directs the totality of our lives together as a society—our political, economic, aesethic, social lives, and more. Worldviews validate and provide reinforcement to basic institutions, values, and goals of a society as they are expressed in the variety of cultural systems and structures.[12] If culture is *religion made visible*, then worldview plays an important mediating function in articulating *how* those religious faith commitments become visible in the cultural life of a society.

Missiological Analysis of North American Culture

With this background we may move toward a missiological analysis of our culture. This involves at least three things: an elaboration of the *religious core* that shapes culture, a narration of the *story* whereby those religious beliefs were formed, and an articulation of the *current religious spirits* at work in the culture. In this brief section we can do no more than offer a brief analysis of North American culture.

---

[12]Conn, "Conversion and Culture," 155.

Religious core of culture. The first necessary step is to unmask the secular bias and expose the religious core, the dominant public *credo* that undergirds the concrete pattern of North American life. We label the religious core of North American culture *confessional humanism.* Two statements arise out of the broader Western story that give vivid expression to this humanist faith. The first is found in the question of Friedrich Nietzsche in his parable of the madman: *"Must we not become gods?"*[13] Nietzsche here asks the obvious question that necessarily arises at the time of the eighteenth-century Enlightenment, when God was pushed to the margins of the public life of Western culture. If there is no God, then there is no Creator to give the meaning to human life, to order the creation and give universally valid standards of right and wrong, true and false, good and bad. Human beings must step into this place of Creator and define the purpose of life, construct order, and become the ultimate arbiter of right, true, and good. Moreover, if there is no God, no sovereign ruler to guide history to its goal and give it meaning, then humanity must take hold of the rudder of history and steer it to its ultimate destination. And, finally, if there is no God, then there is no Savior to liberate our world from evil and misery. Again, human beings must take on that role, and save themselves with their own resources.

The second confession made by Francis Bacon in the seventeenth century makes clear that the humanism of the West is a *scientific* humanism. He says, *"scientia postestas est* [knowledge is power]." Knowledge is power in two ways. First, the scientific method enables humanity to know the laws of the nonhuman creation so they can be translated into technological control in order to dominate nature for our social use. Second, scientific reason reveals to us the laws of the various social dimensions of life so we can fashion a more rational society.

Telling the story that shapes us. To uncover this religious commitment more fully it is necessary to tell the story that shapes us. In *A*

---

[13]For reference to the importance of Friedrich Nietzsche's parable of the madman for an analysis of Western culture, see Michael W. Goheen, *Introducing Christian Mission Today: Scripture, History, and Issues* (Downers Grove, IL: InterVarsity Press, 2014), 321-22; and Bob Goudzwaard, Mark Vander Vennen, and David Heemst, *Hope in Troubled Times: A New Vision for Confronting Global Crises* (Grand Rapids: Baker, 2007), 36-38.

Secular Age Charles Taylor examines how Western culture became secular, and does so by telling a story. "To get straight where we are, we have to go back and tell the story properly. Our past is sedimented in our present, and we are doomed to misidentify ourselves, as long as we can't do justice to where we came from. That is why the narrative is not an optional extra, why I believe that I have to tell a story here."[14] We will identify the religious beliefs of Western culture by sketching the skeleton of a story.

North American confessional humanism has its roots in the European story, and even further back in the religious choices of ancient Greco-Roman culture that set the trajectory of the story. The humanism of Greece and Rome was preserved within Europe in a synthesis with medieval Christianity for close to a millennium. The fifteenth-century Renaissance was a hinge into the modern world as it purportedly "broke the shackles of tradition, religion and superstition with the hammer of humanism forged in Greece and Rome."[15] Romano Guardini helpfully formulates three compass points of the modern humanism that emerged at this time: nature, subject, and culture.[16] The key to understanding all three of these concepts is *autonomy*, an understanding of the nonhuman creation, the human person, and cultural development as all existing apart from God and his authority. Culture is the domination of nature by the human subject to shape it for their purposes.[17] It was this will to dominance that led to the idolatry of science, technology, economic growth, and material abundance in the coming centuries.

The sixteenth- and seventeenth-century scientific revolution gave a method to Western humanity that would enable it to realize its autonomous mastery. At the beginning of the scientific revolution the Christian religious vision was ascendant, yet by the end of this period humanism was the dominant faith. Contributing to this triumph of confessional humanism were two things: the reactionary opposition of the

---

[14]Charles Taylor, *A Secular Age* (Cambridge, MA: Belknap Press of Harvard University Press, 2007), 29.

[15]Philip Sampson, "The Rise of Postmodernity," in *Faith and Modernity*; ed. Philip Sampson, Vinay Samuel, and Chris Sugden (Oxford: Regnum Lynx Books, 1994), 33.

[16]Romano Guardini, *The World and the Person*, trans. Stella Lange (Chicago: Henry Regnery, 1965); originally published as *Welt und Person: Vesuche zur Christlichen Lehr vom Menschen* (Würzburg: Werkbund-Verlag, 1939).

[17]Guardini, *World and Person*, 11.

church to the original fathers of science, which seemed to indicate Christianity's irrelevance; and the religious wars of the seventeenth century, which seemed to prove that the Christian faith only produced violence, while science could achieve unity.[18] As the scientific revolution drew to a close, the "West had 'lost its faith'—and found a new one, in science and in man."[19]

During the eighteenth-century Enlightenment the *credo* of modern humanism was forged. Progress became "the working faith of our civilization."[20] Faith is no longer placed in God but in human ability to progressively build a better world. Ronald Wright refers to this faith in progress as "secular religion."[21] Biblical images of paradise shape the hopeful imagination of the time. The primary characteristic of the good life in paradise is material prosperity and the freedom to pursue and enjoy it. This is the secular paradise toward which the faith and the hope of the West is now directed.

What is the road to this paradise? Humanity "is capable, guided solely by the light of reason and experience, of perfecting the good life on earth."[22] This better world is realized, first, as scientific reason discerns the natural laws of the nonhuman creation and translates them into technological control. In this way humanity could be the "master and possessor of nature."[23] But, second, if scientific reason could discern the laws of politics, society, economics, law, and education, analogous to physical law, then those laws too could be controlled to produce a more rationally ordered society to realize our goals. John Bury describes the spirit in terms of a new social order that "could alter human nature and create a heaven on earth."[24]

---

[18]See Goheen and Bartholomew, *Living at the Crossroads*, 89-91.

[19]Richard Tarnas, *The Passion of the Western Mind: Understanding the Ideas That Have Shaped Our World View* (New York: Ballantine, 1991), 320.

[20]Christopher Dawson, *Progress and Religion: An Historical Inquiry* (Washington, DC: Catholic University of America Press, 2001; originally published 1929), 15.

[21]Ronald Wright, *A Short History of Progress*, CBC Massey Lecture Series (Toronto: House of Anansi Press, 1994), 4.

[22]Carl Becker, *The Heavenly City of the Eighteenth-Century Philosophers* (New Haven, CT: Yale University Press, 1932), 31.

[23]René Descartes, *Discourse on Method*, trans. Donald A. Cress, 3rd ed. (Indianapolis: Hacket, 1993), 3.

[24]John Bagnell Bury, *The Idea of Progress: An Inquiry into Its Origin and Growth* (New York: Dover, 1932), 205.

In this context Adam Smith, an Enlightenment economic philosopher, articulated his vision of progress toward a better world of material prosperity that would arise through discerning and controlling of economic forces. For this to happen, it was necessary to corral two forces—division of labor and accumulation of capital. The market would be the mechanism that would coordinate these forces for the material betterment of humanity. This is the key to the prosperous future of humankind.

If this Enlightenment vision is true, then "the establishment of *new* social institutions is . . . a dire necessity and a high ethical imperative. . . . The narrow way to the lost paradise can only be the way of *social revolution*."[25] The revolutions of the nineteenth and twentieth centuries—Industrial, French, American, Democratic, Marxist—sought to bring society into conformity with this Enlightenment faith. The Industrial Revolution began to implement the Enlightenment economic vision of Adam Smith and the classical economists. But the Industrial Revolution did much more than reorganize economic production. It formed all aspects of culture into a new society ordered around economic life, the world of industrial capitalism, which hit its high point at the end of the nineteenth century.

Discerning the religious spirits today. We can discern three spirits at work in the West today that arose during the twentieth century: postmodernity, economic globalization, and consumerism. The events of the twentieth century delivered some heavy body blows to people's confidence in progress. Environmental destruction, growing poverty, the nuclear threat, economic breakdown, social problems, and psychological disorders all made clear that the religious vision of progress was not working. This widespread challenge to the entire Enlightenment faith is at the heart of postmodernism. Nevertheless, even while a growing postmodern spirit protested the Enlightenment vision, progress remained resilient in its liberal form as the working faith of North American culture. Christopher Lasch suggests that today "it is to Adam Smith and his immediate predecessors . . . that we should look for the inner meaning of

---

[25]Bob Goudzwaard, *Capitalism and Progress: A Diagnosis of Western Society* (Grand Rapids: Eerdmans, 1979), 50-51.

progressive ideology."[26] Indeed, it is his notion of progress as the promise of universal abundance that would endure throughout the twentieth century.

The reason is clear enough. Industrial capitalism had "raised the general standard of living, . . . transformed scarcity into abundance, awakening wants where none had been before, multiplying few into many, bringing more and more varied goods to more people at lower prices, so that what had formerly, if at all, been available only to a few . . . was now in reach of many." Lasch's next words offer insight into the growing global reach of this worldview: "It remained only to complete the capitalist revolution by making the 'blessings of leisure' available to all."[27] Indeed, globalization is the spread of this new economic form of the modern humanist faith around the world. Jane Collier rightly discerns the religious character of this development: "Precisely because the culture of economism is a quasi-religion, with a pretense of encompassing the totality of life and of bringing happiness and fulfilment, we find ourselves obliged from a Christian point of view to denounce it as dehumanizing idolatry."[28]

Economic globalization has generated great wealth but that wealth has been spread unevenly. There is an "asymmetric globalization"[29] in which dire poverty exists alongside an excessive consumer culture. The consumerism of North America "appears to have become part and parcel of the very fabric of modern life. . . . And the parallel with religion is not an accidental one. Consumerism is . . . arguably *the* religion of the late twentieth century."[30] Since the twentieth century, consumerism as a way of life, a consumption of both goods and experiences, is perhaps the most powerful spirit at work in North America as it pervades and shapes all of cultural life. Indeed, "consumer capitalism, both for good and for ill, is a pervasive and foundational reality of our day."[31]

---

[26]Christopher Lasch, *The True and Only Heaven: Progress and Its Critics* (New York: Norton, 1991), 54.

[27]Ibid., 78-79.

[28]Jane Collier, "Contemporary Culture and the Role of Economics," in *The Gospel and Contemporary Culture*, ed. Hugh Montefiore (London: Mowbray, 1992), 122.

[29]Joseph E. Stiglitz, *Making Globalization Work* (New York: Norton, 2006), 62.

[30]Stephen Miles, *Consumerism: As a Way of Life* (Thousand Oaks, CA: Sage Publications, 1998), 1.

[31]Rodney Clapp, "Why the Devil Takes VISA: A Christian Response to the Triumph of Consumerism," *Christianity Today*, October 7, 1996, 21.

The church committed to living out the good news of the kingdom of God in the midst of this kind of culture may not remain content with the status quo. For the consumer culture of the early twenty-first century, the bad news is, "I can't get no satisfaction, and I've tried and I've tried and I've tried."[32] The good news is that true life is found in Jesus Christ, and this can only be offered by a community that believes and embodies the biblical story over against the dehumanizing idolatry of the humanist story.

Missionary Encounter with Culture: Anabaptist or Reformed?

The faithful posture that the North American church must take within this cultural context is that of a missionary encounter. When the gospel is embodied faithfully by the Christian community, a missionary encounter occurs between the gospel and the fundamental beliefs that shape the society. Insofar as the church is faithful, there will be three aspects to this missionary encounter. First, the foundational beliefs shared by a cultural community will be challenged. A missionary encounter is about a clash of ultimate and comprehensive stories—the biblical story centered in the lordship of Jesus Christ and the cultural story. Second, the church will offer the gospel as a noncoercive and credible alternative way of life to its culture. It will embody in its life the coming kingdom of God that will contrast with the life of those within the cultural community. Finally, the attractive lives and words of Christians will be an appealing call for radical conversion, an inviting summons to understand and live in the world in the light of the gospel.

The description that Ian Barns offers of Lesslie Newbigin's work captures the heart of a missionary encounter: "His purpose is not to make a 'space' for Christianity *within* a wide pluralism, but to recover the alternative universalist counter claims of Christianity based on the . . . life, death and resurrection of Jesus."[33] All three adjectives used by Barnes to describe the "claims" of Christianity are important: *alternative*, because

---

[32] Lyrics from The Rolling Stones' song "I Can't Get No Satisfaction."

[33] Ian Barns, "Christianity in a Pluralist Society: A Dialogue with Lesslie Newbigin," *St Mark's Review* 158 (Winter 1994): 29.

the gospel presents another way of understanding and living in the world; *universalist,* because the call of the gospel is valid for all people and claims the whole of human life; and *counter,* because the gospel challenges the story of modernity, calling for repentance and conversion.

A missionary encounter does not mean a polemical or anticultural stance.[34] There is much good about North American culture, and so a missionary encounter will mean a loving involvement and dialogical engagement that appreciates and embraces the creational good while rejecting the idolatrous distortion. A missionary encounter thus involves cultural discernment in light of the comprehensive claims of the gospel.

Among those who agree on the breadth of the church's missional engagement with culture, there remain differences on *how* to witness to Christ's lordship and to his comprehensive salvation. What is the most faithful way to encounter a demonic consumer culture? The Anabaptist approach has become an attractive option in North America, and with good reason.[35] Two important features characterize this view. First, it emphasizes the communal dimensions of missional engagement. This is a reaction against a reduction of mission to the calling of individuals, a reduction that has been characteristic of Christendom. The Anabaptist model emphasizes "the primary task of the church is simply to *be* the church, the *true* community of committed believers which, by its very existence and example, becomes a challenge to society and the state."[36] Second, the critical or negative side of the church's relationship to its culture dominates. The concern is that the church of Christendom has domesticated itself and not been critical of the idolatrous powers of culture. The church must take a countercultural stance and critique the idolatrous status quo. "The church is understood to be an implicit or

---

[34]See Michael W. Goheen, "Is Lesslie Newbigin's Model of Contextualization Anticultural?," *Mission Studies* 19, no. 1 (October 2002): 136-56.

[35]E.g., Stanley Hauerwas and William H. Willimon, *Resident Aliens: A Provocative Christian Assessment of Culture and Ministry for People Who Know That Something Is Wrong* (Nashville: Abingdon, 1989); John Howard Yoder, *The Politics of Jesus: Behold the Man! Our Victorious Lamb* (Grand Rapids: Eerdmans, 1972); Darrell Guder et al., *Missional Church: A Vision for the Sending of the Church in North America* (Grand Rapids: Eerdmans, 1998); Douglas John Hall, *The End of Christendom and the Future of Christianity* (Valley Forge, PA: Trinity Press International, 1997).

[36]David Bosch, "God's Reign and the Rulers of This World: Missiological Reflections on Church-State Relationships," in *The Good News of the Kingdom: Mission Theology for the Third Millennium,* ed. Charles van Engen, Dean S. Gilliland, and Paul Pierson (Maryknoll, NY: Orbis Books, 1993), 92.

latent *critical factor* in society. . . . The church is critical of the status quo, indeed *very* critical of it."[37]

It is not surprising that this approach is appealing in North America. A strong individualism calls forth a biblical emphasis on community. A church deeply compromised by culture—"an advanced case of syncretism"[38]—requires new emphasis on the church's countercultural identity.[39] These renewed emphases are badly needed. The question is whether this way of understanding the church's mission offers resources to scattered believers in their varied callings in the public life of society. Moreover, the church in the West is not as marginalized as the early church; in fact, it holds a great deal of cultural power. The question is how cultural power may be used in a faithful way.

The Reformed approach casts a vision that will equip Christians who hold cultural power to carry out their callings in the world faithfully. With deep appreciation for the emphases of the Anabaptist approach, the Reformational position believes that approach has not adequately addressed the callings of individual believers in society and offered guidance on how to use power responsibly in light of the gospel. And further, the Reformational tradition recognizes the creational good in various cultural structures and is concerned to work toward their renewal. It is just as radical as the Anabaptist model, but it is a radicalism of critical *participation*.

There are dangers. The most obvious is the ever-present and oft-realized danger of domestication. There is pressure to play by the cultural rules of the game, and thereby imbibe the idolatry. The Anabaptist tradition criticizes a Reformational position for this very thing. It believes compromise is inevitable, and therefore urges the church to take a position on the margins. There is also the danger of a nostalgic return to the triumphalism of Christendom. The language of "building God's kingdom" still lingers with the understanding that our cultural endeavors may largely usher in God's kingdom and Christianize society. However, neither of

---

[37]Ibid.

[38]Lesslie Newbigin, *The Other Side of 1984: Questions for the Churches* (Geneva: WCC, 1983), 23.

[39]Cf. Konrad Raiser, "Gospel and Cultures," *International Review of Mission*, 83, no. 331 (October 1994): 623-39; and David J. Bosch, *Believing in the Future: Toward a Missiology of Western Culture* (Valley Forge, PA: Trinity Press International, 1995), 56-57.

these dangers is inherent in the Reformational tradition. And since the church still wields a great deal of cultural power, there is a need to draw on this tradition for resources to equip the church today for its task in the public life of culture.

Different cultural contexts call for different stances. The differing stances that the early church took toward its cultural situation, for example, are revealed in the books of Romans and Revelation. Dean Flemming offers a helpful analysis that compares Romans 13 and Revelation 13, and he argues that "different contexts call for different responses" to the Roman Empire. While the contexts differ, the key is that in both situations the church is called to witness to the breadth of God's kingdom: "Both, in fact, engage their public worlds with a missional goal, but they do so from alternative angles." The book of Romans seems to "encourage Christians to positively participate in the life of society in redemptive ways."[40] Earlier, he notes, "Christians were to live out their calling within the existing structures of Greco-Roman society while displaying a visible internal difference." They were to live within those institutions with a "cross shaped difference" that would lead to transformation from within.[41] On the other hand, Revelation takes a more sectarian stance because of the demonic depths idolatry has reached. Thus Revelation "launches a countercultural critique" and calls the church to a "prophetic and costly witness." In Romans and Revelation "we discover two different but complementary theological visions. Each spotlights one side of the church's relationship to the Empire; each shows sensitivity to the particular needs of the communities they address."[42]

A concern we have about some expressions of the burgeoning Anabaptist tradition, which is more in line with Revelation than Romans, is that the church is not yet marginalized and persecuted to the same extent as the church in Revelation. The church continues to exercise cultural power. Further, the structures of Western culture arguably have not reached the same demonic depth, nor is the cultural attitude toward the

---

[40]Dean Flemming, *Contextualization in the New Testament: Patterns for Theology and Mission* (Downers Grove, IL: InterVarsity Press, 2005), 289-90.

[41]Ibid., 149.

[42]Ibid., 290-91.

church as hostile. We recognize that the church is more and more being marginalized, that global economic structures are increasingly unjust and oppressive, and that hostility to the Christian faith is growing. So it is clear that the rich resources of the book of Revelation will be increasingly important for the North American church.[43] However, we believe that much of the Romans' situation still exists in our context, and that the church must ask how it might participate redemptively in the structures of our culture.

Our changing situation will mean that the church will have to continue to struggle with the shape of its missional engagement with culture. Since the church's calling in culture means participation and involvement, the Reformational tradition can offer insight in how to use its cultural power under the sign of the cross. Since the church's calling in culture means antithesis and resistance, the Anabaptist tradition can offer wisdom in how to oppose cultural idolatry. Loving our neighbor means both positive involvement in cultural development and negative resistance to reigning idolatry that takes both communal and individual form. If the church is to be faithful in its engagement with the public life of Western culture, an urgent task will be to appropriate the insights of both traditions in fresh and creative ways.

Missional Spirituality for North American Cultural Engagement

Given the religious beliefs that profoundly shape North American culture, a robust spirituality for cultural engagement that nourishes and sustains the missional life of the church is vital. This spirituality will seek to flesh out the important role of the communal life of the church, the needed Christian dispositions, and the dynamics of spiritual vitality.

Communal life. We begin by exploring the important role of the church's communal life together. To appreciate the missional importance of the church's communal life for a spirituality of cultural engagement, we must come to terms with the tension the church always faces in its embodiment of the gospel within culture. The gospel is always expressed and

---

[43]See ibid., 266-95. See also Richard Bauckham *The Bible and Mission: Christian Witness in a Postmodern World* (Grand Rapids: Baker, 2003), 83-112.

embodied *in* cultural forms and *by* communities immersed in particular cultures. We cannot speak of the gospel without using the language, symbols, images, or practices of a particular culture. The gospel is not a timeless message quarantined from all cultural "contamination." Rather, the gospel is always embodied in the life and words of a particular culture. There is no such thing as a culturally disembodied gospel.

Both the gospel and human culture are communally embodied. Newbigin laments the tendency to miss this embodiment: "The question of gospel and culture is sometimes discussed as though it were a matter of the meeting of two quite different things: a disembodied message and a historically conditioned pattern of social life."[44] There is no such thing as a disembodied gospel—the gospel is always encountered within a cultural context and as it is embodied by a particular community. The same is true with cultures—they come to us embodied by particular communities with particular ways of life. The religious beliefs that lie at the core of a culture are always embodied in cultural institutions that give expression to these beliefs. These communal embodiments of religious cultural beliefs lend plausibility to the religious beliefs, and function as "plausibility structures" for these beliefs.[45]

Thus, the church will always find itself seeking to incarnate the gospel as a community within the context of a cultural story that has its own religious faith commitments that are embodied by its own institutions and communities. It is into this contested cultural context that the church bears witness to the gospel, as an entirely different but equally comprehensive story about life, embodied by alternative institutions, communities, and practices. This is a recipe for profound tension. Living within this tension and seeking to resolve it together in a community of faith is a vital dimension to the missional task of cultural engagement.

To borrow an image from Peter Berger and Thomas Luckmann, the church in its communal life must seek to function as a laboratory of transformation, where the reality of the gospel is mediated through the

---

[44]Lesslie Newbigin, *The Gospel in a Pluralist Society* (Grand Rapids: Eerdmans, 1989), 188.
[45]Peter Berger and Thomas Luckmann, *The Social Construction of Reality: A Treatise in the Sociology of Knowledge* (New York: Doubleday, 1966), 157.

communal life, stories, and interpretations of reality offered within the Christian community, which are all offered as real alternatives to the reigning plausibility structures within culture.[46] Similarly, John Kavanaugh suggests, we "must turn to a community of shared life-experience which both fosters committed faith and enables the individual to criticize and challenge the programming of the culture."[47]

Not only is this shared way of life necessary for the church to function as a laboratory of transformation, but so are the important ways that local congregations equip, support, and nourish their members for cultural engagement. The local fellowship of believers who support one another in their cultural engagement is vital to this task of the church. The forms of support may vary, depending on context, but certainly should include encouragement, prayer, financial support, insight, and committed wrestling together with Scripture as members seek to be nourished in the gospel and bear witness to the gospel in their particular cultural context. The Jerusalem community in the early chapters of Acts continues to point us to the importance of these forms of support.[48]

In addition to these forms of support, Newbigin highlights the importance of congregational structures that equip members for their task of cultural engagement in their vocational spheres of life. Newbigin highlights four structural features that are particularly needed. The first is regular gatherings where the whole congregation gathers "to find out together what witness and service He wants of them from week to week, as individuals and a body."[49] These gatherings to discern both corporate and individual callings would keep the challenging task of cultural engagement ever before the community as a central part of its missional task in the world. The second is study centers that would carry out the work of doing missiological analysis of culture and resource members with insight and training in the dynamics of cultural engagement on a variety of cultural

---

[46]Ibid., 157-60.

[47]John F. Kavanaugh, *Following Christ in a Consumer Society: The Spirituality of Cultural Resistance*, 2nd ed. (Maryknoll, NY: Orbis, 2006), 148.

[48]Acts 2:42-47; 4:32-35.

[49]Lesslie Newbigin, "Our Task Today" (unpublished address given to the fourth meeting of the diocesan council, Tirumangalam, December 18–20, 1951), 6.

issues and vocational implications.[50] The third is other local initiatives that would be taken up, including conferences and meetings, where congregational members in different vocations would gather to consider the realities of cultural engagement with the gospel and culture at the national and local levels. The fourth is the importance of congregational leadership that equips. For Newbigin, it is a high priority for ministers to train people in their congregations for cultural engagement in their vocational spheres. While gathering the congregation together for worship is part of their role, "the other half is to send them back to their daily tasks equipped to be the salt of the earth and the light of the world. If we forget this second part, the other can be positively dangerous."[51] Newbigin rightly helps us see the importance of congregational and leadership structures that aim to support, equip, and nourish the church in its cultural engagement.

Christian dispositions. A second component of a robust missional spirituality for cultural engagement is the role of Christian dispositions. As we reflect on the unique challenges and opportunities facing the church in its cultural engagement with a consumer culture, three dispositions rise to the surface as particularly important for the church to cultivate among its members.

The first is *gospel freedom*. Newbigin draws our attention to the importance of 1 Peter 2:16 for our cultural engagement: "Live as free people, but do not use your freedom as a cover-up for evil; live as God's slaves."[52] One of the fruits of the gospel is the freedom that Christ has won for those who follow him. Gospel freedom is multifaceted and rich: freedom from condemnation, freedom from the bondage and power of sin, freedom from the wrath of God's judgment on sin, freedom from shame and guilt, and freedom from a life of decay and destruction as we are delivered into the life of the kingdom of God. And because of this freedom, we are now free to become servants of all people. Our freedom *from* the condemnation, bondage, power, judgment, shame, guilt, decay, and destruction of sin

---

[50]Lesslie Newbigin, *Unfinished Agenda: An Updated Autobiography* (London: SPCK, 1993), 119.

[51]Lesslie Newbigin, *The Good Shepherd: Meditations on Christian Ministry in Today's World* (Grand Rapids: Eerdmans, 1977), 80.

[52]Lesslie Newbigin, "Bible Studies: Four Talks on 1 Peter by Bishop Newbigin," in *We Were Brought Together*, ed. David M. Taylor (Sydney: Australian Council for the WCC, 1960), 106.

brings with it a freedom *to* live as a servant of God. As Newbigin comments, "We need to have both of them at full strength and not, as is so often the case, a tasteless mixture of the two. The Christian is a free man. . . . And precisely so, he is the servant of all for Christ's sake."[53]

What is the importance of this disposition for cultural engagement? North American culture, along with other varieties of Western culture, is seeing the proliferation of idolatry. As Tim Keller argues, our contemporary society is not fundamentally different from ancient societies that were filled with shrines built for their favorite deities.

> Each culture is dominated by its own set of idols. Each has its "priesthoods," its totems and rituals. Each one has its shrines—whether office towers, spas and gyms, studios, or stadiums—where sacrifices must be made in order to procure the blessings of the good life and ward off disaster. What are the gods of beauty, power, money, and achievement but these same things that have assumed mythic proportions in our individual lives and in our society?[54]

These idols, or counterfeit gods, are rampant in our North American culture. Keller argues, "A counterfeit god is anything so central and essential to your life that, should you lose it, your life would feel hardly worth living. An idol has such a controlling position in your heart that you can spend most of your passion and energy, your emotional and financial resources, on it without a second thought."[55] There are personal idols in people's lives, cultural idols that shape the religious beliefs of a culture, intellectual idols that function like powerful ideologies; there are idols in every vocational field; "there are idols everywhere."[56]

This dynamic of rampant idolatry is aided by the disintegration of Christendom. This disintegration, Newbigin notes, is "producing an ever multiplying brood of secular messianisms." He continues, noting the missional opportunity,

---

[53]Ibid.
[54]Timothy Keller, *Counterfeit Gods* (New York: Dutton, 2009), xi-xii.
[55]Ibid., xviii.
[56]Ibid., xix-xxi.

The call in our time is for Christian men and women who have been made free as the sons and daughters of God are free, to go wherever this disintegrating culture is going, set free by Christ from every kind of bondage to the spiritual powers which are inherent in these new messianisms, free from fear of all their demonic powers and free from temptation by their illusory promises, in order to be simply at the service of human beings, using modern techniques to serve man but acknowledging no other Lord than the servant-Lord Himself. And that has profound implications for the future pattern of missionary service.[57]

These idols, with their false messiahs, demonic powers, and illusory promises, hold those who serve them in bondage. We tend to love, trust, and obey the idols we serve—both in our personal lives and in our culture as a whole. We look to our idols to give us love, to provide our lives with a sense of beauty, significance, meaning, and purpose. We make "sacrifices" to appease and please our idols, believing they will give us the good life they hold out for us. We look to idols to provide us with confidence, security, and hope. Before we realize it, the idols we worship exercise their control over us.

We are free in Christ from all of these. This life of freedom from the false, secular messiahs and their "demonic powers" and "illusory promises" will be nourished in the life of the church through the regular practice of repentance and rejoicing. As Keller suggests, these two belong together. The gospel freedom that Christ has won for us invites us to honestly identify and turn from the idols we are tempted to serve. The kind of cultural analysis suggested above is critical for a spirituality of cultural engagement that helps the church identify the idols of our day.

This identification of idols must also move beyond cultural analysis into the personal and corporate practices of repentance. And this repentance must be coupled with a life of rejoicing in the freedom that Christ has won for us in the gospel. Repenting without rejoicing will lead us down the path of introspection and despair, while rejoicing without repenting is a shallow exercise that will not lead to deep change.[58] But when

---

[57]Newbigin, "Bible Studies," 106.
[58]Keller, *Counterfeit Gods*, 172.

the two come together, we experience the freedom of the gospel—a freedom that is the key to lasting change and a spirituality that resists the powerful idols rampant in our culture.

A second needed disposition is *faithful endurance*. Cultural engagement will bring with it the inevitability of suffering. The faithfulness of our missional engagement with the New Testament "may perhaps be in part judged by the place which we accord to suffering in our understanding of the calling of the Church."[59] Newbigin continues to explain why suffering is a mark of missional faithfulness:

> No human societies cohere except on the basis of some kind of common beliefs and customs. No society can permit these beliefs and practices to be threatened beyond a certain point without reacting in self-defense. The idea that we ought to be able to expect some kind of neutral secular political order, which presupposes no religious or ideological beliefs, and which holds the ring impartially for a plurality of religions to compete with one another, has no adequate foundation. The New Testament makes it plain that Christ's followers must expect suffering as the normal badge of their discipleship, and also as one of the characteristic forms of their witness.[60]

Part of the "self-defense" we can expect from societies whose idolatrous beliefs and practices are threatened is the backlash of the powers at work in that society. North America is no exception. The backlash from our North American society will lead inevitably down the path of suffering for those who threaten the reigning beliefs and structures of this society.

In light of this, a spirituality of suffering is vital for the church in North America to recover. Again, Keller has helped the church tremendously in this regard with his recent work on suffering. Keller notes that when it comes to understanding and handling suffering, "our own contemporary secular, Western culture is one of the weakest and worst in history at doing so."[61] Our secular Western culture gives us no explanation for suffering, very little guidance on how to deal with it, and as a result we are

---

[59]Lesslie Newbigin, *Trinitarian Faith and Today's Mission* (Richmond, VA: John Knox, 1964), 42.
[60]Newbigin, *Trinitarian Faith*, 42.
[61]Timothy Keller, *Walking with God Through Pain and Suffering* (New York: Dutton, 2013), 14.

left more shocked and undone by suffering than any other culture throughout history.[62]

In contrast, Keller points to the resources within the Christian tradition. These resources of the Christian faith constitute bedrock for developing a spirituality of suffering, whether that suffering comes through loss or cultural backlash. First, Christians believe in a personal, wise, inscrutable God who controls the affairs of the world. We are delivered from the fates to which we must blindly submit in the face of suffering. Second, Christians believe in a God who entered our world, who came and suffered with and for us in the person of Jesus Christ. God is not detached from our pain and suffering, but enters into our suffering with us. Third, Christians believe that through faith in Christ, we are given the assurance of salvation from the endless cycle of suffering. The power of karma is broken by the power of Christ's salvation. And, at the same time, there is greater room for expressions of sorrow and grief as we see and experience the love of God in Christ. Fourth, Christians believe in the future bodily resurrection and restoration of the material world, which also means that all that we lose in this life will not be lost to us forever.[63]

Building on this foundation, Keller points us to some of the important practices of a spirituality of suffering for the church today. To begin, we are invited to "move through suffering without shock and surprise, without denial of our sorrow and weakness, without resentment or paralyzing fear, yet also without acquiescence or capitulation, without surrender or despair."[64] Suffering that comes as a part of cultural engagement should not shock us. As we learn to walk through it, our walking is grounded in the biblical promise of a God who is committed to walk beside us through the suffering we experience.

Second, we are invited to weep in the darkness that suffering inevitably brings with it.[65] Whether suffering is related to loss, rejection, or persecution, the experience of darkness accompanies those who suffer. While there is a long tradition in the church of minimizing expressions of sorrow

---

[62]Ibid.,15.
[63]Ibid., 42-58.
[64]Ibid., 226.
[65]Ibid., 246-49.

and lament, a robust spirituality of suffering will renew our practices of learning to grieve, to weep, to lament as we experience the anguish of suffering.

Third, we are invited to trust in a God whose ways are often hidden from us in the midst of suffering. Suffering is often accompanied by an invitation to trust in a God whose ways we do not understand and whose presence can sometimes even seem hidden from us.

Fourth, we are invited to practice what Keller describes as the disciplines of "thinking, thanking, and loving." Christian peace in the face of suffering, argues Keller, "comes not from thinking less but from thinking more, and more intensely, about the big issues of life. . . . Peace comes from a disciplined thinking out of the implications of what you believe."[66] The discipline of thanking is to learn to live out the invitation of Philippians 4:6, where Paul says, "Do not be anxious about anything, but in every situation, by prayer and petition, with thanksgiving, present your requests to God." This, Keller explains, is the discipline of thanking a sovereign God for whatever he sends our way, even if we do not understand it.[67] Loving is an invitation to allow our experience of suffering to expose the ways we have ordered the loves of our heart. Keller comments, "Here, then, is what we must do when we suffer. We should look around our lives to see if our suffering has not been unnecessarily intensified because there are some things that we have set our hearts and hopes upon too much. We must relocate our glory and reorder our loves."[68] Particularly in a post-Christendom world, the church in North America may discover some disordered loves exposed by finding itself suffering on the margins of society.

Finally, we are invited in the face of suffering to walk in hope. This is a hope that is rooted in the future life of the kingdom, where we believe that all our desires and loves will be fulfilled, all that we have lost will be restored, no perpetrator of injustice will get away with anything, and all wrongdoing will be put down. "If the death of Jesus Christ happened for

---

[66]Ibid., 299-300.
[67]Ibid., 302.
[68]Ibid., 307.

us and he bore our hopelessness so that now we can have hope—and if the resurrection of Jesus Christ happened—then even the worst things will turn into the best things, and the greatest are yet to come."[69]

This leads us to consider a third needed disposition: *provocative hope.* The apostle Peter speaks of the missional importance of hope for the Christian community when he writes, "But in your hearts revere Christ as Lord. Always be prepared to give an answer to everyone who asks you to give the reason for the hope that you have. But do this with gentleness and respect" (1 Pet 3:15). This "living hope," was something that distinguished the early church communities. Newbigin describes the power of living by this hope. He says,

> The hope is the inexplicable thing, for everything visible will speak of trouble and conflict and loss. . . . Hope was the thing the pagan world could not understand. It was . . . a mere delusion which men might follow who were foolish enough to imagine that it led anywhere. . . . But for Peter, as for all the apostles, hope is the keynote of everything.[70]

The Christian hope is an unshakable confidence in God's future kingdom coming to earth, of heaven and earth being united as one—a confidence rooted in the reality of Christ's resurrection victory over all the powers of evil and death. As Peter expresses it, we have a "living hope through the resurrection of Jesus Christ from the dead" (1 Pet 1:3). This unshakable disposition of hope nourishes the church for its cultural engagement with a confidence that is much needed. Newbigin comments, "The Christian is always looking forward, most sure of victory just when everything looks most hopeless; basing his actions in each situation upon the sure certainty of God's kingdom coming, when all the evidence seems to point to its receding."[71]

Such hope in North American culture today will be provocative; it will provoke questions, inviting explanations for the hope we have in the gospel. Such an explanation must avoid the dualism that reduces the gospel to the private realm of life and reduces hope to the afterlife.

---

[69]Ibid., 318.
[70]Newbigin, "Bible Studies," 113.
[71]Ibid.

Rather, it is an explanation that is rooted in the good news that in the person and work of Jesus Christ, God is restoring his rule over the whole of creation and every aspect of human life. Our hope of salvation in the gospel is one of creation being restored and made to flourish under the loving and gracious rule of Christ, who rescues the creation from the twisting power of sin. This must lead the church not to a place of passively wishing God's rule to manifest itself in the world, but rather "to 'involvement,' or engagement with the world—with the whole of human life in all its dimensions."[72] A dualistic hope that sanctions living out certain areas of our lives within the hope of Christ's lordship, while living out other areas of our lives under the idolatrous religious beliefs shaping North American culture, is nothing less than an abandonment of our calling as Christians. To live with such hope in our troubled times is and will remain a powerful, provocative witness for the church in North American culture.[73]

Nourishing spiritual vitality. A final aspect of missional spirituality for cultural engagement is the importance of practices for nourishing spiritual vitality in both the corporate and personal aspects of Christian life. The corporate life of the local congregation is essential for the nourishment of spiritual vitality among its members. The local fellowship of believers is vital to nourish the life of Christ through the practices of proclaiming the Word and the celebration of the sacraments. These are the means through which the power and presence of God himself is mediated to the church. Newbigin asks, "Are we placing these in the very centre of our church life? . . . Do we understand, do our congregations understand, that when the Word is truly preached and the sacraments duly administered, Christ himself is present in the midst with all His saving power?"[74]

Together, the Word, sacraments, and the entirety of the corporate practices of worship nourish the local congregation for its task of cultural engagement. The gathered community for Sunday worship is nourishment in the power of the gospel and the life of Christ for the

---

[72]G. C. Berkouwer, *The Church: Studies in Dogmatics*, trans. James E. Davison (Grand Rapids: Eerdmans, 1976), 395-96.
[73]See Bob Goudzwaard et al., *Hope in Troubled Times*, for a robust and timely exposition of how the Christian hope informs cultural engagement in areas of pressing global concern.
[74]Newbigin, "Our Task Today," 4.

engagement of its members in their scattered witness Monday through Saturday. It is only as the life of Christ flows to us through the Spirit that it will be possible to endure the painful tension of bearing witness to the gospel and therefore challenging the idolatrous powers and beliefs at work in North American culture.

Along with these corporate practices in the local congregation, the personal life of the believer must continually be renewed in the gospel for spiritual vitality to be sustained. Two aspects can be highlighted. The first is the importance of cultivating gospel renewal in the heart. We need the Spirit to bring the gospel home to our hearts so that we experience the love and power of Christ and are renewed regularly by God's grace.[75] Personal renewal takes place at the level of the heart, which the Scriptures, particularly the book of Proverbs, make clear in their description of the human heart. The heart is the core root of human nature. That is where we see the motivational structure to our thoughts, our emotions, and our wills; all that we are and all that we do flows out of the heart. The heart is the "control center" of our lives; it is in the heart where we find the foundational commitments we make and that give shape to every aspect of our lives. It is therefore in our hearts where the Spirit needs to do his renewing work in our lives. Keller describes the Spirit's work:

> The Holy Spirit's job is to unfold the meaning of Jesus' person and work in such a way that its infinite importance and beauty are brought home to the mind and heart. This is why in the letter to the Ephesians Paul hopes that Christians, who already know rationally that Christ loves them, will have "the eyes of [their] heart . . . enlightened" (1:18) so they will "have power . . . to grasp how wide and long and high and deep is the love of Christ" (3:17-18). Paul's prayers in Ephesians show that Christians can expect the Holy Spirit to continually renew their boldness, love, joy, and power as they go beyond merely believing in the things that Jesus has done to experiencing them by the work of the Spirit.[76]

Second, the practice of prayer is critical for spiritual vitality. Prayer is the primary means by which we are joined to Christ and find his "life-giving

---

[75]Timothy Keller, *Center Church* (Grand Rapids: Zondervan, 2012), 60.
[76]Ibid.

sap" to empower and nourish us for mission.[77] Without this, the church dries up and bears little fruit. Indeed, prayer is how the kingdom of God advances, as we see in the book of Acts.[78] All our missional efforts are futile without prayer; prayer is central to the Christian's life and the church's missional engagement. Prayer emboldens the Christian and protects the integrity of our missional witness in North American culture. As N. T. Wright puts it, "Those involved at the leading edge of the church's mission to bring healing and renewal to the world, should be people of prayer, invoking the Spirit of Jesus daily and hourly as they go about their tasks, lest they be betrayed into the arrogance of their own agendas or into the cowardice of relativism."[79]

Conclusion

C. S. Lewis rightly claims, "There is no neutral ground in the universe: every square inch, every split second, is claimed by God and counter-claimed by Satan."[80] The Christian church joins the side of God in this battle, and if they are obedient, it will mean a missional engagement with every square inch of culture. If the church in North America has any hope of being faithful to this calling, it will require a rich spirituality that will emphasize the important role of the communal life of the church, will cultivate the needed Christian dispositions, and will nourish spiritual vitality with communal and personal devotional practices.

---

[77]Newbigin, *Good Shepherd*, 140.
[78]See the centrality of prayer in Acts, e.g., Acts 1:14; 2:42; 3:1; 6:3-4; 13:2-3; 16:22-26.
[79]N. T. Wright, *New Tasks for a Renewed Church* (London: Hodder & Stoughton, 1992), 86.
[80]C. S. Lewis, *Christian Reflections*, ed. Walter Hooper (Grand Rapids: Eerdmans, 1967), 33.

6

Welcome to Paul's World

THE CONTEXTUAL NATURE OF
A MISSIONAL SPIRITUALITY

Gary Tyra

THE FACT THAT MISSIONAL MINISTRY is highly contextual in nature is widely acknowledged.[1] The bold thesis of this chapter is that a fully faithful missional endeavor requires not only a ministry *methodology* that is context sensitive, but a *spirituality* as well. To be more precise, the chapter will argue that, while the biblical exhortation found in Jude 3 to "contend for the faith" should always be observed, the implicit call of the apostle Paul in 1 Corinthians 9:20-22 to keep contextualizing the gospel for various cultural contexts can be interpreted to suggest that *we should expect the spirituality (as well as the methodology) of missional communities to necessarily differ from one ministry location to the next.*

The first of the three sections making up this chapter provides a couple of important conceptual clarifications that,

---

[1]For example, see Darrell Guder, ed., *Missional Church: A Vision for the Sending of the Church in North America* (Grand Rapids: Eerdmans, 1998), 11; Alan J. Roxburgh and M. Scott Boren, *Introducing the Missional Church: Why It Matters, How to Become One* (Grand Rapids: Baker Books, 2009), 87; Craig Van Gelder, *The Missional Church in Context: Helping Congregations Develop Contextual Ministry* (Grand Rapids: Eerdmans, 2007), 32, 34, 40, 42-43.

when taken together, not only frame the discussion overall, but also forge a foundational presupposition critical to it. The second section of the chapter presents a theological discussion supportive of the notion that a particular type of ministry contextualization is required if the transformative power of the gospel is to be fully realized by means of it. The final section explores the way the missionary practices of ancient Celtic Christianity support the contention that a ministry spirituality that is both theologically and missionally faithful will necessarily differ from one ministry context to another.

My hope is that the arguments presented in this chapter will serve to inspire as well as inform, encouraging missional practitioners to cultivate a context-sensitive ministry spirituality that, precisely because it strives to do justice to both the apostolic understanding of the Christian faith and the contemporary cultural context, will enable an engagement in ministry contextualization that is both faithful and fruitful vis-à-vis the *missio Dei*.

Two Conceptual Clarifications

Though the multiple authors contributing to this collective work have approached their respective topics with a shared understanding of mission and spirituality in place, the editors have wisely allowed the contributors to fill out the concept of a missional spirituality in ways appropriate to their assigned topics. In my case, the charge is to elaborate on the relationship between a *missional spirituality* and *ministry contextualization*. Toward this end, the reader will find in this initial section of my essay some foundational clarifications of what I have in mind when I refer to these two cardinal concepts.

The dual nature of a missional spirituality. From the outset, I want to underscore the fact that Christian spirituality can be thought of in two different ways. First, the phenomenon of Christian spirituality can be understood in an *indicative* sense as the observable *effects* of a Christian's relationship with God. Second, Christian spirituality can also be construed in an *instrumental* sense as the *means* by which the follower of Christ endeavors to cultivate his or her relationship with God. In other words, Christian spirituality can either be conceived of as the manifestation of a disciple's experiential relationship with God in terms of his or her convictions, attitudes, priorities, and actions; or it can be conceived of as those practices intentionally engaged in by Christian disciples so as to put themselves in a place where the Holy Spirit can form within them the actions and attitudes of the Christ they claim to follow.

Now, with respect to the topic at hand—a *missional* spirituality—it should be obvious that this same duality applies. While it is appropriate to conceive of missional spirituality indicatively as the *attributes* that characterize the lifestyle of Christians who take their "sentness" seriously,[2] it is also possible to think in instrumental terms of those devotional, formational, and ministry *activities* in which some Christ-followers purposefully engage so as to shape, empower, and effect a fruitful participation in the mission of God. The point is that for reasons that will be elaborated on in a succeeding section of the essay, *the reader should expect to find in this chapter a special focus on the need for a missional spirituality that is instrumental as well as indicative in nature.*

The dual sensitivity a theologically and missionally faithful engagement in ministry contextualization requires. In the same way that it is important from the outset to acknowledge how this essay will approach the topic of *missional spirituality,* also needed is a careful articulation of what the chapter has in mind when it refers to the *ministry contextualization* endeavor.

As I have suggested elsewhere, at the heart of the missional endeavor is a commitment to *faithfully* translate the truth of the Christian gospel into diverse, unique cultures so that those living in those cultures might be formed by the gospel within their cultures.[3] The technical term for the translation process so important to missional ministry is *contextualization.* Indeed, missional authors Michael Frost and Alan Hirsch provide one of my favorite definitions of contextualization:

> Contextualization, then, can be defined as the dynamic process whereby the constant message of the gospel interacts with specific, relative human situations. It involves an examination of the gospel in light of the

---

[2]For more on the missional theme lying behind this turn of phrase, see Kim Hammond and Darren Cronshaw, *Sentness: Six Postures of Missional Christians* (Downers Grove, IL: InterVarsity Press, 2014).
[3]Gary Tyra, *The Holy Spirit in Mission: Prophetic Speech and Action in Christian Witness* (Downers Grove, IL: IVP Academic, 2011), 23.

respondent's worldview and then adapting the message, encoding it in such a way that it can become meaningful to the respondent. Contextualization attempts to communicate the gospel in word and deed and to establish churches in ways that make sense to people with their local cultural context. It is primarily concerned with presenting Christianity in such a way that it meets peoples' deepest needs and penetrates their worldviews, thus allowing them to follow Christ and remain in their own cultures.[4]

Though this definition is pregnant with insight into what is (or should be) involved in Christian ministry contextualization, I want to point out just a couple of ways it provides some implicit support for the notion that an engagement in this "dynamic process" may be more or less *faithful*. On the one hand, we should note how the reference to "the constant message of the gospel" resonates with the concern for a theological faithfulness expressed in Jude 3.

> Dear friends, although I was very eager to write to you about the salvation we share, I felt compelled to write and urge you to contend for the faith that was once for all entrusted to God's holy people.

On the other hand, also worth noting is the fact that the definition's focus on how "the gospel interacts with specific, relative human situations" calls to mind 1 Corinthians 9:20-22 and its implicit call for a *missional faithfulness*—that is, Christian ministers continually contextualizing the gospel concerning Christ for various people groups.

> To the Jews I became like a Jew, to win the Jews. To those under the law I became like one under the law (though I myself am not under the law), so as to win those under the law. To those not having the law I became like one not having the law (though I am not free from God's law but am under Christ's law), so as to win those not having the law. To the weak I became weak, to win the weak. I have become all things to all people so that by all possible means I might save some.

It is on the basis of both of the passages just cited that I contend that a *theologically and missionally faithful* engagement in ministry

---

[4]Michael Frost and Alan Hirsch, *The Shaping of Things to Come: Innovation and Mission for the 21st-Century Church* (Peabody, MA: Hendrickson, 2003), 83.

contextualization will be one that strives to be sensitive to both the *biblical text* and the *cultural context*—that is, faithful to both Jude's call to remain true to the apostolic understanding of the Christian gospel, and Paul's call to keep contextualizing the faith for ethnically and culturally diverse people groups.

Unfortunately, not all attempts at ministry contextualization succeed at manifesting the theological and missional faithfulness just described. Though in another work I focused on the failure of many progressive evangelicals to maintain a sufficient degree of sensitivity to Jude 3, and the failure of many traditional evangelicals to do the same with respect to 1 Corinthians 9:20-22, the emphasis was more on the former than the latter.[5] In this chapter, the emphasis will be reversed. While remaining ever mindful that there exists the possibility of overcontextualizing the gospel—accommodating too much to the cultural context—*the burden of this chapter is to indicate why a missional spirituality can and should be quite contextual in nature.* Because the final section of the chapter will explore a historical/missiological case study supportive of this thesis, I will simply observe here that, while there are many passages in the Pauline corpus that resonate strongly with the concern for Christian orthodoxy expressed in Jude 3 (e.g., see 1 Tim 1:10, 4:16; 2 Tim 1:13; 4:3; Titus 1:9; 2:1), it is also true that Paul's practice of ministry contextualization, as indicated in 1 Corinthians 9:20-22, seems to have involved some remarkable flexibility in not only his ministry methodology but the instrumental spirituality he employed as well.

The upshot of all this, which is crucial to the argument presented in this chapter, is the following foundational presupposition: *a proper recognition of the dual nature of missional spirituality, combined with a serious commitment to maintain the dual sensitivity required of a theologically and missionally faithful contextualization of the gospel, virtually mandates a missional spirituality that, while remaining true to historic Christianity, is highly contextual in nature.* Given the importance of this presupposition to the chapter's thesis, the remaining sections of the essay will provide, in turn,

---

[5]See Gary Tyra, *A Missional Orthodoxy: Theology and Ministry in a Post-Christian Context* (Downers Grove, IL: IVP Academic, 2013).

theological and missiological support for each of the conceptual clarifications presented above.

Support for a Ministry Contextualization That Is Both Theologically and Missionally Faithful

Not a few missiologists have suggested that the most appropriate theological model for gospel contextualization is the incarnation of Christ.[6] Going so far as to refer to Jesus as a contextual theologian, Alan Roxburgh and Scott Boren comment on the significance of Jesus' incarnation to his revelatory ministry thusly:

> John tells us in his Gospel, "The Word became flesh and dwelt among us" (John 1:14 NKJV). Eugene Peterson paraphrases this verse, "The Word became flesh and moved into the neighborhood" (Message). John uses *Word* to communicate a radical message: the Word is Jesus and the Word came to earth and showed us who God is. Jesus' way of being a theologian was to embody God in a local setting. He came to earth not in an ideal time, an ideal way, or with an ideal plan. He did not come to all people at all times in some kind of universal way of the mystics or philosophers. He came in a very particular way to a particular people at a particular time in history. He moved into the neighborhood of Galilee and demonstrated there who God is.[7]

According to this quote, the root idea behind an incarnational approach to ministry is that of "moving into the neighborhood." But the issue here is not merely geographical proximity but something much more significant: a radical *identification* with the members of the target community that, when combined with a divinely enabled *differentiation*, makes possible a

---

[6]For example, see David J. Bosch, *The Transforming Mission: Paradigm Shifts in Theology of Mission* (Maryknoll, NY: Orbis, 2011), 464-65; Ross Hastings, *Missional God, Missional Church: Hope for Re-Evangelizing the West* (Downers Grove, IL: IVP Academic, 2012), 38, 82, 148-89; Guder, *Missional Church*, 11, 14; Roxburgh and Boren, *Introducing the Missional Church*, 32; Frost and Hirsch, *The Shaping of Things to Come*, 35-41; Alan Hirsch, *The Forgotten Ways: Reactivating the Missional Church* (Grand Rapids: Brazos Press, 2006), 128-29, 131-47; Ed Stetzer, "Why We Should Use the Term 'Incarnational Mission' (Part 1)," *The Exchange* (blog), June 20, 2011, www.edstetzer.com/2011/06/incarnational-mission-part-1.html; Ed Stetzer, "Incarnational Mission (Part 2)" *The Exchange* (blog), July 21, 2011, www.edstetzer.com/2011/07/incarnational-mission -part-2.html; Ed Stetzer, "Incarnational Mission (Part 3)," *The Exchange* (blog), July 25, 2011, www .edstetzer.com/2011/07/incarnational-mission-part-3.html.

[7]Roxburgh and Boren, *Introducing the Missional Church*, 94. See also Guder, *Missional Church*, 13-14.

powerful *transformation* (in the lives of individual members and the community as a whole). It is important to keep in mind that the end goal of Jesus' ministry was not merely to identify with sinful humanity but to heal, transform, and re-create it. However, and this is crucial, in order to bring about this *transformation*, Jesus first embedded himself deeply within a particular historical cultural context (*identification*), while maintaining his integrity as the divine Son of God (*differentiation*).

It is probably safe to say that the consensus among most missional authors is that, figuratively speaking, just as Jesus' ministry approach was incarnational, so should be that of his followers.[8] Some tacit biblical support for this bold assertion may be found in Jesus' high priestly prayer, in which Jesus says to his Father, "As you sent me into the world, I have sent them into the world" (Jn 17:18). Missional authors are also fond of citing John 20:21, which indicates that some of Jesus' final words to his disciples included, "As the Father has sent me, I am sending you." The suggestion is that in each of these passages we find an indication that Jesus expected the gospel proclamation ministry of his followers to somehow follow an incarnational—identification-differentiation-transformation—model.

Moreover, some additional support for the incarnational approach to ministry contextualization described above may be adduced by observing how the bishops at the Council of Chalcedon (AD 451) resolved the question of how the two natures of Christ—human and divine—relate to one another, and the importance of this relationship to the transformational power of the Christ event. At the risk of greatly oversimplifying matters, the question that those participating in this ecumenical council were dealing with was essentially as follows: *How do we understand Jesus being human and divine at the same time?* Several perspectives were on offer, some of which *abjectly denied* the inherent divinity of Christ (adoptionism) or his actual humanity (Docetism), and some that *merely downplayed* the divinity of Jesus (e.g., Nestorianism) or his humanity (e.g., Apollinarianism). In a nutshell, the tack taken by the bishops was to reject

---

[8]For example, see Darrell L. Guder, *Be My Witnesses: The Church's Mission, Message and Messengers* (Grand Rapids: Eerdmans, 1985), 24-32; Guder, *Missional Church*, 14; Frost and Hirsch, *The Shaping of Things to Come*, 35-41.

all of the perspectives just presented and, instead, to affirm a union (rather than a division or conflation) between the two natures of Christ. Thus, at the heart of what is known as the "Chalcedonian definition" is the doctrine of the *hypostatic union*, "the belief in a perfect union of two distinct but never separate natures—one human and one divine—in one integral eternal divine person."[9] In sum, the Chalcedonian definition calls for the faithful to maintain a delicate balance as it relates to Christ's two natures. The church fathers seemed to be convinced that a theologically coherent conception of the revelatory and redemptive ministries of Christ required a "both-and" rather than "either-or" relationship between Jesus' divinity and humanity. Put differently, we might say that the church fathers recognized that in order for the *transformation* of fallen, sinful human beings to have been achieved through the Christ event, a simultaneous *identification* with and *differentiation* from fallen, sinful humanity on the part of the incarnate Christ had to have occurred.

Now, it is my suggestion that there exists a conceptual analogy between the perfectly balanced Christology hammered out at Chalcedon and an engagement in Christian ministry contextualization that is theologically and missionally faithful (precisely because of its balanced commitment to both Jude 3 and 1 Corinthians 9:20-22). This theory of correspondence is prompted by two observations and a critical question produced by them. The first observation is that the dynamic of ministry contextualization, like the dual nature of Christ, involves two components. The *divine* component is the gospel itself—the faith once for all entrusted to God's holy people. The *human* component is comprised of the "conditions on the ground"—the matrix of sociocultural realities at work in each slightly unique ministry locale. The second observation has to do with the lamentable fact that, when engaging in the ministry contextualization endeavor, it is possible to fail to do justice to both of these components at the same time. Indeed, the history of Christian mission seems to indicate that, despite our best intentions, we seem to possess a persistent capacity to *deny* or *downplay* one or the other of

---

[9]Roger Olson, *The Mosaic of Christian Belief: Twenty Centuries of Unity and Diversity* (Downers Grove, IL: IVP Academic, 2002), 227.

these dual components in our missional endeavors. The critical question these two observations produce is this: Could it be that, just as a particular (fully incarnational, balanced) Christology is crucial for a theologically coherent understanding of the revelatory and redemptive ministries of Christ, a particular (fully incarnational, balanced) missiology (engagement in ministry contextualization) is crucial for a practical unleashing of the transformational power of the gospel in the lives of the people inhabiting the neighborhoods missional Christians feel called to reach? If there is even the possibility that the answer to this critical question is yes, then what we find in the Chalcedonian definition is some tacit support for the importance of an engagement in ministry contextualization that is both theologically and missionally faithful.

Support for a Missional Spirituality That Is Instrumental in Nature

It is time now for a more nuanced discussion of what I have in mind when I refer to the possibility of a "contextualized spirituality." Speaking broadly, we might think of a contextualized Christian spirituality as a way of being Christian (understood in terms of the disciple's attitudes and actions) that interacts creatively and appropriately with its historical context. But, once again, the need to understand the duality inherent in Christian spirituality becomes apparent. For, though it is possible, in an indicative sense, to conceive of a Christian spirituality contextualized merely in that it has *been influenced by* the surrounding culture, it is also possible to envision, in an instrumental sense, a Christian spirituality contextualized in that it has been cultivated in an intentional manner so as to *exert a transforming influence* on the surrounding culture. It is this recognition that warranted, in my mind at least, the discussion presented in the previous section. It is also at the heart of my bold contention that *while it is true that no spirituality can avoid being contextual in the indicative sense, a truly missional spirituality will be one in the instrumental sense—a "ministry spirituality" that is deliberately cultivated in order to, with the help of the Holy Spirit, effect the identification-differentiation-transformation ministry contextualization process described above.*

Is there any historical/missiological support for this bold contention? As a matter of fact there is. By conducting a brief survey of one of the most successful missional endeavors in the history of Christian missions, this section of the chapter will provide some historical/missiological support for the importance of a missional spirituality that is instrumental in nature to a theologically and missionally faithful contextualization of the Christian faith. In the process, it will also serve to indicate why a missional spirituality that functions as a ministry spirituality can be expected to differ from one context to another.

The ministry methodology of the Celtic Christian movement. Due in no small part to the publication of *The Celtic Way of Evangelism* by George G. Hunter III,[10] the connection between Celtic Christianity and missional spirituality has been pronounced.[11] The reason for this is that the story of Patrick bringing Christianity to the Irish is not only renowned but instructive as well. As Hunter's work indicates, the Celtic Christian movement is replete with insights about how to contextualize the Christian faith for a thoroughly non-Christian culture in a theologically and missionally faithful manner.

Having grown up in northeast England and possessing nothing more than a nominal Christian faith, at sixteen years of age (ca. AD 400), Patrick was kidnapped by a band of Celtic pirates, taken to Ireland, and sold into slavery. Over time, three dramatic changes occurred in Patrick's life. First, his devotion to Christ became intense. Second, he developed a deep, existentially impactful understanding of the Irish Celtic culture. Third, he developed a profound love and missional concern for the Irish people as a whole.[12]

After about six years of captivity, Patrick was able to escape and return to England where, after studying for the priesthood, he served for a couple of decades as a parish priest. Eventually, Patrick sensed a

---

[10]See George G. Hunter, *The Celtic Way of Evangelism: How Christianity Can Reach the West...Again*, 10th anniversary ed. (Nashville: Abingdon Press, 2010).

[11]For example, in addition to many online blog postings, one might see Michael Frost, *The Road to Missional: Journey to the Center of the Church* (Grand Rapids: Baker Books, 2011) or Roger Helland and Leonard Hjalmarson, *Missional Spirituality: Embodying God's Love from the Inside Out* (Downers Grove, IL: InterVarsity Press, 2011).

[12]Hunter, *Celtic Way of Evangelism*, 1-2.

"call" to take the Christian faith to the Celtic peoples back in Ireland. According to tradition, Patrick formed what might be referred to today as a "missional team" made up of priests, seminarians, laymen, and laywomen. This missional team or community arrived in Ireland around 432.[13]

History reveals that Patrick's mission to Ireland was amazingly successful, not simply because of its team approach, but because of its utilization of a contextualized ministry model that was quite novel at the time. Heretofore, the "Roman perspective" called for the *civilization* of barbarian people groups before their *Christianization*. According to Hunter,

> The perspective of the ancient Roman Christian leaders can be baldly stated in two points: (1) Roman Christian leaders assumed that some civilizing had to come *first*. A population had to already be civilized enough to become Christianized; some degree of civilization was a prerequisite to Christianization. (2) Then, once a sufficiently civilized population became Christian, they were expected in time to read and speak Latin, to adopt other Roman customs, to do church the Roman way, and in other ways to become culturally Roman people.[14]

As should be apparent, the Roman perspective was hardly contextual, at least not in the sense of how ministry contextualization is construed today. Though the goal was a *transformation* of sorts, it focused almost entirely on the dynamic of *differentiation*, virtually ignoring the need for any sort of *identification*.

To state simply that the missional approach of Patrick and his ministry successors differed dramatically from the Roman perspective constitutes a colossal understatement. What follows is a cursory treatment of what has come to be known as the Celtic way, *paying special attention to the manner in which it employed the identification-differentiation-transformation process*.

Identification. Undergirding the entire approach was the foundation provided by a pronounced degree of cultural understanding. Hunter observes that

---

[13]Ibid., 2-3.
[14]Ibid., 5.

the fact that Patrick understood the people and their language, their issues, and their ways serves as the most strategically significant insight that was to drive the wider expansion of Celtic Christianity and stands as perhaps our greatest single learning from this movement. There is no shortcut to understanding the people. When you understand the people, you often know what to say and do and how. When the people know the Christians understand them, they infer that maybe Christianity's High God understands them too.[15]

Now in Patrick's case, this fundamental cultural awareness derived from the time he had spent among the Irish as a kidnapped slave. But Patrick also modeled for his ministry team (and missionary successors) a missional methodology that emphasized the need for some significant rather than perfunctory cultural exegesis, and that at a micro as well as macro level. Thus, we are given to believe that one of the first things that Patrick's ministry team did, having moved into a neighborhood (so to speak), was to "meet the people, engage them in conversation and in ministry."[16] Though one of the aims of this initial relationship building was to *identify* people who appeared to be receptive,[17] it also enabled the contextualization dynamic we are referring to as *identification.* Speaking of Patrick, Thomas Cahill writes, "his love for his adopted people shines through his writings, and it is not just a generalized 'Christian' benevolence, but a love for individuals as they are.... He worries constantly for his people, not just for their spiritual but for their physical welfare.... Patrick has become an Irishman."[18]

Though references to the identification dynamic are scattered throughout *The Celtic Way of Evangelism,* the topic is discussed most extensively in a chapter explaining those factors that enabled Patrick and his team to communicate the gospel to a pre-Christian audience in a manner that was highly impactful. Greatly simplifying a somewhat complex, multilayered argument, I will suggest one huge takeaway from

---

[15]Ibid., 8.

[16]Ibid., 9.

[17]Ibid.

[18]Thomas Cahill, *How the Irish Saved Civilization: The Untold Story of Ireland's Heroic Role from the Fall of Rome to the Rise of Medieval Europe* (New York: Doubleday, 1995), 109, as cited in Hunter, *Celtic Way of Evangelism,* 58.

Hunter's discussion of "How Celtic Christianity Communicated the Gospel." Among the biggest reasons for the fruitfulness of the ministry contextualization endeavor engaged in by the Celtic Christian movement was their willingness to identify with the Irish in some remarkable ways. The legitimacy of this takeaway is supported by the following summary of Hunter's treatment of this topic.

Having reminded his readers that the communication model presented in Aristotle's *Rhetoric* suggests that "public influence occurs from an interaction between the *ethos* of the communicator, the *logos* of the message, and the *pathos* of the audience," Hunter makes the following assertion straightaway: "I believe that much of the unusual communicative power of the Celtic Christian movement was attributable to the ethos of its communicators and its communities."[19] Hunter goes on to explain that when speaking of the communicator's ethos, Aristotle had in mind the notions of intelligence, character, and good will.[20] Pressing on, Hunter points out how that the German theologian Helmut Thielicke identified credibility as an essential component of a communicator's ethos.[21] Hunter then makes the point that, according to both Søren Kierkegaard and Kenneth Burke, yet another factor crucial to a communicator's ethos is identification—the "closeness that members of an audience experience between themselves and the communicator."[22] Then, citing Burke specifically, Hunter explains that the type of rapport crucial to effective communication calls for the communicator to not only speak the audience's language and communicate within their thought patterns, but also to indicate a capacity to personally identify with some of their beliefs, attitudes, values, needs, issues, and struggles.[23]

Putting all of these observations together, and considering them in the light of what we have come to know about how Patrick's radical identification with the Irish earned him a tremendous degree of ministry credibility, Hunter offers the following conclusion: "So, from the case of Patrick

---

[19]Hunter, *Celtic Way of Evangelism*, 47.
[20]Ibid., 49.
[21]Ibid., 50.
[22]Ibid., 51.
[23]Ibid., 51-52.

of Ireland, we can appreciate the musing of Aristotle and Burke that, among the three modes of persuasion—ethos, logos, and pathos—ethos plus identification are essential in transformational communication."[24]

Of course, this is not to say that the elements of *logos* and *pathos* were not also important in the conversion of the Irish. And yet, Hunter's description of how the message (*logos*) Patrick proclaimed, along with his ability to successfully engage the particular fascinations and passions (*pathos*) of his Irish auditors, only serves to reinforce the crucial importance of the identification dynamic. For example, with respect to the logos of Patrick and his team, Hunter observes, "The biblical revelation was primary, but understanding the people's cultural and historical context helped them to know what in Scripture to feature first, and how to 'translate' it for the people."[25] And, with respect to the Irish pathos, Hunter suggests that it was the Celtic Christian movement's willingness to identify with the Irish that empowered Patrick and his successors to: (1) connect the message of the gospel to the deepest concerns of the Irish; (2) serve as vivid proof of the fact that, "in contrast to the indifference of their capricious gods, . . . their feelings mattered to the triune God of Christianity"; (3) minister to the Irish in such a way as to convince them that, because of God's providence, they could experience "victory over terror and other destructive emotions"; and (4) provide them with "outlets for expressing their constructive emotions through indigenous oratory, storytelling, poetry, music, dance, drama, and so on in God's service."[26]

In other words, the tremendous communicative success the Celtic Christian movement experienced among the Irish was due in no small part to the significant commitment on the part of Patrick and his associates to truly understand this pagan people group from the inside out. Through intimate conversation and simply doing life together, Patrick and his team came to thoroughly understand the hopes, fears, imaginations, fascinations, and modes of intellection at work in this ministry

[24]Ibid., 58.
[25]Ibid., 72.
[26]Ibid., 64-65.

context. This observation yields the missiological insight that for a fully faithful and fruitful Christian ministry contextualization to occur, the endeavor must begin with some serious identification. Indeed, Hunter concludes the final chapter of his book—a chapter titled "The Celtic Future of the Christian Movement in the West"—with the following bold statement:

> The supreme key to reaching the West again is the key that Patrick discovered—involuntarily but providentially. The gulf between church people and unchurched people is vast, but if we pay the price to understand the unchurched, we will usually know what to say and what to do. If they know and feel we understand them, by the tens of millions they will risk opening their hearts to the God who understands them.[27]

Differentiation. Given the emphasis on identification in the ministry approach employed by the ancient Celtic Christians, and the fact that Hunter nowhere employs the term *differentiation* in his discussion of it, one might assume that Patrick and his team were guilty of neglecting this critical contextualization dynamic. However, in a way other than direct reference, Hunter assures his readers that the *differentiation* dynamic was not completely absent from how Patrick and his team engaged in missional ministry. Indeed, we have reason to believe that the ministry posture of the ancient Celtic missionaries actually had a fairly powerful prophetic (culture-confronting) quality about it.

For one thing, my read is that while Patrick's presentation of the gospel to the Irish was quite context sensitive, his essential message was thoroughly evangelical. As a result, the *missional orthodoxy* presented to the Irish was not only comprehensible and compelling, but inherently challenging as well. The evangelical nature of the message is evidenced by the fact that, according to Hunter, "the salient goal of the mission to each settlement was to plant a church" and the "founding of a church would have involved a public service in which the church's first *converts* were

---

[27]Ibid., 130.

baptized into the faith."[28] It is fairly clear that some serious disciple making was being practiced by Patrick and his ministry team.

Furthermore, it appears that the missional way the Celtic missionaries exposed the Irish to the powerful effects of the gospel, while evidencing a passionate commitment to identification, displayed a strong yet compelling degree of differentiation also. Patrick's missionary successors, having adopted his "principle of indigenous Christianity," modified it by introducing the dynamic of monastic communities.[29] I will immediately suggest that, by definition, the formation of a monastic community presumes some degree of differentiation from the surrounding society. However, as the history of the Celtic missionary movement indicates, the purpose of a monastic community might be evangelical as well as formational in nature. Indeed, according to Hunter, the Celtic communities functioned as "mission stations," not only "preparing people for ministry to pre-Christian populations,"[30] but as actual hubs of ministry activity themselves. Hunter begins his discussion of this crucial topic explaining that

> in significant contrast to contemporary Christianity's well-known evangelism approaches of Lone Ranger one-to-one evangelism, confrontational evangelism, or the public preaching crusade. . . . Celtic Christians usually evangelized as a team—by relating to the people of a settlement; identifying with the people; engaging in friendship, conversation, ministry, and witness—with the goal of raising up a church in measurable time.[31]

Then, providing a bit more detail about how the monastic community's hospitality toward outsiders was designed to function evangelistically, Hunter notes how that non-Christian guests of the community would "learn some Scripture" and "worship with the community." Moreover, one or more members of the community would "share the ministry of conversation" with each guest and pray with them daily. Finally, says Hunter, after some days or weeks it was not unusual for non-Christian guests to find

---

[28]Ibid., 10. Emphasis added.
[29]Ibid., 16.
[30]Ibid., 17.
[31]Ibid., 36.

themselves "believing what these Christians believe." It was only at that point that receptive *converts* would be invited to commit their lives to Christ and his will for their lives.[32]

I have written elsewhere of the need in our day for a more relational "taste and see" (Ps 34:8; cf. 1 Pet 2:3) or "come and see" (see Jn 1:35-41) approach to Christian apologetics.[33] This Spirit-empowered, relationship- and experience-based approach to evangelism occurs when spiritually hungry people not currently professing the Christian faith are encouraged to "belong in order to believe"—that is, to participate with a missional community in its praying, indwelling of Scripture, worshiping, serving the poor, and so forth, essentially giving the risen Christ the opportunity to reveal himself to them by his Spirit in the process. What we seem to observe in Hunter's treatment of the way the Celtic monastic communities functioned as dynamic ministry centers is an ancient version of this contemporary missional ministry practice! In the next subsection of this essay I will draw some special attention to the instrumental ministry spirituality required of a missional community in order for it to employ the "taste and see" ministry approach just described. At this stage in the discussion, my point is simply this: *the dynamic of differentiation had to have been at work in the Celtic missional communities, albeit in a compellingly winsome manner, for this type of Spirit-empowered, experience-based evangelistic ministry to occur among them.*

Transformation. Beyond dispute is the fact that the missional ministry effected by Patrick and his missionary successors succeeded in seeing transformation occur not only in the lives of a multitude of individual converts, but in the Irish culture as a whole. According to Hunter, "Patrick and his people launched a movement," baptizing "tens of thousands" of pagan converts and planting upward of seven hundred churches.[34] Moreover, "Patrick's apostolic achievement included social dimensions" as well. For example, we understand Patrick to be "the first public European leader to speak and crusade against slavery,"[35] and this crusade

---

[32]Ibid., 42.
[33]See Tyra, *Missional Orthodoxy*, 151, 153, 285, 366, 368.
[34]Hunter, *Celtic Way of Evangelism*, 11.
[35]Ibid.

was not without effect. Citing Cahill, Hunter states that, "within Patrick's lifetime, or soon after, 'the Irish slave trade came to a halt, and other forms of violence, such as murder and intertribal warfare, decreased,' and his communities modeled the Christian way of faithfulness, generosity, and peace to all the Irish."[36]

In the end, Hunter asserts, "In two or three generations, all of Ireland had substantially become Christian, and . . . Celtic monastic communities became strategic 'mission stations' from which apostolic bands reached the 'barbarians' of Scotland, much of England, and much of western Europe."[37] Indeed, due to the success Celtic Christian missionaries had in winning to Christ the "barbarians" who invaded western Europe, the movement launched by Patrick has been credited with not only transforming Ireland, but bringing Europe out of the Dark Ages and saving western civilization![38] All of this seems to argue in favor of the bold assertion that *the missional ministry of the ancient Celtic Christians not only evidenced the identification and differentiation dynamics included in a theologically and missionally faithful engagement in ministry contextualization, but the transformation aspect dynamic as well.*

The ministry spirituality of the Celtic Christian movement. As previously stated, the central thesis of this chapter is that a missional spirituality that is instrumental in nature cannot help but differ from one ministry context to another. In this final subsection, I will explore how missional spirituality that characterized and was employed by the ancient Celtic Christians verifies this premise.

Given the significant numbers of converts baptized and churches planted by Patrick and his associates, one would think that the ecclesial leaders in England (and Rome) who had commissioned the mission would have been highly supportive of it. But this was not the case.

Why?

It appears that the biggest reason for this lack of support was some serious institutional concern regarding the highly contextual nature of

---

[36]Cahill, *How the Irish Saved Civilization*, 110, quoted in Hunter, *Celtic Way of Evangelism*, 12.
[37]Ibid., 24.
[38]See Cahill, *How the Irish Saved Civilization*.

the Celtic Christian movement's missional spirituality. Hunter explains that "Irish Christianity was geographically beyond the reach of Rome's ability to shape and control, so a distinctively Celtic approach to doing church and living out the Christian life and witness emerged."[39] Specifically, Hunter indicates that British church leaders took issue with Patrick, an ordained bishop, spending so much time with barbarian pagans and sinners rather than church members.[40] Hunter also suggests that a visitor from Rome to an Irish tribal settlement targeted by one of Patrick's ministry teams would have been struck by the rather noninstitutional ethos of the missional enterprise, finding there a movement that strongly promoted the involvement of laity in ministry, and that, when compared with the Roman model, "was more imaginative and less cerebral, closer to nature and its creatures, and emphasized the immanence and providence of God more than his transcendence."[41] Most significantly, says Hunter, Celtic settlement or parish churches broke the "Roman imperial mould" [sic] in the way they included settlement-situated monastic communities that functioned missionally.[42] One of the effects of this pairing was that the missional spirituality practiced in the monastic community was able to exercise a huge influence on how the members of the settlement church lived out the Christian life. Thus, the ethos of the Celtic churches tended to be more missional/incarnational than institutional, in significant contrast to the state of Roman churches elsewhere. Apparently, it was due largely to the missional spirituality employed by Patrick and his missionary teams that they were rather soundly criticized rather than supported by "the folks back home." One cannot help but be reminded at this point of the antagonism the apostle Paul seems to have experienced from some Jewish Christians over the manner in which he contextualized the gospel when ministering in Gentile contexts (see Acts 15:1-5; cf. Gal 4:21-29; 5:11-12; 6:12-17).

Now, since many books have been written about the distinctive nature of Celtic spirituality, my focus here has been on how its missionality

---

[39]Hunter, Celtic Way of Evangelism, 14.
[40]Ibid., 12-13.
[41]Ibid., 14.
[42]Ibid., 14-15.

(or instrumentality) fairly mandated that it differ from what characterized the Christian way of life practiced in Rome and virtually every other ministry context that existed at the time. Actually, because the argument is not all that complicated, it can be stated rather simply: since the Celtic approach was to introduce non-Christians to the faith by inviting them to participate with the missional community as it engaged in its spiritual practices (worship, study, prayer, community, service, etc.), essentially viewing these practices as means to an end rather than as ends themselves, *the Celtic Christian missionaries considered it appropriate to indigenize their approach to these spiritual practices rather than feel compelled to follow a devotional template provided by the church in England or Rome.* This is not to say that Celtic Christian missionaries completely abandoned the idea that the end result of Christian spirituality should be an increased capacity to know, love, and serve God in an ever more faithful (Christ-centered, biblically-informed, and Spirit-empowered) manner. It only meant that in order for their missional spirituality to prove to be both comprehensible and compelling (as well as challenging), it (like their presentation of the gospel) had to resonate with the particular hopes, fears, imaginations, fascinations, and modes of intellection present within their ministry context. This, I suggest, is a writ-large explanation for many of the distinctives for which Celtic Christian spirituality is famous. Rather than view these devotional distinctives as indications of an abject assimilation of the Christian faith to a previously pagan Irish culture, it is possible to find in them some historical/missiological proof of the fact that an instrumental missional spirituality cannot help but differ from one context to another.[43]

Conclusion

In this chapter's introduction I indicated that my goal was to inspire as well as inform—to encourage missional practitioners to cultivate a context-sensitive spirituality that, precisely because it strives to do justice to both

---

[43]In truth, additional verification for this chapter's premise is provided by the global growth of Pentecostalism in the modern era. However, because I have written elsewhere of the relationship between a theologically real spirituality and the success at ministry contextualization that missional Pentecostals are experiencing worldwide (see chapter three in Tyra, *The Holy Spirit in Mission,* 102-28), I have chosen to focus my attention in this essay on the support provided by the Celtic Christian movement.

the apostolic understanding of the Christian faith and the contemporary cultural context, will enable an engagement in ministry contextualization that is both faithful and fruitful vis-à-vis the *missio Dei*. Toward this end I devoted a discussion to the nature of and need for a ministry contextualization that is both theologically and missionally faithful. I have also made use of the story of Patrick's conversion of the Irish as an illustration of the nature of and need for a missional spirituality that is instrumental as well as indicative in nature. I am hopeful that these two discussions have indeed proved to be at least somewhat encouraging.

And yet, I want to conclude the chapter with an important caveat and brief word of exhortation. Ironically, it is possible for missional practitioners to baptize Celtic spirituality *in toto*, treating it as if it were the consummate approach to a spirituality that is missional, and using it as a one-size-fits-all template for missional endeavors wherever.[44] Though there are certainly valuable lessons to be learned from the way the Celtic Christian movement contextualized the gospel and Christian spirituality for its time and place, what is actually needed with respect to both the proclamation of the message and an embodying of it is ever and always a recontextualization that is careful to manifest a balanced sensitivity to both the current cultural realities on the ground and the faith that was once for all entrusted to the saints.[45] It is only a theologically and missionally faithful recontextualization of the Christian faith that, precisely because it corresponds with the consubstantiality inherent in Christ's incarnation, possesses the spiritual power required for a genuine transformation of individuals and cultures to occur.

And this is what we are about, right? Not simply being different in our ministry approach, but actually making a difference for the glory of God and the good of the world? To the degree this type of God-honoring difference making is indeed the goal of missional ministry, it is imperative

---

[44]It should be pointed out that even though Hunter refers to Celtic spirituality as an "enduring treasure" and "our 'once and future' resource" (Hunter, *Celtic Way of Evangelism*, 95), he also felt the freedom/need to critique Celtic Christianity at points (e.g., see ibid., 84-86), thus avoiding the divinizing dynamic I am warning against.

[45]Some implicit support for this contention can be found in Roxburgh and Boren, *Introducing the Missional Church*, 24. For more on the need for a "recontextualization" of the gospel, see chapter three in Tyra, *A Missional Orthodoxy*, 64-123.

that those of us who take our "sentness" seriously come to terms with the contextual nature of not only our ministry methodology but our ministry spirituality as well. By all means, let us heed the exhortation presented in Jude 3. But, at the same time, let us also recognize that striving to do justice to the call implicit in 1 Corinthians 9:20-22 will sometimes have us living out our faith in ways the folks back home might not, at first, be completely comfortable with.[46] We should do this anyway. After all, we are in good company. Welcome to the world of the apostle Paul!

---

[46]For more on the importance of a "careful boldness" to a properly contextualized ministry endeavor, see Tyra, *Missional Orthodoxy*, 323-25.

7

Lament *as* Appropriate Missional Spirituality

Soong-Chan Rah

SEVERAL YEARS AGO I RECEIVED promotional material from a US-based Christian relief agency. The nicely packaged DVD had the words, "The poor will not always be with us" emblazoned on the cover. The incongruity with the actual words of Scripture caught my attention. Further examination of the contents of the material revealed a loose interpretation of Matthew 26:11 to assert the specific role of the US church in fixing the problem of extreme poverty. While confronting poverty offers a noble and worthwhile cause, the material inferred that American exceptionalism should compel the American Christian to give generously. The DVD material exemplifies the American church's self-perception of privilege and the subsequent assertion as the saviors of the world. This type of exceptionalism and triumphalism betrays a dysfunctional spirituality that undermines a more holistic missional theology and spirituality.

Sections of this chapter appeared in the 2012 *Christian Community Development Association Theological Journal*. Used with permission.

The assumed exceptionalism and excessive triumphalism of the American church conflicts with the biblical call for humility as evidenced by lament. The practice of lament in the Bible confronts our American Christian assumptions. Biblical lament calls for honesty and truth telling about the broken state of society and the individual. As such, the excessive triumphalism of American society has nearly quashed a necessary countercultural practice. Not even missional ecclesiology is exempt from expressions of an unbiblical triumphalism and exceptionalism. The belief that God has called us to an exceptional mission and that we are responsible for the fulfillment of that mission can lead to a significant arrogance. Missional ecclesiology could be derailed by a hubris that characterizes the theological language and imagination of those who are caught up in American ecclesial triumphalism. One of the casualties of this triumphalism is the practice of lament.

In *Journey Through the Psalms*, Denise Hopkins notes that among the major liturgical traditions in America, "the majority of Psalms omitted from liturgical use are the laments."[1] In *Hurting with God*, Glenn Pemberton notes that lament constitutes 40 percent of all psalms, but in the hymnal for the Churches of Christ, laments make up 13 percent; in the Presbyterian hymnal, they make up 19 percent, and in the Baptist hymnal, 13 percent.[2] Christian Copyright Licensing International (CCLI) licenses and tracks church usage of contemporary worship songs. CCLI's list of the top one hundred worship songs in August of 2012 reveals that five of the songs could qualify as a lament.[3] Most of the songs reflect themes of triumph and victory: "How Great Is Our God," "Happy Day," "Friend of God," "Glorious Day," and "Victory in Jesus." Majority culture's infatuation with success narratives and the American church's avoidance of lament results in a severe deficiency in our ecclesiology and the loss of the underlying narrative of suffering. We forget the reality of suffering and pain.

---

[1] Denise Hopkins, *Journey Through the Psalms* (St. Louis: Chalice Press, 2002), 5-6.
[2] Glenn Pemberton, *Hurting with God: Learning to Lament with the Psalms*, Kindle ed. (Abilene, TX: Abilene Christian University Press), loc 441-45 .
[3] "CCLI Top 100 Songs," www.praisecharts.com/ccli-top-100.

The fullness of the story of God's work requires a remembering of suffering and a willingness to enter into lament. Lament calls for an authentic encounter with the fullness of truth. The dysfunctional exceptionalism and triumphalism of American Christianity reveals the need for the reclamation of lament. An alternative narrative is required to stretch the theological imagination of a Christianity that has drunk too deeply from a cultural captivity to triumphalism. In this chapter, we examine the historical development of the narrative of triumphalism and exceptionalism that developed specifically in US evangelicalism in the latter part of the twentieth century in the United States. The biblical practice of lament will be offered as an appropriate response to this historical narrative. Additionally, the humility of lament may serve as a necessary corrective, even to those who pride themselves on not being encumbered to the tether of US evangelicalism, by evoking a claim in the stream of missional spirituality. Missional spirituality requires the embracing of lament in order to offset an entrenched triumphalism and exceptionalism.

The Rise of Triumphalistic US Christianity

Throughout the twentieth century, US evangelicalism struggled with its place in the larger culture. This ambivalent relationship found two key expressions: (1) the prioritizing of personal evangelism over against expression of social justice, thereby diminishing missional ecclesiology, and (2) a growing suspicion of the academy and a lack of intellectual engagement, resulting in a corresponding anti-intellectualism. Both of these expressions limited evangelical embodiment of missional ecclesiology. A dysfunctional twentieth-century American ecclesiology hindered robust missional spirituality. This dysfunctional ecclesiology emerged from expressions of exceptionalism and triumphalism found in the culture as well as in the church.

The first historical stream reveals the disengagement of twentieth-century evangelicals from American society. This disengagement took the form of separating the act of personal evangelism from acts of social justice. Twentieth-century evangelicalism's disengagement with the culture reflects a significant departure from the social-cultural engagement and activism of nineteenth-century evangelicalism. Timothy Smith in *Revivalism and Social Reform* argues, "Far from disdaining earthly affairs, [nineteenth-century evangelicals] played a key role in the widespread attack upon slavery, poverty, and greed."[4] In the nineteenth century, Christianity in the United States exhibited significant concern for social issues. Revivalism and social justice were joined in holy matrimony. Nineteenth-century evangelicalism embodied this union. Twentieth-century evangelicalism witnessed a painful divorce.

This split mirrored a theological rift that developed in American Christianity. George Marsden reveals that a "deep crisis was brewing over theological issues. . . . Twentieth century American Protestantism began to split into two major parties . . . between conservatives and liberals in theology."[5] The widening rift between the theologically liberal and the theologically conservative segment of the American church resulted in a divergence of emphasis between the two groups. Theologically conservative fundamentalists prioritized individual spirituality over social transformation preferred by the theologically liberal modernists. Suspicion of theological liberalism and its link to the social gospel resulted in personal evangelism becoming the primary expression of Christian outreach for fundamentalists.

The theological contention between fundamentalists and modernists reflected a growing fissure in how Christians viewed the church's relationship to the larger culture. The fundamentalists viewed the world as a hostile and evil place, worthy only of rejection and damnation. Spurred by a growing mistrust of the world, fundamentalists rejected the trappings of modern culture. In the language of H. Richard Niebuhr, fundamentalists took on the posture of Christ against the culture.[6] Meanwhile, the modernist branch of American Christianity saw culture through a more optimistic point of view, believing that Christ could be *of* the culture. This disparate framework of how the church relates to the culture

---

[4]Timothy L. Smith, *Revivalism and Social Reform: American Protestantism on the Eve of the Civil War* (1958; reprint, Eugene, OR: Wipf and Stock, 2004), 8.

[5]George M. Marsden, *Understanding Fundamentalism and Evangelicalism* (Grand Rapids: Eerdmans, 1990), 30.

[6]H. Richard Niebuhr, *Christ and Culture* (New York: Harper and Row, 1951).

yielded the creation of two camps: the personal evangelism camp and the social justice camp, the "Christ against culture" camp and the "Christ of culture" camp.

Fundamentalists were disheartened by a perceived sense of rejection by American society (particularly following the public embarrassment of the Scopes Trial). Dispensational eschatology provided additional fodder for fundamentalist separatism. As Randall Balmer posits, "Evangelicals suddenly felt their hegemonic hold over American society slipping away. . . . The teeming, squalid ghettoes, . . . festering with labor unrest, no longer resembled the precincts of Zion that postmillennial evangelicals had envisioned earlier in the century. . . . Faced with this wretchedness, American evangelicals looked to alter their eschatology."[7] Dispensational eschatology fit this emerging worldview. The world had become uninhabitable for the good Christian. A drastic change from above would be required to stop the flood of secularism and societal decay. Balmer explains, "With their embrace of dispensationalism, evangelicals shifted their focus radically from social amelioration to individual regeneration. Having diverted their attention from the construction of the millennial realm, evangelicals concentrated on the salvation of souls and, in so doing, neglected reform efforts."[8] Theologically conservative Christians moved increasingly toward a rejection of social transformation efforts with a focus on dispensational eschatology reflecting a "Christ against culture" perspective.

Theological liberals embraced a contrasting position on the relationship between the church and the culture, which resulted in a contrasting view on the role of the church in the world. Theological liberalism shifted away from a focus on personal conversion and stressed social transformation.[9] In 1932 Harvard professor William Hocking spearheaded a

---

[7] Randall Balmer, *The Making of Evangelicalism: From Revivalism to Politics and Beyond* (Waco, TX: Baylor University Press, 2010), 33.

[8] Ibid., 36.

[9] Robert Wuthnow notes that "the question of whether to engage in direct action or to try to influence individual consciences was inevitably associated with differences in theological orientation—and here it did parallel to some extent the earlier division between modernists and fundamentalists." Robert Wuthnow, *The Restructuring of American Religion: Society and Faith Since World War II* (Princeton, NJ: Princeton University Press, 1988), 148.

research report called *Rethinking Mission,* which launched rigorous debate among the mainline churches. Gerald Anderson quotes the report's proposal: "The report proposed that the . . . missionary 'will look forward, not to the destruction of these [non-Christian] religions, but to their co-existence with Christianity.'"[10] *Rethinking Mission* proposed a departure from traditional forms of mission that seek conversion of non-Christians, but instead reflected the belief in the pursuit of righteousness within every religion. The Hocking Report sent reverberations throughout mainline denominations. The implication for missions for theological liberals was the prioritization of works of social justice. Missions would be the fulfillment of the kingdom of God in the human realm through good works.

In contrast, early twentieth-century fundamentalism prioritized individual spirituality over social transformation. While fundamentalists did not shy away from the exploitation of cultural tools,[11] they emphasized engaging the culture for the sake of saving individuals. Personal evangelism became the primary expression of Christian faith at the expense of concern for social problems. George Marsden notes that the "'Great Reversal' took place from about 1900 to about 1930, when all progressive social concern, whether political or private, became suspect among revivalist evangelicals and was relegated to a very minor role."[12] David Moberg asserts, "A great reversal early in [the twentieth] century led to a lopsided emphasis upon evangelism and omission of most aspects of social involvement."[13]

Evangelicalism in the United States continued this disproportionate emphasis on personal evangelism inherited from fundamentalism. Many evangelicals continued the belief that involvement in social concerns would distract from the central work of personal evangelism. "There was a deep, deep individualism that lay at the heart of the evangelical project.

---

[10] Gerald Anderson, "American Protestants in Pursuit of Mission: 1886-1986," *International Bulletin of Missionary Research* 12 (July 1988): 106.

[11] See Joel Carpenter, *Revive Us Again: The Reawakening of American Fundamentalism* (New York: Oxford University Press, 1997), and Matthew Avery Sutton, *Aimee Semple McPherson and the Resurrection of Christian America* (Cambridge, MA: Harvard University Press, 2007).

[12] George M. Marsden, *Fundamentalism and American Culture,* new ed. (New York: Oxford University Press, 2006), 86.

[13] David O. Moberg, *The Great Reversal: Evangelism Versus Social Concern* (Philadelphia: Lippincott, 1973), 25-26.

This individualism is best exemplified in the doctrine of personal regeneration. . . . When translated into a social ethic, this meant that the conversion of individuals led to the transformation of society."[14] This approach reveals a belief in the primacy of the individual to affect change and how the efforts of exceptional individuals change the world. The emphasis on individuals among evangelicals[15] contributes to an exceptionalism that shapes the evangelical ethos. Evangelical ecclesiology was rooted in a dysfunctional elevation of individualism and the false hope of an exceptional individual who was set apart from a broken and fallen world but would persevere and triumph over the world.

Academic Disengagement

Fundamentalism's rejection of secular culture extended into the realm of the academy and intellectual engagement. Marsden states, "Fundamentalism was the response of traditionalist evangelicals who declared war on these modernizing trends. In fundamentalist eyes the war had to be all-out and fought on several fronts."[16] Fundamentalism took seriously the perceived challenge from the academy. Darwinism, scientific challenges to the Bible, and a modern worldview were seen as originating from the academy and providing fierce opposition to assumed biblical norms and values. Withdrawal from the larger culture and from the academy seemed to be an appropriate response. Fundamentalism's withdrawal made the movement susceptible to charges of anti-intellectualism. Fundamentalism would be perceived as unable to provide intellectual answers to society's questions, furthering its alienation from society and furthering the perception of anti-intellectualism.

The assumed anti-intellectualism of fundamentalism gave way to a more culturally astute evangelicalism. However, despite evangelicalism's ability to tap into contemporary culture for the sake of personal evangelism, evangelicalism still had difficulty finding an academic voice in response to the changes occurring in American society. Mark Noll notes,

---

[14]Peter Goodwin Heltzel, *Jesus and Justice: Evangelicals, Race and American Politics* (New Haven, CT: Yale University Press, 2009), 138.
[15]Soong-Chan Rah, *The Next Evangelicalism* (Downers Grove, IL: InterVarsity Press, 2009), 27-45.
[16]Marsden, *Reforming Fundamentalism*, 4.

"Within a generation, the cities had mushroomed; older churches no longer seemed able to preserve a vital witness in those cities; immigration brought vast numbers of new Americans and great problems of social cohesion; mammoth factories sprang up and their owners achieved unrivaled influence in public life; freed slaves were forced back in and the South and allowed a mere subsistence in the North."[17] Noll recognizes that evangelicalism lacked intellectual resources to deal with these seismic changes in American society. He describes the situation: "When Christians turned to their intellectual resources for dealing with these matters, they found that the cupboard was nearly bare.... Almost no one had been engaged in ... a process of consistent Christian thinking."[18]

For decades, fundamentalism and evangelicalism had focused on an individual spirituality for the sake of personal evangelism. When American society required a deeper theological response from theologically conservative Christianity, the answer provided by evangelicals proved to reflect anti-intellectualism, a theological shallowness, or a hyperindividualism. Noll notes that "the descendants of orthodox evangelicalism ... did hold on to basic Christian truths, but in order to do so they fled the problems of the wider world into fascination with inner spirituality or the details of end-times prophecy."[19] While a broken society sought answers for a broken system, evangelicalism provided shallow theological answers focused on the individual.

Evangelicals' disengagement with culture and with the academy could find theological justification and rationalization. Evangelicals perceive themselves to be heirs to historical orthodoxy. As the self-perceived inheritors of historical orthodoxy, US evangelicals would feel a particular pressure to maintain the purity of the church. As the bearers of orthodox Christianity, evangelicals would seek to preserve the integrity of the gospel in the midst of a changing world. While eschewing the wisdom of the world, evangelicals would embrace what they perceived to be intellectual foundations for their theological convictions.

---

[17]Mark A. Noll, *The Scandal of the Evangelical Mind* (Grand Rapids: Eerdmans, 1994), 106.
[18]Ibid.
[19]Ibid., 107.

Evangelical theology operates from certain key intellectual assumptions. Historian George Marsden points out that Scottish Common Sense philosophy plays a prominent role in the formation of evangelical theology. Scottish Common Sense philosophy operates under presuppositional assumptions. As Marsden summarizes, "According to Common Sense philosophy, one can intuitively know the first principles of morality as certainly as one can apprehend other essential aspects of reality."[20] A theology that relies on Common Sense philosophy is prone to have a bias toward one's own point of view. If evangelicals assume that a divinely sanctioned "common sense" shapes one's point of view, then there is an underlying assumption that one's point of view is intuitively and correctly derived. The danger of Common Sense philosophy is to attribute nonnegotiable status to Enlightenment assumptions. If "common sense" becomes the measure of biblical faith, then rational assumptions can take the place of God's ordering of creation.

The individual that follows the line of reasoning offered by evangelical doctrine could deduce that their perspective (presumably obtained using reason and logic) produces the definitive position for the entire community that perfectly mirrors the biblical perspective. Since the individual gained this understanding through reason and logic, all other options can be eliminated. Evangelical theology assumes a level of reasonableness and perspicuity. Even as the culture around them changes, evangelicals assert a positive self-perception of the thought processes that formed evangelical theology, revealing the foundation for exceptionalism.

Missional ecclesiology attempts to correct the historical problem in American Christianity of a social and cultural disengagement. Exceptionalism and triumphalism served as contributing factors to a historical dysfunction in the American church. In particular, the evangelical church asserted a particular worldview that assumed the possession of truth. The assumption of serving as the guardians of an inherited tradition contributed to a "common sense" derived worldview where the salvation of the exceptional individual became paramount. That individual would

---

[20]Marsden, *Fundamentalism and American Culture*, 15.

triumph victoriously over a fallen world. An unhealthy view of the world and a disengagement with the world followed. For most of the twentieth century, therefore, among evangelical Christians, there was a conspicuous divorce between social justice and personal evangelism.

In the twenty-first century, many Christians are attempting to reverse "the great reversal." Missional ecclesiology can be seen as an important move within that stream. More and more Christians are seeking to integrate justice into the missional life of the church. While this desire is noble and well-intentioned, even the best of intentions can go awry. If the missional impetus arises from a truth-possessed assumption that leads to exceptionalism and triumphalism, missional ecclesiology will be thwarted. The pursuit of justice and a missional ecclesiology needs to be situated in our biblical-theological reflection. In other words, our missional spirituality needs to go deeper and engage the practice of lament beyond a cultural captivity rooted in exceptionalism and triumphalism.

Suffering, Celebration, and the Need for Lament

Lament theology presents an important contrast to the narrative of American triumphalism and exceptionalism and potentially contributes to a healthy missional spirituality. The term *missional* has the negative potential of becoming a hackneyed and ambiguous term that perpetuates a hubristic self-perception for the American church. Missional ecclesiology could degenerate into an expression of the elite and the privileged to further marginalize the voices that are often unheard. Assumptions about who are the legitimate and important voices need to be confronted. The resurgence of a missional perspective on the role of the church could present an opportunity to engage a more robust spirituality. Marginalized and suffering voices can be raised to teach and challenge the assumptions of the dominant culture. The practice of lament could challenge the exceptionalism and triumphalism of American Christianity. Missional spirituality, therefore, needs to engage the lost practice of lament.

Walter Brueggemann writes about the contrast between a theology of the "have-nots" versus a theology of the "haves." The "have-nots" develop a theology of suffering and survival. The "haves" develop a theology of celebration. Those who live under suffering live "their lives aware of the acute precariousness of their situation." Worship that arises out of suffering cries out for deliverance with "a vision of survival and salvation." Lament marks the story of suffering.[21] Those who live in celebration "are concerned with questions of proper management and joyous celebration." Instead of deliverance, they seek constancy and sustainability. Brueggemann says, "The well-off do not expect their faith to begin in a cry, but rather, in a song. They do not expect or need intrusion, but they rejoice in stability." Praise marks the story of celebration.[22]

Praise seeks to maintain the status quo, while lament cries out against existing injustices. Christian communities arising from celebration do not want their lives changed, because their lives are in a good place. They want their extravagant individual lifestyles to be affirmed by the narrative of success and victory expressed in the church. The celebration of success would reveal an American Christianity that would triumph over all of societal ills. A celebration-only church would elevate the narrative of an exceptional individual in an exceptional community triumphing over a fallen world. Lament, however, recognizes the struggles of life. The status quo is not to be celebrated but instead must be challenged. Lament challenges the status quo of injustice.

American Christians that flourish under the existing system seek to maintain the status quo and remain in the theology of celebration over and against the theology of suffering. To only have a theology of celebration at the cost of a theology of suffering is incomplete. The intersection of the two threads provides the opportunity to engage in the fullness of the gospel message. Lament and praise must go hand in hand.

Walter Brueggemann asks the question,

> What happens when appreciation of the lament as a form of speech and faith is lost, as I think it is largely lost in contemporary usage? What happens when the speech forms that redress power distribution have been silenced and eliminated? The answer, I believe, is that a theological

---

[21]Walter Brueggemann, *Peace*, Understanding Biblical Themes (St. Louis: Chalice Press, 2001), 26-28.
[22]Ibid., 28-32.

monopoly is reinforced, docility and submissiveness are engendered, and the outcome in terms of social practice is to reinforce and consolidate the political-economic monopoly of the status quo.[23]

According to Brueggemann, the dominant culture seeks to maintain existing power structures—insuring the ongoing cultural captivity of the American evangelical church. Toward that end, lament must be suppressed by the dominant culture in power.

For American evangelicals riding the fumes of a previous generation's Christendom assumptions, a triumphalistic theology of celebration and privilege rooted in a praise-only narrative is perpetuated by the absence of lament and the underlying narrative of suffering that informs lament. The suffering narrative is considered inferior and should be ignored or removed from the dominant narrative of success. Stories of successful church plants and growing megachurches with huge budgets are front and center in how we tell the story of American Christianity. Conferences must bring in big-name speakers—usually young, hip, white pastors who meet the ideal of a typical American success story as entrepreneurs and "thought leaders" with a missional vision.

These trends further perpetuate the triumphalistic narrative of white American evangelicalism. Other forms of Christianity can be portrayed as inferior to the successful formula for ministry put forth by white evangelicals. A narrative of success propels white evangelicalism over and above other expressions of Christianity.

For the complete biblical narrative to take root in our community, lament has to become a part of our story. Praise and lament must intersect. Lament calls us to examine the work of reconciliation between those who live under suffering with those who live in celebration. Lament challenges our celebratory assumptions with the reality of suffering. The real-life struggles experienced by marginalized communities should not be swept under the rug, but instead embraced as an important aspect of the gospel.

---

[23]Walter Brueggemann, *The Psalms and the Life of Faith*, ed. Patrick D. Miller (Minneapolis: Fortress, 1995), 102.

The Hope of Lament Is That All the Voices Are Heard

The book of Lamentations offers the possibility of a missional spirituality for our contemporary context. The text responds to the aftermath of the destruction of Jerusalem and the exile of many of its literate and able-bodied residents. The remnant in Jerusalem responds to this tragedy with a lament expressed by the community. Lamentations demonstrates that our suffering is not in isolation but experienced as a community. As the body of Christ, suffering in one part of the body means suffering exists in the entire body. Communal lament calls the ones living under the blessings of celebration to engage with those living under the pain of suffering. Our understanding of the gospel is incomplete if both suffering and celebration are not embraced. The stories of suffering that arise out of the marginalized communities reflect an essential narrative for the fullness of the American Christian story. A missional spirituality that reverts to an individualism that lifts up the exceptional individual will serve to undermine the fullness of missional theology. A communal lament is necessary in order to combat our tendency toward prioritizing the narrative of the exceptional individual.

Lamentations offers both communal and individual laments to reveal the breadth of suffering. Individual laments affirm the communal experience. Individual laments are not spoken in isolation, separate from each other. F. W. Dobbs-Allsopp notes a reason for the range of individual voices in Lamentations: "These very concrete and specific instances of suffering have been intentionally gathered together, each strung, as it were, like individual pearls on a necklace . . . ensur[ing] that they mean [something] cumulatively as well as individually."[24] The individual laments in Lamentations point to the communal grieving experienced by all segments of the community.

A central characteristic of the book of Lamentations is the employing of a myriad of voices. While seemingly reflecting the perspective of Jeremiah, the text draws from the spectrum of Jerusalem's residents to reflect the full story of Jerusalem's fall. As Adele Berlin notes, "In order to

---

[24]F. W. Dobbs-Allsopp, *Lamentations*, Interpretation: A Biblical Commentary for Teaching and Preaching (Louisville, KY: John Knox Press, 2002), 41.

show how far-reaching the suffering was, the poet refers to its effect on various elements of the population, for example, young and old, priest and prophet, women and children."[25] In other words, the fullness of the biblical testimony requires a variety of voices to be heard.

Furthermore, much of the suffering in Lamentations reflects a woman's voice. Jerusalem is personified as a woman who has experienced tremendous suffering and pain. Kathleen O'Connor states, "The poetry focuses on her (Zion's) female roles—widow, mother, lover, and rape victim. . . . By making Jerusalem a woman, the poetry gives her personality and human characteristics that evoke pity or disdain from readers."[26] Lamentations may prove to be the most important book of the Bible with a feminine voice.

In the face of tremendous suffering, the voices of women rise up to express the depth of sorrow experienced by the community. The voices of suffering women can offset the triumphalistic tendencies of American Christianity. Lamentations does not survive without the female voice. By silencing women's voices, we project our inadequacy on our under-standing of the biblical message. We gravitate toward the silly triumpha-listic tendencies of an unfettered masculinity without the necessary balance of alternative narratives found in the Bible.

My deep disappointment with American Christianity is that the stories of the latest evangelical superstar with a megachurch consistently rise to the top. We love to hear from the hotshot pastor with the hip haircut, tattoos, cool glasses, and Ed Hardy shirts. We worship at the altar of the latest and greatest American evangelical icon, who regales us with stories of the exploits of their cutting-edge ministry. Our ears have been tuned to hear the call for successful pastors who will go and conquer the world with a mis-sional theology. Even as we strive to be missional, we may ignore the stories of suffering and oppression. We have a deficient theology that trumpets the triumphalistic successes of American Christianity while failing to hear the stories of suffering that often tell us more about who we are as a community. This deficiency is to our great loss as a Christian community.

---

[25] Adele Berlin, *Lamentations,* The Old Testament Library (Louisville: Westminster John Knox, 2004), 13.
[26] Kathleen O'Connor, *Lamentations and the Tears of the World* (Maryknoll, NY: Orbis Books, 2002), 14.

The expression of suffering through the genre of lament does not imply hopelessness. While Lamentations does not end with a happy resolution, the possibility of hope remains. The presence of lament actually gestures toward the presence of hope. To lament before God is to petition the Almighty. Hope is built into the practice of lament. Lament breaks the narrative of an oppressive triumphalism.

The very real suffering of God's people is presented in Lamentations in vivid, even gory details for the world to hear. But in the process of expressing that suffering, hope is offered. Recognizing suffering is an affirmation that God is still there and still concerned with his people. Even if the explicit promise is not offered, the freedom to voice despair portends hope. "Lamentations' very bleakness expresses fidelity. Its bitter accusations reveal profound yearning for God.... It voices truth without which relationships cannot prosper."[27] The hope is in the relationship, not merely in words spoken or promises made, but that God offers reconciliation to even his most bitter enemies. The hope of reconciliation rests in a relationship with God.

Hope is not found in the human ability to come up with the solutions. Hope is found in the steadfast character of God. Lamentations 3 reminds God's people that the steadfast love of the Lord never ceases and that his mercies never come to an end. Despite the suffering expressed throughout the book of Lamentations, the character of God remains unchanged. The confirmation of God's character leads to the possibility of appealing to God. Equipped with a deep belief and faith in YHWH, the voice of Jeremiah moves toward a corporate confession. "Let us examine our ways and test them, and let us return to the LORD" (Lam 3:40); "Let us lift up our hearts and our hands to God in heaven, and say: We have sinned and rebelled" (Lam 3:41-42). The beginnings of spiritual renewal emerge as God's people engage in a corporate confession of sin. A sincere repentance moves the community toward a changed and renewed life.

The communal lament offers the possibility of moving from suffering to celebration. The petition of lament has the very real promise of

---

27Ibid., 125.

becoming a psalm of praise. Claus Westermann notes that "the beginnings and transitions to praise of God are seen even in the laments of the people and of the individual."[28] Lament leads to petition, which leads to praise for God's response to the petition. Brueggemann summarizes, "The intervention of God in some way permits the move from plea to praise [and] . . . the proper setting of praise is as lament resolved."[29] Praise follows lament. However, in a cultural context that upholds triumph and victory but fails to engage with suffering, praise replaces lament. We skip the important step of lament and offer supplication in a contextual vacuum.

The absence of an immediate promise of restoration should not be taken as a lack of hope. The power of the lament is the ability to sustain a deeply troubled narrative. Implicit in the privilege of expressing that suffering lies the hope that the speaking of that suffering is not in vain. In a triumphalistic world, Lamentations makes no sense. The theology of celebration will always be more attractive than the theology of suffering. But if lament were offered to a suffering world, the hope that is woven into lament will shine brighter than our tendency toward exceptionalism and triumphalism.

Conclusions

Missional ecclesiology offers an opportunity to reverse the great reversal. The negative impact of separating works of social justice from personal evangelism efforts lingered into the twenty-first century. The emphasis on personal evangelism betrays a faith in the heroic individual narrative. The exceptional individual hero would be able to triumph over a fallen world. This narrative encompassed a worldview that marked clear boundaries for twentieth-century evangelicals. Because evangelicals viewed themselves as inheritors of a received faith, they could cling to the notion of a truth possessed. The assumption of a truth possessed would exasperate the tendency toward exceptionalism and triumphalism.

While missional ecclesiology confronts the problem of the great reversal, the underlying tendencies could still find an outward expression.

---

[28]Claus Westermann, *Praise and Lament in the Psalms* (Louisville, KY: Westminster John Knox, 1987), 155.
[29]Brueggemann, *The Psalms and the Life of Faith*, 99.

Lament, therefore, becomes a necessary expression of spirituality, particularly given our tendency toward exceptionalism and triumphalism. Triumphalism seeks the quick fix and exceptionalism assumes the capacity to find the quick fix. Missional theology should not allow for the quick fix brought about by human effort. Instead, the ultimate hope of triumph rests on the power of a sovereign God. The spiritual practice of lament acknowledges the source of hope. Lament helps the people of God find hope even in the midst of suffering.

The practice of lament introduces a spirituality that is more communal in its trajectory. Individual voices are heard but they collectively offer a more fully orbed perspective on the reality of human suffering. Lament does not simply explain away suffering. Instead, lament allows for the suffering to speak and contribute to the larger story. The narrative is not merely an expression of the privileged and the powerful but of the humble. Lament is not a passive act, but a subversive act of protest against the status quo. Missional spirituality requires lament.

8

Godly Love

THE PRIMARY MISSIONAL VIRTUE

Diane Chandler

Introduction

Mother Teresa exemplifies a Christian humanitarian whose unquestionable love for Jesus translated into active service to thousands around the world. For seventeen years, Mother Teresa gave herself to teaching geography and history at St. Mary's School in Calcutta, as overseen by the Sisters of Our Lady of Loreto. Her life continuously developed as an emblem of love, commitment, and devotion to God. However, while taking the train from Calcutta to Darjeeling to participate in a season of spiritual retreat at age thirty-six, Mother Teresa sensed God speaking to her to leave the convent school and work full-time among the poor on the streets of Calcutta. Calling this "a call within a call," Mother Teresa embarked on an unknown journey that would lead to her establishing the Order of Missionaries of Charity, a ministry to the poor, sick, and dying around the world.[1]

---

[1] See Becky Benenate and Joseph Durepos, *No Greater Love: Mother Teresa* (Novato, CA: New World Library, 1989); George Gorée and Jean Barbier, eds., *The Love of*

How could an unknown Catholic nun become such a powerful global emblem of Christ's love? Simply, Mother Teresa's intimate relationship with Christ, and her engaging in spiritual practices that continually deepened that relationship, positioned her to hear God's unique calling for an ongoing life of obedience. Her daily rhythms of prayer and contemplation in silence and solitude cultivated communion with her Lord and Savior. She continually heard the Lord's voice speak personally to her.

Prayer was Mother Teresa's lifeline to God and the source of love both for God and for others. She wrote, "Real prayer is union with God, a union as vital as that of the vine to the branch. . . . We need that union to produce good fruit."[2] She viewed becoming more like Jesus as her highest goal, so that divine love would flow to and through her to others. She continued, "It is not a matter of doing but being. It is the possession of our spirit by the Holy Spirit breathing into us the plenitude of God and sending us forth to the whole creation as His personal message of love."[3] Truly, Mother Teresa exemplified this profound reality. Her influence was bound by the love she received from God and then expressed to others throughout her lifetime.

Sadly in the contemporary church, we have isolated Christian spiritual formation from active participation in God's mission in and to the world, a grievous bifurcation that is contrary to the teachings of Jesus. To follow Jesus means not only to become more like him but also to do the works of Christ. Godly virtue is who we are. Mission is what we do. Virtue and mission belong together in Christian spiritual formation, discipleship, and outreach values and practices. Misunderstanding the mission of Christ and his expectations for his followers has bred serious consequences, including uncommitted, lukewarm, and compromising believers who lack a powerful witness in the world and deplete the church's effectiveness.

Whatever happened to the two clarion calls of Jesus through both the Great Commandment *and* the Great Commission? Did Jesus give us a choice to select one over the other or to dismiss them both altogether?

Christ, Spiritual Counsels: Mother Teresa of Calcutta (San Francisco: Harper & Row, 1982); Brian Kolodiejchuk, M.C., ed., *Mother Teresa: Come Be My Light* (New York: Image, 2007).

[2] See the chapter "Prayer" in Benenate and Durepos, *No Greater Love*, 11-16. The quote is found on page 11.

[3] Ibid., 13.

Certainly not! Like two wheels on a bicycle, both the Great Commandment and the Great Commission integrally link to move the individual believer and the church further as a Christ-centered witness in and to the world under the auspices of God's overarching mission. In order to fulfill Christ's mission, his followers must receive divine love in order to enact the Great Commandment and be empowered by the Holy Spirit to engage in the Great Commission. Following Christ as the perfect *imago Dei*, we too are to grow increasingly into the image of Jesus, becoming like Christ in word and deed in order to advance the *missio Dei* through the Great Commission.

This chapter presents four primary claims: (1) godly love expressed in the Great Commandment is the highest virtue; (2) *the missio Dei*, or Christ's mission in and to the world, frames the Great Commission, which, as love in action, is inseparable from the Great Commandment; (3) Christ-centered missional spirituality is every believer's calling—extending witness and service in the world; and (4) the Holy Spirit undergirds godly love received and extended, as well as mission advance. By addressing each claim, I argue for a reevaluation of our lives and ministries in order to bring them into greater conformity with Christ's life and mission. We begin by addressing the Great Commandment, with godly love as the highest virtue.

The Great Commandment: Godly Love as the Highest Virtue

Responding to a Pharisee's question concerning which commandment was the greatest, Jesus drew on two Scriptures from the Hebrew Bible: the Shema in Deuteronomy 6:4-5 and Leviticus 19:18. Each Synoptic Gospel relates Jesus' reply with a slight variation (Mt 22:34-40; Mk 12:28-34; Lk 10:25-28). The Shema states, "Hear, O Israel: The LORD our God, the LORD is one. Love the LORD your God with all your heart and with all your soul and with all your strength." Leviticus 19:18 states, "Do not seek revenge or bear a grudge against anyone among your people, but love your neighbor as yourself. I am the LORD." The Great Commandment, also termed the double-love command, frames the bedrock of the Christian faith.

In answering a crooked question, Jesus provided the vision statement that his followers were to obey for all subsequent generations.[4] By its very nature, godly love was and is to infuse one's relationship with God and with others.[5] As New Testament scholar Victor Furnish argues, "In Jesus' teaching, love is not just *commended* as a prudent or noble way of life; it is actually *commanded* as the rule of the Kingdom."[6] Essentially, divine love is the language of the kingdom. Moreover, service to others "is the watch-word of this ethic and the visible expression of the love Jesus commands."[7] The Great Commandment unequivocally declares the basis for relationship with God and others—godly love evidenced through godly character.

Godly love deserves definition. Elsewhere, I have defined godly love as "the essence of God's character and personality, proceeding from the Father as demonstrated by the Son through the work of the Holy Spirit, which unconditionally upholds the highest good of others and fosters the same altruism and benevolence in human relationships without regard for personal sacrifice."[8] Godly love is trinitarian, other focused, and self-sacrificial; and as Jeffrey Greenman emphasizes, "for the sake of the world."[9] Thus, Greenman concludes that spiritual formation and its undergirding theology "equips the saints to obey the Great Commandment, loving God with all our being . . . and our neighbors as ourselves."[10]

Godly love is the very character of God (i.e., "God is love," 1 Jn 4:8, 16). By its inherent nature, godly love expresses the trinitarian relationship of God between the Father, Son, and Holy Spirit as it reaches out to

---

[4]Luke's account follows this exchange by including a second question by the Pharisee. Jesus responds by articulating the parable of the good Samaritan (Lk 10:29-37), instructing the Pharisee to "go and do likewise."

[5]For viewing spiritual formation through the lens of the Great Commandment, see Scot McKnight, *The Jesus Creed: Loving God, Loving Others* (Brewster, MA: Paraclete Press, 2004).

[6]Victor Paul Furnish, *The Love Command in the New Testament* (London: SCM Press, 1973), 69.

[7]Ibid. Furnish asserts that love stands in close connection with both faith and hope because love is "the content and context of faith," making faith possible (94).

[8]Diane J. Chandler, *Christian Spiritual Formation: An Integrative Approach to Personal and Relational Wholeness* (Downers Grove, IL: IVP Academic, 2014), 20. God creates, redeems, and sanctifies humanity because of divine love.

[9]Jeffrey P. Greenman, "Spiritual Formation in Theological Perspective: Classic Issues, Contemporary Challenges," in *Life in the Spirit: Spiritual Formation in Theological Perspective*, ed. Jeffrey P. Greenman and George Kalantzis (Downers Grove, IL: IVP Academic, 2010), 25.

[10]Ibid., 34.

others to uphold God's highest intentions for them. Theologian Donald Bloesch captures this essence: "The focus of true spirituality is on God's holy love, not on humanity's spiritual fulfillment."[11] Unlike our contemporary culture, godly love evidences in humility, deference, and self-sacrifice on behalf of others.

As such, godly love is cruciform, meaning that God's love is shaped and filtered through the cross of Christ, as God's ultimate demonstration of divine love for humankind. In his account of the apostle Paul's spirituality, Pauline scholar Michael Gorman emphasizes that God is a cruciform God, meaning that God's love passes through the cross in expression and revelation to humankind.[12] Our conformity to Christ through the cross, therefore, is what Gorman refers to as "cruciformity," or what comprises God's sacrificial character. Throughout Paul's letters, godly love is situated at the very core of his theology. Paul repeatedly exhorts the churches to love one another (Rom 13:8, 1 Thess 4:9), pursue love (1 Cor 14:1), view love as all that counts (Gal 5:6), allow love to overflow (Phil. 1:9) and be compelling (2 Cor 5:14), express love as the fruit of the Spirit (Gal 5:22), and possess love's attributes (1 Cor 13:1-8). Godly love, as a hallmark of Christian virtue, must be enacted to be effectual.

In Christian ethics, agape love is considered a superlative virtue.[13] Virtue reflects an inner disposition demonstrated by excellence in moral conduct.[14] For a follower of Jesus, virtue always is predicated on God's Word, with the goal of loving God and others. For this reason, the need

---

[11]Donald G. Bloesch, *Spirituality Old and New: Recovering Authentic Spiritual Life* (Downers Grove, IL: InterVarsity Press, 2007), 29.

[12]Michael J. Gorman, *Cruciformity: Paul's Narrative Spirituality of the Cross* (Grand Rapids: Eerdmans, 2001), 17. For addressing expressions of cruciform love, Gorman cites being other centered by attending to others' spiritual, emotional, and physical needs, being inclusive of all peoples, liberating victims of violence and revenge, and seeking mercy and justice (389-94), all of which are expressions of loving one's neighbor as oneself.

[13]See Paul Tillich, *Morality and Beyond* (New York: Harper & Row, 1963), where Tillich asserts that love is both the "ultimate principle of morality" (43) and "the ultimate principle for social ethics" (45). See also Richard A. Burridge, *Imitating Jesus: An Inclusive Approach to New Testament Ethics* (Grand Rapids: Eerdmans, 2007), 107-15.

[14]The contemporary retrieval of virtue ethics can be attributed to Alasdair MacIntyre, *After Virtue: A Study in Moral Theory*, 3rd ed. (Notre Dame, IN: University of Notre Dame Press, 2007). Also see Stanley Hauerwas and Charles Pinches, *Christians Among the Virtues: Theological Conversations with Ancient and Modern Ethics* (Notre Dame, IN: University of Notre Dame, 1997).

for grace is great, according to ethicist Gilbert Meilaender, who maintains that "the very fact that virtues are habits of behavior engrained in one's character may suggest that they become our possession and that the moral life is not continually in need of grace."[15] God's grace, therefore, enables virtue to become a part of a believer's character through holiness and obedience. Jesus' exhortation, "If you love me, keep my commands" (Jn 14:15), elicits the importance of obedience as a response to receiving the love and grace of God. Living a life of holiness that is pleasing to God reflects love and shapes virtue (Heb 12:14). Interestingly, eighteenth-century theologian and revivalist Jonathan Edwards believed that divine love was the sum of all virtue.[16]

The Great Commandment, as the acid test of love, extends even to one's enemies, causing the very character of God to manifest in and through the life of the believer. Christian spirituality, then, derives its very nature from trinitarian love that works through individuals as well as the believing community in loving God and others, notably through expressions of service. Thus, the church, as Stanley Grenz argues, "reflects God's character in that it lives as a genuine community—as it lives in love—for only as the community of love can the church mirror the nature of the triune God" and effect "the reconciliation of the world."[17] If what Grenz asserts is true, then the Christian ethic of love is likewise an ethic of salvation, which is at the very heart of the *missio Dei*, the mission of God.

God's mission is to redeem the world. As Christ was sent into the world to seek and save that which was lost, so we are to follow in Jesus' footsteps to declare in word and deed God's message of saving love. This was Christ's mission, as he was sent by the Father to extend this life-transforming message to the world. Before there can be a Great Commission, however, we must turn to the overarching mission of God from which the Great Commandment derives.

---

[15]Gilbert Meilaender, *The Theory and Practice of Virtue* (Notre Dame, IN: University of Notre Dame Press, 1984), 36.

[16]Jonathan Edwards, "Love: The Sum of All Virtue," *Charity and Its Fruits: Living in the Light of God's Love—Jonathan Edwards*, ed. Kyle Strobel (Wheaton, IL: Crossway, 2012), 37-56. Edwards asserted that divine love was best revealed through God's redemptive activity for all to see.

[17]Stanley J. Grenz, *The Moral Quest: Foundations of Christian Ethics* (Downers Grove, IL: InterVarsity Press, 1997), 296.

The *Missio Dei*: Love in Action

The very mission of God underlies all human kingdom activity. So what exactly is the mission of God? From a biblical perspective, Gorman clarifies the term *missio Dei* as

> the conviction that the Scriptures of both Testaments bear witness to a God who, as creator and redeemer of the world, is already on a mission. Indeed, God is by nature a missional God, who is seeking not just to save "souls" to take to heaven some day, but to restore and save the created order: individuals, communities, nations, the environment, the world, the cosmos. This God calls the people of God assembled in the name of Christ—who was the incarnation of the divine mission—to participate in this *missio Dei*, to discern what God is up to in the world, and to join in.[18]

Rather than an emphasis on human initiatives in extending God's kingdom either through individual or corporate efforts, theologians and missiologists have shifted their emphasis *from* viewing individuals and the church as the locus of mission *to* the very triune God—Father, Son, and Holy Spirit. Rather than human initiatives as catalyzing mission, God is clearly the initiator who invites human participation in all kingdom missional activity. As missiologist Lesslie Newbigin emphasizes, "It is of the greatest importance to recognize that it remains his mission."[19] And as a result, the Great Commission entails not primarily obedience to a command but rather an expression of explosive joy, resulting in the realization of good news that must be shared.[20] Through divine love, the Father sent the Son who obediently fulfilled his calling for the joy set before him (Heb 12:2) through the power of the Spirit and continues this ongoing mission to bring salvation to the world.[21]

---

[18]Michael J. Gorman, *Elements of Biblical Exegesis: A Basic Guide for Students and Ministers*, rev. ed. (Grand Rapids: Baker Academic, 2009), 155.

[19]Lesslie Newbigin, *The Gospel in a Pluralist Society* (Grand Rapids: Eerdmans, 1989), 177.

[20]Ibid., 116.

[21]Michael J. Gorman, *Becoming the Gospel: Paul, Participation, and Mission* (Grand Rapids: Eerdmans, 2015), 23. This book, the third in his trilogy on the apostle Paul, was prompted in part by David W. Congdon's concern that Gorman's second book, *Inhabiting the Cruciform God: Kenosis, Justification, and Theosis in Paul's Narrative Soteriology* (Grand Rapids: Eerdmans, 2009), did not adequately address the theme of mission relative to Pauline theology. Congdon's justified critique focused on Gorman's unintentional separation of being from acting, as well as union with God from mission (*Becoming the Gospel*, 3-4), which prompted Gorman to write this third volume. See Congdon's "Why I Think Missional Theology Is the Future of Theology, or, Why I Think Theology Must Become Missional or Perish,"

In the words of influential missiologist David Bosch, "God is a missionary God."[22] In his seminal work *Transforming Mission*, Bosch emphatically asserts that mission is a movement from God to the world, with the church as the instrument, not the catalyst, of this mission: "There is church because there is mission, not vice versa. To participate in mission is to participate in the movement of God's love toward people, since God is a fountain of sending love."[23] Therefore, the *missio Dei* is worldwide in scope, with the church witnessing to God's kingdom rule and reign by upholding divine love and authority in its struggle to defeat the powers of evil, sin, and darkness. "This is the deepest source of mission. . . . There is mission because God loves people."[24] Bosch rightly emphasizes God's divine love as the source of the *missio Dei*, with divine love being the primary missional virtue on which other virtues and mission itself are built.

Moreover, God is a sending God. To fully understand the *missio Dei*, we need to view God's mission through the life of Jesus as the One being sent. The mission of sending love clearly emerges in John's Gospel. "For God so loved the world that he gave his one and only Son, that whoever believes in him shall not perish but have eternal life" (Jn 3:16). The starting place of mission is God's eternal love, with salvation as God's prescient disposition for all humankind. From the beginning, God in Christ "became flesh and made his dwelling among us" (Jn 1:14) in order to reveal the Father's highest intention for humankind. Over forty times, John's Gospel addresses Jesus being sent by the Father.[25] Here's a sampling of verses (emphasis added):

Theology & Praxis, August 2008, https://theologyandpraxis.files.wordpress.com/2008/08/why-i
-think-missional-theology5.pdf.

[22] David J. Bosch, *Transforming Mission: Paradigm Shifts in Theology of Mission*, 20th anniversary ed. (Maryknoll, NY: Orbis, 2011), 400.

[23] Ibid. Bosch explains that while previously the *missio Dei* was viewed as God the Father sending Jesus, and then the Father and Jesus sending the Spirit, a fresh perspective emerged, as reflected in Karl Barth's essay *Die Theologie und die Mission in der Gegenwart* and later developed at the International Missionary Council's Willingen Conference in 1952. Here the Father, Son, and Holy Spirit sent/sends the church into the world. As a result, missionary initiatives became fused with the incarnate and crucified Christ, with the cross as central.

[24] Bosch, *Transforming Mission*, 402.

[25] Dean Flemming, *Recovering the Full Mission of God: A Biblical Perspective on Being, Doing, Telling* (Downers Grove, IL: IVP Academic, 2013), 114.

- John 4:34: "'My food,' said Jesus, 'is to do the will of him who *sent* me and to finish his work.'"

- John 5:36: "The works that the Father has given me to finish—the very works that I am doing—testify that the Father has *sent* me."

- John 6:38: "For I have come down from heaven not to do my will but to do the will of him who *sent* me."

- John 13:20: "Very truly I tell you, whoever accepts anyone I send accepts me; and whoever accepts me accepts the one who *sent* me."

- John 17:18: "As you *sent* me into the world, I have *sent* them into the world."

- John 20:21: "As the Father has *sent* me, I am *sending* you."

These declarations of Jesus' mission proceeding from the Father are crystal clear. The Father's sending Jesus reflects the internal character and disposition of our loving God who is always reaching out. As David Congdon notes, "Our understanding of mission has to flow from God's own mission in Jesus."[26] As the perfect example, Jesus became the penultimate missionary, leaving heaven's pristine paradise for earth's dusty domain. God's being and acting come into perfect alignment in and through Jesus. Being completely dependent on the Father, Jesus' mission was first and foremost to remain attached in loving relationship to the Father (Jn 15:9-10). Being precedes doing. Like the Father, Jesus' actions comprise the carbon copy of his being. Doing, then, flows out of being. God's internal character and external actions completely align. It is impossible for God to not act out of his divine character.

God's being, doing, and telling comprise what Flemming calls "a mission of love."[27] This mission is to witness to the Father's love demonstrated in (1) forgiveness, (2) salvation, (3) reconciliation, (4) teaching, (5) demonstration, and (6) healing. In John's Gospel these six purposes evidence in Jesus ministering to a broad cross-section of people: the seeking Pharisee, Nicodemus (Jn 3:1-21), the Samaritan woman at the

---

[26]Congdon, "Why I Think Missional Theology Is the Future of Theology," 5.
[27]Flemming, *Recovering the Full Mission of God*, 113.

well (Jn 4:1-42), the man healed at the Bethesda pool (Jn 5:1-14), the five thousand who were miraculously fed (Jn 6:1-16), the restitution of the woman caught in adultery (Jn 8:1-11), and the raising of Lazarus (Jn 11:38-44). These acts were often accompanied by "telling," teaching and declaring the truths of God about who he was and why he came (Jn 7:14-24).

Even in washing the disciples' feet, Jesus showed them "the full extent of his love" such that divine love was actualized for the sake of others as an example for all future disciples. Yet, Jesus was careful to remind them that they were to love one another as *he* had loved them (Jn 13:34; 15:12, 17). This love signifies the essence of the kingdom. Thus, Jesus' being, doing, and telling in that Upper Room interlude would only be superseded by his self-sacrificial death on the cross, where laying down his life for his friends became actualized (Jn 15:13).

The sending of God's Son and his model of a ministry of servanthood to the very end impregnated the church to carry on this mission mantle shaped by the cross. The church's identity derives from Jesus' divine, self-emptying love—so tangible in the early church's experience. As Jesus shared with his disciples, those who love him will obey his commands (Jn 14:21, 23). Obedience would require faith, faith in the One who promised to be with us through the power of the Holy Spirit. The apostle Paul shines as one who was called into the reality of divine love in Christ and sent to be a witness by God, as the *missio Dei* extended through the conduit of the Great Commission.

Paul's calling on the Damascus Road punctuated the preaching of the cross that he proclaimed as a witness to the truth. The Lord said to Ananias, "Go! This man is my chosen instrument to proclaim my name to the Gentiles and their kings and to the people of Israel. I will show him how much he must suffer for my name" (Acts 9:15-16). Paul also received this word in Acts 22:14-15: "The God of our ancestors has chosen you to know his will and to see the Righteous One and to hear words from his mouth. You will be his witness to all people of what you have seen and heard." Paul was sent as a witness, conveyed by Luke in Acts 26:17-18: "I am sending you to them to open their eyes and turn them from darkness to light, and from the power of Satan to God, so that they may receive forgiveness of sins and a place among those who are sanctified by faith in me."

Paul's sense of being through ongoing reception of God's love led to his championing the Great Commission by going into the entire world to preach the gospel. Interestingly, worship preceded Jesus' final recorded words in Matthew's Gospel: "All authority in heaven and on earth has been given to me. Therefore go and make disciples of all nations, baptizing them in the name of the Father and of the Son and of the Holy Spirit, and teaching them to obey everything I have commanded you. And surely I am with you always, to the very end of the age" (Mt 28:18-20). The worship of Jesus, a love response, fosters the Great Commandment.[28] The "go" of the gospel appears throughout Scripture, beginning with the call of Abram to the Great Commission, as it is enacted in each generation.

As Abraham was blessed to be a blessing to the nations, so God's people are to be a blessing to the nations.[29] As Paul was sent to preach the gospel and declare the love and grace of God through the cross, we too are to embrace this global mission, reminiscent of John Stott's words, "Mission arises from the heart of God himself and is communicated from his heart to ours. Mission is the global outreach of the global people of a global God."[30] The *missio Dei*, God's sending mission of love in action to reach the world, infuses the Great Commission to go into all the world, to declare God's forgiveness of sin, and to invite those in darkness to receive the light of the gospel.

In the words of Mother Teresa, "Our mission is to convey God's love—not a dead God but a living God, a God of love."[31] Similarly, Bosch simply concludes, "It [the *missio Dei*] is the good news of God's love, incarnated in the witness of a community, for the sake of the world." The

---

[28]See Congdon, "Why I Think Missional Theology Is the Future of Theology," 8-9.

[29]See Christopher J. H. Wright, *The Mission of God: Unlocking the Bible's Grand Narrative* (Downers Grove, IL: IVP Academic, 2006), 208-21. Emphasizing the Old Testament, Wright traces the mission of God theme throughout the Scriptures, concluding that biblical theology is inherently missional: "Mission is, in my view, a major key that unlocks the whole grand narrative of the canon of Scripture" (17).

[30]John Stott, *The Contemporary Christian: An Urgent Plea for Double Listening* (Downers Grove, IL: InterVarsity Press, 1992), 335.

[31]Quoted in Benenate and Durepos, *No Greater Love*, 52.

Great Commandment and the Great Commission comprise the two-sided coin of the mission of God to redeem the world. Our relationship with Christ provides the bedrock of missional spirituality.

Christ-Centered Missional Spirituality: Every Believer's Calling

Every believer is to engage in missional spirituality by remaining attached to Christ in communion, while simultaneously extending Christ's witness through personal service in the world.[32] This seeming dichotomy between the contemplative life and the active life has been compared to breathing in and breathing out. Both are necessary for life; one without the other is indeed problematic. Breathing out is only possible by breathing in; whereas breathing in is only possible by breathing out. In this analogy, breathing in is likened to the contemplative, or spiritual communion that fosters a deeper relationship with Christ, as we are being conformed into his image (Rom 8:29). On the other hand, breathing out is likened to reaching out in mission in the areas to which we are called. As M. Robert Mulholland observes, "No healthy spiritual formation in Christ is possible apart from mission with Christ. Similarly, no transformative mission with Christ is possible apart from formation in Christ."[33] Through the virtue of love, a vibrant union with Christ fosters the very impetus for serving in the world.

Similarly, missional spirituality relates to what missiologists describe as the centripetal and centrifugal dimensions of the Christian life.[34] Centripetal refers to the force drawing inward toward the center; whereas centrifugal relates to the force moving away from the center. These descriptors envision the contemplative life, giving rise to the active life of mission. The apostle Paul referred to this as the love of Christ compelling him into the ministry of reconciliation because of Christ's sacrifice (2 Cor 5:14).

---

[32]See chapter thirteen in Scott W. Sunquist, *Understanding Christian Mission: Participation in Suffering and Glory* (Grand Rapids: Baker Academic, 2013), 396-411.

[33]M. Robert Mulholland, "Spiritual Formation in Christ and Mission with Christ," *Journal of Spiritual Formation and Soul Care* 6, no. 1 (Spring 2013): 11.

[34]See Martin Reppenhagen and Darrell L. Guder's conclusion, "The Continuing Transformation of Mission," in Bosch, *Transforming Mission*, 549. The terms *centripetal* and *centrifugal* were first coined by Dutch scholar Johannes Blauw, describing the missional pilgrimage of demonstrating God's love in Christ to the world.

Spiritual formation leads to mission, and mission leads to spiritual formation. This reciprocal interdependence resulting in intimacy and fruitfulness shines brightly through the apostle Paul, who identified with the crucified Christ as a humble servant (Phil 2:6-8). This posture is what Madge Karecki affirms as giving "witness to the transformative love of Christ available to all people."[35] Hence, spiritual formation supports mission through spiritual practices designed to draw us to and make us more like Christ. These practices include reading and meditating on Scripture, prayer, worship, and fasting, among others.

Thus, a continual cycle of drawing on the grace of God weaves communion with God (the contemplative) with mission (the active). The contemplative propels us to God and outward to others, whereas involvement in mission exposes our weaknesses and launches us back into the grace of God in dependence to be further transformed.[36] The cultivation of this tandem is the basis for many individuals and groups extending the love of God around the world through the witness of the church.

Historical examples abound related to missional spirituality expressing godly love in word and deed. These Spirit-directed initiatives counter what Matt Jenson recaps from Saint Augustine as *homo incurvatus in se* (Lat. "incurvature of the soul")—referring to the self turning inward.[37] Rather expressions of divine love reach out, move out, and give out.[38] Three specific individuals noted here highlight those who actualized the Great Commandment and the Great Commission because of the *missio Dei*, just the opposite of incurvature of the soul: (1) Saint Patrick, Englishman turned missionary to the Irish; (2) Count Zinzendorf and the Moravians, through a historic prayer-missions movement; and (3) Amy Carmichael, missionary to India.

---

[35]Madge Karecki, "Mission Spirituality in Global Perspective," *Missiology: An International Review* 60.1 (January 2012): 33.

[36]For a discussion of how spiritual formation impacts mission and conversely how mission influences spiritual formation, see Kenneth Berding, "At the Intersection of Mission and Spiritual Formation in the Letters of Paul," *Journal of Spiritual Formation and Soul Care* 6.1 (Spring 2013): 18-37.

[37]Matt Jenson, *The Gravity of Sin: Augustine, Luther and Barth on homo incurvatus in se* (London: T&T Clark, 2007), 2.

[38]Also see Barry D. Jones, *Dwell: Life with God for the World* (Downers Grove, IL: InterVarsity Press, 2014), 59.

Saint Patrick and the Irish. First, we turn to Saint Patrick (386–461), who is a stellar example of missional spirituality. Born presumably around 386, he was taken captive at age sixteen from his home in northeast England to Ireland by Irish pirates. He was then sold into slavery. During his six years in captivity, Patrick learned the language and customs of his Irish captors, but more providentially developed a relationship with God while serving long hours alone tending sheep. In his confessions, Patrick recounted the extensive hours he spent in prayer and how his love of God grew.

> I prayed frequently during the day. More and more the love of God increased, and my sense of awe before God. Faith grew, and my spirit was moved, so that in one day I would pray up to one hundred times, and at night perhaps the same. I even remained in the woods and on the mountain, and I would rise to pray before dawn in snow and ice and rain. I never felt the worse for it, and I never felt lazy—as I reali[z]e now, the spirit was burning in me at that time.[39]

Then one night, Patrick heard a voice telling him that he would return to his native country. Subsequently, he left in "the strength of God"[40] and boarded a ship headed for England. After a perilous journey, Patrick arrived back to his hometown and, after studying for the ministry, led a parish for almost twenty years. In one stunning turn of events, Patrick had a "vision in the night" in which he heard many voices with an Irish accent appealing to him. In Patrick's words: "They called out as it were with one voice: 'We beg you, holy boy, to come and walk again among us.'"[41] Deeply touched with the love of God for a people who had enslaved him, Patrick embraced this Macedonian call at age forty-seven. According to one account, he planned to return to the exact town where he had been held captive in order to share the love of Christ with Miliuc, the man who purchased him from the slave traders.[42]

---

[39]Saint Patrick, *St. Patrick's Confessio* (online version, Royal Irish Academy, 2011), chapter sixteen, www.confessio.ie/etexts/confessio_english#01.

[40]Ibid., chapter seventeen.

[41]Ibid., chapter twenty-three.

[42]George G. Hunter, III, *The Celtic Way of Evangelism: How Christianity Can Reach the West...Again,* 10th anniversary ed. (Nashville: Abingdon Press, 2010), 49.

As a consecrated bishop, Patrick's legacy of love for the Irish people led him to preach, teach, baptize, and minister in Ireland until his death at age seventy-five. He built scores of churches, trained church leaders, and continued in a simple devotion to God and service to others. His legacy of loving his enemies could not be more Christlike. Patrick's life demonstrates missional spirituality at its core, where love of God and love of others propelled him to risk his life in the spreading of the gospel to an entire nation. The Great Commandment and the Great Commission found their home in his life and ministry.

Count Zinzendorf and the Moravians. Fast forward to the eighteenth century for another example of missional spirituality at its finest. In 1722, a small group of persecuted Christians from Moravia, today's Czech Republic, traveled to Saxony, or modern-day Germany, seeking refuge. They received permission from Count Nicholas Ludwig von Zinzendorf (1700–1760) to settle on his land. Soon afterward, Christians from other regions and backgrounds, including Catholic, Reformed, Anabaptist, and Lutheran believers, joined this band of settlers. They named the town Herrnhut, which means to "abide under the Lord's watch."[43]

Eventually, this growing community became contentious. Speaking different languages and having different creeds, they argued over issues of liturgy, communion, pastoral responsibilities, and their relationship to the local Lutheran church. Dissension turned to disunity, which threatened their community existence.

The twenty-six-year-old Count Zinzendorf wisely intervened to establish harmony and provided leadership within the Herrnhut community. In remembering his pledge as a fifteen-year-old to love all people, Zinzendorf made the decision to step back from his state duties so that he could personally visit each family in the Herrnhut community. Through these personal exchanges and his neutrality, the count won people's trust, and unity slowly was reestablished. To solidify their change of heart in 1727, each person signed a *Brotherly Agreement*, stating, "Herrnhut shall stand in unceasing love with all children of God in all Churches, criticize

---

[43]See Jeff Fountain, *The Little Town That Blessed the World* (Seattle: YWAM Publishing, 2007), 36-40 [quote on 38].

none, take part in no quarrel against those differing in opinion, except to preserve for itself the evangelical purity, simplicity and grace."[44]

After admonishing them to settle their differences, Count Zinzendorf asked them to walk together down a road on the property to the chapel. During that walk, the Spirit of God fell mightily on them, resulting in confession, sincere repentance, and praise—with signs, wonders, and miracles following. Within a few weeks of the Spirit's outpouring, twenty-four men and twenty-four women covenanted together to pray for one-hour periods around the clock. The move of the Holy Spirit had baptized them into one love—the love of Christ.[45]

Their spirituality, characterized by loving obedience to forgive one another, eventuated into one of the longest sustained prayer movements in history: a "24/7" prayer ministry that lasted for over one hundred years. Furthermore, they met three times daily for Scripture reading, prayer, and worship. Their commitment to the Great Commandment naturally led to their enacting the Great Commission to fulfill God's *missio Dei*. With the Word of God central to their worship and prayer time as anointed by the Spirit, they initially sent out one hundred missionaries "to the Caribbean and Surinam, to Lapland and Greenland, to Morocco and South Africa, to Russia and Turkey, to Georgia and to Pennsylvania."[46] Amazingly, this occurred fifty years before William Carey's modern missions movement began. Within sixty-five years, the Moravians had dispatched a total of three hundred missionaries around the world.

Accounts report that Moravian missionaries were so passionate about sharing the gospel through love to the lost that they sold themselves into slavery in order to reach slaves on ships in the West Indies. On one ship sailing to America in 1735, a group of Moravians worshiped God during a violent storm. John Wesley overheard them and marveled at their faith. Two years later, Wesley came to Christ in a meeting room at Aldersgate Street in London and later credited the Moravians for guiding him to true faith in Christ. The love of God poured out on a rag-tag band of

---

[44]Ibid., p. 39.
[45]Diane J. Chandler, "*Missio Dei*: Where Spirituality and Mission Meet," in *Cosmic Christ, Contemporary Church, Changing Culture*, ed. Johnson T. K. Lim (Singapore: Word N Works, 2015), 14-19.
[46]Fountain, *The Little Town That Blessed the World*, 40.

believers—the Moravians—and catalyzed a world mission movement, not out of compulsion but out of joy. The Great Commandment married the Great Commission to fulfill God's *missio Dei*.

Amy Carmichael and Indian children. From the late nineteenth into the twentieth century, Amy Carmichael (1867–1951) serves as another exemplar of missional spirituality whose personal relationship with God led to her loving response in obedience to God's call. Born in Northern Ireland, Amy was the eldest of seven children. After her father died when she was seventeen, Amy had the experience of helping an old woman who lived within her city of Belfast. At this juncture, Amy overcame fear of what others thought about her when ministering to the marginalized. Moreover, she poured her life into those in need, especially young people, and "was more than ready to take on risks for the sake of others."[47]

Over time, Amy's love for God and hunger for biblical truth took her to a Keswick meeting in Glasgow. The meeting produced a decisive shift in her perspective, and she began to distance herself from worldly things to align her life around spiritual priorities. Then at another meeting, Amy heard Hudson Taylor of the China Inland Mission speak about those who had never heard of the love of God in their native land. In addition, she met Mr. Robert Wilson, cofounder of the Keswick Convention, who would become a father figure and mentor to her.

Mr. Wilson would later invite her to one particular Keswick meeting, where she recommitted her life to Christ's service. Four years later, she noted that God was speaking "Go ye."[48] After intense wrestling with the prospect of leaving Mr. Wilson, who adopted her as his daughter, Amy served in Japan for fifteen months. Then she traveled to India, where her life's work actually began. She established the Dohnavur Fellowship, a home for destitute children, and a refuge for young girls forced into temple prostitution in southern India. For over fifty-five years, Amy served in India without a furlough, becoming the hands and feet of Jesus.

---

[47]Elisabeth Elliot, *A Chance to Die: The Life and Legacy of Amy Carmichael* (Old Tappan, NJ: Fleming H. Revell, 1987), 32.
[48]Ibid., 52.

Her prolific writings testify of a woman whose anchor was prayer,[49] as the Dohnavur Fellowship itself was a faith work.[50] Missional spirituality brought the Great Commandment and the Great Commission together in joyful partnership. Her love for God outpoured in compassion for the weak and abused. Selflessly, she laid her life down for those she served.

These exemplars, Saint Patrick, Count Zinzendorf and the Moravians, and Amy Carmichael, highlight missional spirituality—a deepening relationship with God, fueled by spiritual practices, which in turn led to outreach to others in mission. The love of God and others (the Great Commandment) undergirded their obedient response to God's unique calling on their lives (the Great Commission), which supported the *missio Dei*. It was through the power of the Holy Spirit that they fulfilled their calling, which leads us to the fourth section of this chapter.

The Holy Spirit, Divine Love, and Mission Advance

The Holy Spirit activates divine love, which in turn advances the *missio Dei*. As Congdon notes, "In the Spirit, the mission of God is held together."[51] And by love, the Spirit empowers for mission.[52] Highlighted below are three examples of the Spirit's activity in saving the lost through Jesus, the apostle Paul, and the church.

We turn first to Jesus. The life and ministry of Jesus demonstrates his dependence on the Spirit, being empowered by the Spirit at his baptism (Lk 3:21-22), led by the Spirit into the wilderness (Lk 4:1-13) and advancing the message of the kingdom through Spirit-directed preaching, teaching, healing, delivering from evil spirits, and transforming relationships.[53] When Jesus stood up in the Nazareth temple and read from Isaiah 61 (Lk 4:14-21), he masterfully announced the *mission Dei* that would become the conduit for transformative ministry. God's mission to seek and save the lost required Spirit empowerment (Is 61:1a), offering hope

---

[49]Of Carmichael's thirty-five published books, perhaps her most well-known is *Things as They Are: Mission Work in Southern India* (London: Morgan and Scott, 1905). The free ebook is available at www .gutenberg.org/files/29426/29426-h/29426-h.htm.

[50]See the Dohnavur Fellowship website for how the work continues: http://dohnavurfellowship.org.in/.

[51]Congdon, "Why I Think Missional Theology is the Future of Theology," 15.

[52]Berding, "At the Intersection of Mission and Spiritual Formation in the Letters of Paul," 22.

[53]See chapter eight in Sunquist, *Understanding Christian Mission*, 230-80.

to the poor (Is 61:1b), a divine exchange of joy for despair (Is 61:3), and a restoration of favor. Emboldened with a mandate, Jesus accomplished his mission because of the Spirit's empowerment, leaving all subsequent followers with the primary source for mission advance after his resurrection. The same Spirit likewise "thrust the disciples into mission."[54]

Second, we turn to the apostle Paul. Paul expressed the compelling love of God through the cross as the very source of God's mission: "For Christ's love compels us, because we are convinced that one died for all, and therefore all died. And he died for all, that those who live should no longer live for themselves but for him who died for them and was raised again" (2 Cor 5:14-15). Paul's sense of drive because of the reality of Christ's sacrifice for him thrust him into the same self-sacrificial ministry as his Lord's.

Confronting opposition and severe suffering only highlighted his passion to reach the lost at any cost. Paul commented, "I will very gladly spend for you everything I have and expend myself as well" (2 Cor 12:15). For everything Paul did was for the sake of building up through love those in the churches he planted (2 Cor 12:19). As Raymond Brown proffers regarding Paul, "If the love of God was manifested in the self-giving of Christ, how could the love of Christ be shown to others except in the same way?"[55] To the Corinthians, Paul's love overshadowed their unruliness. As Gorman observes, "Paul's love is greater than the chaos at Corinth that he addresses throughout the letter" (1 Cor).[56]

Similarly, Paul's address to other churches mirrored his love for them. To the Thessalonians, he wrote, "Because we loved you so much, we were delighted to share with you not only the gospel of God but our lives as well" (1 Thess 2:8). In describing his relationship to them, he likens his missional love to that of a nursing mother and an encouraging father. Simply, Paul's love abounded for them, which served as a catalyst for them to love one other (1 Thess 3:12).

---

[54]Bosch, *Transforming Mission*, 115.
[55]Raymond E. Brown, *An Introduction to the New Testament* (New York: Doubleday, 1997), 448.
[56]Gorman, *Cruciformity*, 180.

Third, we turn to the church. The Spirit prompts the ministry of the church. The outpouring of the Spirit at Pentecost released the power of God that propelled the early church to be Jesus' witnesses in Jerusalem, Judea, Samaria, and the ends of the earth (Acts 1:8). As Bosch describes, this baptism released the gift of the Spirit for "becoming involved in mission, for mission is the direct consequence of the outpouring of the Spirit."[57] Hence, the growth of the church results from "the active power of the Spirit drawing men and women to recognize in this human weakness the presence and power of God."[58] Thus, the church becomes the heart, hands, and feet of Jesus by the Spirit. As Darrell Guder insists, the Spirit equips the church for missional purpose as a "unified witness of God's love in Christ" in being sent into the world, whereby God's mission cannot be separated from the church's existence.[59] Simply, the church serves God's mission—not the other way around.[60] The Holy Spirit through divine love fuels mission advance.

Conclusion

This chapter presented four primary claims. First, godly love as expressed in the Great Commandment is the highest Christian virtue. Second, the *missio Dei* frames the Great Commission. Third, Christ-centered missional spirituality is every believer's calling in extending witness and service in the world. Fourth, the Holy Spirit extends godly love through mission advance. Do our lives and ministries evidence the love of God characterized by transformation into Christlikeness? Do we view the Great Commission as being a part of God's overarching mission to redeem humankind, as predicated on the Great Commandment? Do we operate out of the reality that our spirituality is not to be isolated from our calling to further Christ's mission in the world? Are we inviting the Holy Spirit into all aspects of our lives, as they are lived out in obedience and holiness through Christian witness and service?

---

[57]Bosch, *Transforming Mission*, 115.
[58]Newbigin, *The Gospel in a Pluralist Society*, 119.
[59]Darrell Guder, "*Missio Dei*: Integrating Theological Formation for Apostolic Vocation," *Missiology: An International Review* 37, no. 1 (January 2009): 63-74 [quote on 68].
[60]See Dwight J. Zscheile, "A Missional Theology of Spiritual Formation," in *Cultivating Sent Communities: Missional Spiritual Formation*, ed. Dwight J. Zscheile (Grand Rapids: Eerdmans, 2012), 6.

Our love and our work need to be inseparably intertwined. Mother Teresa had it right when she wrote, "The work that we are called to accomplish is just a means to give concrete substance to our love for God."[61] Likewise, Paul's prayer to the Philippians testifies that spirituality and mission frame "fruits of righteousness" where "love may abound more and more in knowledge and depth of insight" (Phil 1:9-10).

---

[61]Quoted in Benenate and Durepos, *No Greater Love*, 147.

9

Missional Spirituality *and* Worship

Gordon T. Smith

THE MISSION OF GOD in the world cannot be understood and appreciated apart from the liturgical life of the church. A truly missional church is a worshiping church. We note, in Matthew 28, that the early disciples were in worship when they received the call of Christ to make disciples of the nations (see Mt 28:16-20). The elders were in worship, in the church in Antioch, when they were called of the Spirit to set aside Paul and Barnabas for the missional work to which the Spirit was calling them (Acts 13:1-3). Neither of these is mere coincidence. Mission cannot be understood or undertaken except by a worshiping people.

In what follows my primary focus will be on the collective—the corporate worship of the people of God, the liturgy—the shared worship of the gathering of the saints. And yet, much of what is offered in these comments applies equally well to our personal prayers, reflecting the observation that just as the shared liturgy of the church informs and animates the mission of the church, in like manner our personal prayer and worship is an essential counterpart to the work to which we are called as we fulfill our individual vocations. However, as noted, in what follows the focus will be on the church gathered in worship. I will consider what it means to speak of the missional church as a worshiping community.

The Nature of the Church: Liturgical, Catechetical, and Missional

Any consideration of the relationship or connection between worship and mission necessarily needs to be located within an understanding of the nature and identity of the church. We cannot speak of worship and mission, for the church, without first reflecting on what it means to be the church. And while it is not the only way to think about the church, it is surely helpful and consistent with both the biblical witness and the historic understanding of the church to speak of the church as having a threefold identity in light of its central and defining practices.

The church is a liturgical community. First and foremost—and it is noteworthy that we begin here—the church finds its identity and purpose for being in her call to offer unbounded praise and adoration to the Creator and Redeemer of all things. The Father seeks those who would worship him in Spirit and in truth (Jn 4). Thus mission, in many respects, is nothing but witnessing, in word and deed, to the world with this end in view: that all would come to worship the true God. Thus, there is no integrity, no meaning, really, to mission if the church is not first a worshiping community.

The church is a catechetical community. Second, and equally essential to what it means to be the church, is that the church is a teaching-learning community—that is, a catechetical community, in that the teaching and learning has a particular intent: it is religious instruction and learning, with a view toward formation and maturity. Disciples are made through teaching (Mt 28). The early church devoted itself to the apostles' doctrine (Acts 2:42). While the word "catechesis" speaks most specifically to the religious instruction that precedes and informs the rite of baptism, in a very real sense catechesis never stops for the church. The Christian community grows and matures as it engages effective instruction—the teaching that is pivotal to knowing the truth and the renewal of the mind.

The church is a missional community. The church is a people in mission, whose very identity and purpose is to be salt and light and specifically to witness and word and deed to the reign of Christ, the kingdom of God. The Christian community is invited and called to participate in the purposes of God in and for the world: to speak the Gospel, to live out the Gospel identity and, in so doing through word and deed, to be instruments of God's peace and work of reconciliation.

The church is a liturgical, catechetical, and missional community. In what follows, this threefold identity will be the basis on which everything is offered, even though the particular focus will be the connection between worship and mission. Both, it must be stressed, are informed and sustained by the teaching-learning ministry of the church.

And yet, before we continue, it is essential that we stress the following.

First, each of these is integral and thus essential and *each* gives integrity to the other. Thus, the church cannot be the church in mission unless it is a church that worships; and, conversely, the church cannot be truly a liturgical community unless and until it is engaged in the purposes of God in the world, in mission.

And second, the only way that this can be appreciated and sustained—this threefold identity—is if each has integrity in its own right. In other words, liturgy must be liturgy and worship, worship. When "worship" is nothing more than catechesis or when it is used instrumentally for mission, it is no longer truly worship. Thus it is imperative that to appreciate the call to mission, and the connection between worship and mission, we affirm unequivocally that the church is a worshiping community in its own right. And then from that position or perspective, we can consider the relationship between worship and mission.

Worship and Mission in Dynamic Counterpoint

As noted, the church cannot be in mission unless it is a liturgical community and it cannot be in worship unless it is in mission. We need to stress this point. Each—worship and mission—gives meaning and integrity to the other. They are distinct and it is important that they be kept distinct and that we respect the integrity of each. And yet, they are mutually interdependent. And thus, as will be stressed below, the church is only truly in mission and faithful to its call if mission is animated by and informed by worship. We are in the world, engaged with the world, witnessing in word and deed to the reign of Christ as worshipers.

But then, the reverse is also true. The church is only truly in worship, in the adoration of the Creator and Redeemer, if that worship is informed by the work of God and the work of the church in the world. We come to worship as those who are in the world (Jn 17:15-17), engaged with the purposes of God and agents of God's peace in the world. And this should be patently evident in our worship: we worship as those whose worship is deeply informed by our experience of the world, in all its joys and sorrows, both the signs that God is good and that his reign is at hand and, just as surely, by the deep fragmentation of the world. We come to worship not to escape the world; rather, we come to worship as those who are truly engaged, who see and feel the full force of the dislocation of God's creation and the suffering of humanity, as those who through their days seek to witness and word and deed to the reign of Christ. We come to worship as those who are "in the trenches."

And you can tell. Or, better put, you should be able to tell; it *should* be evident in our worship. Thus the problem, and it is a huge problem: so much contemporary worship in evangelical Christian communities is escapist. Nice, pleasant songs are sung and everyone is happy and seemingly at peace with themselves. One has little sense that these people, who have gathered for worship, actually live in the world that is depicted in the morning newspaper.

I am going to propose that part of the genius of worship—true and authentic liturgy—is that it fosters a deep and resilient hope; it is a means of grace by which we come and go from the world not with despair, given that so much is so very wrong, but with a deep and resilient hope, a hope that is fueled by our encounter with Christ in worship. And yet, if our worship is escapist, if we do not truly worship as those who have felt the full force of the dislocation of our universe, it is nothing but sentimentality.

It has no redemptive power or any capacity to inform and animate the church as it participates in the mission of God.

When worship is nothing but nostalgia for a previous time, or when it is triumphalistic, it is nothing but hype, and thus does not truly call the church to be in the world or equip the church to be in the world as it *actually* is rather than as we wish it to be.

Thus, the church that is to be truly liturgical worships as those who are in the world. And this is evident, at the very least, in two fundamental acts of worship. The first of these is the prayers of the people, that point in the liturgy when prayers of thanks and praise and adoration are offered but also, just as surely, intercession for the mercy and grace of God to intersect the world and bring hope and healing. And thus the church prays for peace, with particular reference to those areas of the world where war is raging. We pray for migrants, with particular reference to where the daily news is speaking of those who are fleeing from war or economic dislocation, and we pray for protection and healing, particularly for those areas of the world that are threatened with illness or plague. We pray for the persecuted church. We pray very specifically for the things that matter in our lives: the economy and our bankers, our schools and those who teach within them, our city streets and the taxi drivers who ply their routes. That is, we come to worship as those who are very much in the world.

Second, it will be evident in this: our worship is penitential. We do not come to worship as those whose actions in the world, even those acts done in the name of Christ, are somehow pure and unaffected by the fragmentation of our world. Rather we know and feel that as we come to worship and pray "your kingdom come" (Mt 6:10), we also necessarily must pray "and forgive us our debts, as we also have forgiven our debtors" (Mt 6:12). In other words, we refuse to assume that we are somehow beyond the mission of the church, as though we have somehow "arrived." Rather, true worship reflects an awareness that as those who are in the world, we have not always been faithful, we have not always been consistent, and we know that while we had the best of intentions to witness in word and deed to the reign of Christ, we have fallen short. And surely if we come to worship, we then come with a penitential disposition. But more, we recognize that if we are missional, prayers of confession are integral to our worship.

As an example of what I mean, visit an Anglican/Episcopalian church on the first Sunday of Lent, when typically—not always, but typically—the Great Litany is said. It is but one example, though a powerful one, of what it means to come into worship as those who are very much in the world: no sentimentality, no nostalgia, no escapism. We name and feel the full force of the fragmentation of our world in its current expression. It is of course not the world as we wish it were; but that is not the point. The issue at hand is that this is the world to which we are called. And thus, we eschew sentimentality—"happy clappy" songs that are nothing more than trite diddies. We reject all forms of nostalgia, those songs—seemly religious— that harken back to a previous time in the life of the church ("old time religion"). And instead, we engage liturgies that bring ancient wisdom, liturgical wisdom, to bear on the contemporary life of the church.

Worship That Animates and Informs Mission

As the mission of God and of the church informs our worship, we can consider the ways in which worship sustains mission. And it needs to be stressed again: worship is only truly worship if our liturgies ultimately—perhaps not immediately, but ultimately—encourage us and equip us for the work to which we are called as the people of God.

The grace we seek through our worship, simply put, is to be God's people in the world in all the manifold ways in which we are called to fulfill our vocations and, together, to be the church in our community, our city, our country, and our world. This happens as the people of God once more meet, in real time, with the risen and ascended Christ; again, in real time they hear the voice of Christ as Christ himself receives our worship and our prayers, and then, through Word and Spirit, equips and empower us, in the name of Father, Son, and Spirit.

As a rule, two things happen. First, the burden of the world is lifted, perhaps ever so slightly—but the burden is indeed eased. We give thanks and our faith is strengthened. We are reminded that we do not carry the weight of the world on our shoulders, but rather that Christ and Christ alone is Messiah and good shepherd. Our hope is renewed. Our confidence in the purposes and timing of God is reaffirmed.

Second, we see the world more clearly and discern more nearly how we are called to act in word and deed. We are not called to do everything. Worship, true worship, frees us from the need to be little messiahs, little heroes. Rather, we better discern how we are being called, for such a time as this, to be the people of God in our world.

We might wish that it would happen so neatly and clearly as it seemingly happened for the church in Antioch. There we read that the elders were together in prayer and worship and that they recognized the call of the Spirit to set aside Paul and Barnabas for work that would take them to Asia Minor. And yet, while it may not actually, in practice, be so clear cut, if we are faithful in worship, we do grow in our capacity to discern well and to see our world as God sees it and to recognize the particular ways we are called to be and to act. Ideally, of course, every element in worship would be this grace to the people of God.

Songs of praise and adoration, hymns and anthems are sung, by which hearts are once more aligned to the wonder that Christ is on the throne of the universe. The creed is said, and it becomes a deep and powerful reminder of the ancient truths that transcend all cultures and nation states. And the Word is read and preached.

The genius of preaching, at its best, is two things. First, we are once more drawn into a greater sense of the story of God—the purposes of God and the ways of God, so that we can once more appreciate better what God is doing in the world. Preaching calls us into a greater appreciation of the work of the Creator and Redeemer, and to the significance of the great acts of redemption: incarnation, cross, resurrection, ascension, and the sending of the Spirit—all in anticipation of the consummation of all things at the revelation of the Christ. We are brought into the God story.

And second, our faith, through the Word, is strengthened. Preaching can so easily be demoralizing when it is nothing but mere moral instruction—how to be a good father (on Father's Day) and how to manage your finances, and how to do this or that and, of course, how to be a morally upright citizen of society. But what is most urgently needed, week in and week out, is the reminder that in the midst of it all, Christ is on the throne of the universe. Our greatest need is that our faith would be strengthened. Every week. That our confidence would be restored that God will indeed fulfill God's purposes in the world. That good will triumph over evil. That, indeed, God will do God's work in God's time.

Then, of course, the sacraments are celebrated. Nonsacramental traditions and Christian communities as a rule do not fully appreciate the potential of the sacramental acts of the church to be a powerful means by which the church affirms and sustains its missional identity.

Baptism, ideally within the context of the liturgy, is the essential counterpart to teaching and catechism (Mt 28:19-20). It is the visual counterpart, the symbolic partner, of the preached Word.

The Lord's Table is in like manner the essential complement to the Word, the visual and gestural equivalent to the verbal proclamation of the gospel. In this act, not merely in the words of institution, but in the act itself, Christ through the church and through this meal declares afresh the gospel, the good news of the mercy and love of God for a sin-sick world. The table is the great declaration of God's love (Jn 3:16) and God's radical hospitality for those who feel that they have no hope apart from God, who has acted for them in Christ and who is calling them to God's very self through the ministry of the Spirit. The table, each time we gather, is a reminder of the hope of the church—the gathering of all of the elect at the marriage supper of the Lamb (Rev 19:9).

Then also, the table is a means of grace: through this simple act, with God's people, the church's hope is renewed, and the church is strengthened for the road. This is her spiritual meat and drink, sustaining the church in mission.

There is an ancient expression for all of this, attributed often to the Psalms, but applicable to all worship: in worship we know the ordering of the affections. We grow in faith, hope, and love. Through worship, as those who are truly engaged with the world, we move from despair to hope, from fear to love. Our faith is strengthened. The nerve of cynicism is cut. Any proclivity toward despair, in the face of setback and disappointment, is thwarted.

Then, worship also grants clarity of vision—or, better put, *greater* clarity of vision. We see more clearly the context and setting to which we are called. As noted, we see Christ on the throne and thus are freed from the need to be heroes and thus freed to discern and embrace our particular callings, the specific ways we are being called to contribute, in word and deed, to the coming of the reign of Christ.

"The Love of Christ Urges Us On"

The reference to seeing Christ on the throne is a vital and essential way of speaking of worship. There is a huge and palpable difference between worship that is mere *remembrance* of Christ, and worship that *encounters* Christ in real time. The church confesses that in her worship, the church is in dynamic communion with the risen Lord—no less a communion, and encounter, than that which the eleven experienced prior to the ascension, to the mission to make disciples of the nations, referenced in Matthew 28:17.

In the Lord's Supper, for example, we are not merely remembering Christ, in the sense that all that is happening is that we are thinking about the past tense event. Rather, the Lord's Supper and all of worship is an encounter with the ascended Lord—in real time. What animates the church in mission is not ultimately a christological principle or idea, but rather the encounter with Christ himself. Theological convictions we have about Christ are tremendous good news, as we see from the doxology to Christ in Colossians 1:15-20. And the ancient creeds are tremendously important, vital to our worship, grounding our worship and our faith in the truth. And yet, what sustains the church, week in and week out, through opportunity and through setback, is not so much the thinking we do *about* the truth of Christ as rather the *experience* of Christ, the encounter with Christ's very self and the wonder of God's radical hospitality in Christ.

What propels us in mission is not a conviction of truth, though this is terribly important; rather, what sustains us, through all the challenges of life and mission, is that we have found mercy, grace, and love at the cross of Jesus. This is not merely an idea or a conviction, but something that is encountered afresh each week in the liturgy. We feel, and that is the imperative and operative word, we *feel* the full force of the gospel.

The intimate and intense autobiographical reflections found in 2 Corinthians 2–7 provide a profound insight into the missional heart of the apostle Paul. We can read these reflections wondering what it was that moved and animated him, sustained him, and kept him going—so that he would persevere through all the trials he describes so eloquently in these chapters. At one point he speaks poignantly of how, in mission, "death is at work in us, but life is at work in you" (2 Cor 4:12). He speaks of how "we do not lose heart. Though outwardly we are wasting away . . ." (2 Cor 4:16). He speaks of how no one is viewed from a human point of view (2 Cor 5:16) and then, almost climactically, how in all his afflictions, his joy knows no bounds (2 Cor 7:2). One naturally asks how, for one so engaged in mission, who again and again through his apostolic witness and ministry came up against the forces of darkness and evil, the apostle is able to sustain such a spiritual centeredness, clarity, and, yes, even joy. What is clear from any reading of these chapters by Paul is that the fundamental orientation he had was the vision of the ascended Christ: "the knowledge of God's glory displayed in the face of Christ" (2 Cor 4:6). And more specifically, it was the encounter with the love of Christ, as he speaks of how Christ's love urges us on (2 Cor 5:14). It was this that gave him the grace to carry on—living in the love of God in Christ.

Nothing so undergirds and sustains the work of the church, in mission, in her engagement with the world, as the love of Christ. The church in worship is the church that comes afresh into the presence of the one who loves the church and loves the world; and more, the encounter in and through worship is precisely and intentionally a fresh encounter with the love of God, in Christ, specifically in the face of Christ (2 Cor 4:6).

Pentecost, The Mission of God, and Spirit-Infused Worship

And yet, there is a crucial piece—an essential and vital understanding or perspective—without which all that is said so far is an inconceivable ideal: the Holy Spirit, third person of the Trinity.

The operative agent in the mission of God and thus the mission of the church is not the church itself, but the Spirit of God. Mission is inconceivable apart from Pentecost. The church in mission is the church filled by the Spirit, guided by the Spirit, walking in the Spirit, a church that overcomes divisions by maintaining the unity of the Spirit and that in the end is bearing the fruit of the Spirit (see Gal 5:13-26).

Yet, what makes this possible is surely that the church prays in the Spirit (Eph 6:18). Until and unless we learn to pray—to worship—"in the Spirit," both worship and mission will be nothing more than human constructs. Mission will be nothing more than human strategizing, human endeavor to accomplish human designs on fixing the world. The genius of mission is an appreciation of the work of the Spirit, hovering over the world, infusing the church with grace, equipping the church for the work to which it is called, nurturing within it love, joy, and peace, and then guiding the church into the very specific ways in which it is called to witness to Christ in word and deed.

What the church urgently needs is an appreciation of the immediacy of the work of the Spirit in the church's life and mission—to see and feel the force of what the church in Antioch experienced when, we read, the elders were together in worship and they recognized coming out of their worship the specific calling of the Spirit for them to lay hands on Barnabas and Paul and commission them for the work to which the Spirit was calling them in Asia Minor. This kind of *immediacy* of the Spirit's work in mission arises from and is sustained by a similar immediacy in worship itself. If worship is going to foster Spirit-infused and guided mission then worship—the liturgy—needs to be itself a Spirit-infused and guided encounter with Christ.

Spirit-infused mission is not an approach to mission that discounts the importance of clear thinking and well-designed strategies. It is rather a realization that these strategies and approaches to mission necessarily are done "in the Spirit." In like manner, to speak of worship as "praying in the Spirit" does not mean that formal liturgy is discounted. To the contrary, we read that the early church, post-Pentecost, devoted itself to the apostles' teaching and the fellowship, the breaking of bread and the prayers (Acts 2:42). Rather, it means that the liturgy, however formal or informal, however structured or planned, assumes both the *prior* work of the Spirit, guiding the church in the design of her liturgies, and the *immediate* work of the Spirit present and operative in the liturgy.

This needs to be made explicit. We give thanks for the liturgy recognizing that while human agency is evident in all its components, this form and structure and content of our worship is a gift of God to the church. Ancient liturgies are not so much artifacts as Spirit-inspired guides to those who design the worship of the contemporary church, so that we can lean into the teaching ministry of the Spirit who superintends the church in worship.

Then, in worship, we call on the Spirit, invoking the Spirit's presence in each element or movement of the liturgy. Each element, but two elements in particular: Word and sacrament. Surely we only come to the ministry of the Word—the readings and then the exposition and proclamation of the Word—with a prayer that is spoken, not merely understood. This is the aptly termed "prayer for illumination," the explicit declaration by the church that the Word is just words, with no power, only the letter, apart from the gracious work of Spirit illuminating both preacher and hearer, rekindling our cold hearts and renewing our strength. Yes, it is very much through the Word, but it is the Spirit at work, in and with and through the Word, that is the crucial and essential dynamic to this dimension of our worship.

I stress that this needs to be made explicit—this crucial work of the church, the ministry of the Word, is done in and through the grace of the Spirit. If we do not make it explicit, it is too easily assumed that what sustains the church is the rhetoric of the preacher who moves people and empowers them through careful exegesis and study, timely illustrations, and a "wonderful way with words."

The Lord's Table is also a crucial venue in which we affirm, yet again, that this encounter with Christ, at the table, is a Spirit-superintended meeting between Christ and his people. Thus the very best of liturgies and the wisest of liturgists know that the "epiclesis" is the essential invocation of the Spirit's presence at the table, infusing and anointing the elements, the people, the act itself, so that these elements are, indeed, "the gifts of God for the people of God." Liturgies or worship leaders that either downplay or simply fail to make reference to the Spirit are in practice making a subtle but no less staggering assumption: that the church can manage this on its own. We might insist that to the contrary we of course do not believe this. And yet, ancient liturgical wisdom suggests that we do not appreciate this until and unless we make it explicit.

Thus I stress that if we truly believe that the only mission of the church is the mission that is guided by and infused by the work of the Spirit, then this must necessarily be evident in our worship. I say to pastors and worship leaders, if you want your people to be fully engaged in the world as eager participants in the purposes of God for the world, doing so in the grace and power of the Spirit, then it only makes sense that in turn you assure that the worship itself is guided by and infused with the work of the Spirit.

Worship in the Academy

If this is our vision—our understanding—of the connection or relationship between worship and mission, then surely it should be evident in the institutions that are likely as formative as any other to the understanding and experience of the church. A case could be made that Christian universities, colleges, and seminaries are the most formative agencies of the church, shaping the perspective and orientation of the next generation of Christian leadership for the church and for the society. Yes, of course, it is so very crucial that all that we have said so far be evident in the weekly worship of a congregation. And yet, likely nothing in this regard is so formative as the university and college and seminary that has made it explicit that their educational mission and vision is the equipping of women and men for service in the world. In other words, the university, college, or seminary that self-identifies itself as Christian typically, and appropriately so, views itself as in the business of formation: education, training, equipping, and inspiriting women and men to engage the world with a vision for the purposes of God for the world.

Contemporary Christian institutions of higher education engage the whole purpose of God for the world—yes, the work of religious leadership for congregations and for apostolic witness, but also for the diverse ways in which the Spirit of God is calling women and men into the arts, into education, into business, into the professions of law, medicine, and engineering and into the trades as carpenters, electricians, and nurses. And, of course, it is the assumption of Christian universities and seminaries that their graduates will do the good work to which they are called to the glory of God, for the sake of the reign of Christ, and do so in the grace and power of the Holy Spirit.

Our assumption as often as not is that those who finish their studies at these institutions will engage the world through the lens and thus with the perspective that is shaped and informed by worship and liturgy. They live in the world with hope and not despair, with love rather than fear, with a courage that is informed and animated by the experience of the love of Christ. What we surely hope for is that our graduates will be women and men who have a deep appreciation in the rhythms of their own lives of the essential counterpart, for the sake of their lives and their work, of worship and mission. They see and feel that if they are truly going to be all that God is calling them to be in the world, then they need to be worshipers.

Thus, while the academy is first and foremost a teaching-learning community, it is also a liturgical community; the liturgy is fundamental to the mission and vision of institutions of higher education that self-identify as Christian. Those who give leadership to this dimension of an academic institution, perhaps the campus chaplain, need to understand the importance of liturgy for the fulfillment of the institution's mission, and also have the liturgical savvy to implement liturgical rhythms in the life of the university and seminary. And more, presidents, senior administrators, and faculty signal this as well by stressing the vital place of worship in the institution and by their own modeling for their students that this matters, not only to them personally, but to the work of the academic. Worship and chapel is not a nice convenient break to an otherwise demanding day of rigorous research, study, and teaching; it is rather the essential and animating force in the academy—the very practice or exercise that makes the university and the seminary truly Christian.

This is so because in the end, it is not merely a christological idea or even a "Christian worldview" that makes the university or seminary Christian. Rather, what animates and informs and infuses the academic program with a deeply Christian identity is the encounter with Christ—in real time—that is fostered in worship.

Thus, dynamic academic communities have a delightful rhythm to them, moving from the library to the chapel, and back, from the classroom to the shared liturgy and back again, with each informing the other. We worship as those who are in the classroom engaged in the academic process; and we come to our studies as those who have and are meeting Christ together in worship. And what all of this signals, of course, is that worship then becomes for the graduates of our schools something that is integral to their lives and to their understanding of their individual vocations and to the ways they understand and participate in the mission of God in the world.

Conclusion

I have stressed that worship and mission are not only inseparable but also that they are distinct. While mission and worship inform and animate each other, this is only possible if each has integrity in its own right. Worship must be worship if it is to truly inform and animate the work of the church in the world. It cannot be co-opted by mission concerns; it is a distinct act of the church.

Yet, there is no avoiding, nor should there be any attempt to avoid, recognizing that the worship of the church is in many cases an essential means by which God is drawing men and women to Christ. The liturgy itself has very often been a vehicle by which the Spirit of Christ as attended to the hearts and minds of those who are seeking the salvation of God.

A compelling example of this was the role of the liturgy in the coming to faith of Simone Weil. In *Waiting for God* she speaks of the impact of several encounters with liturgy in different contexts and settings, including the procession of fishermen wives on the coast of Portugal, singing ancient hymns, of being deeply struck by the beauty of the Catholic liturgy when she visited Milan and Florence. Then finally, the critical turning point, when during Holy Week she visited a Benedictine abbey in northeastern France, and how there she found deep consolation through the liturgy, and knew intimately the love of Christ in the midst of her own personal pain and suffering.[1] Particularly noteworthy for her was the celebration of the Eucharist, where she knew that she was being drawn directly into the very presence of the Christ who loved her so deeply.

All of this is a reminder that on any given Sunday and for any given chapel service on the campus of the university, there are those who are on the way—inquirers, seekers, those who are trying to make sense of their lives, but who have yet to know the love of God in Christ.

Some conclude that therefore, given that there are those who have yet to accept Christ as Lord, we should evangelize in the worship service. But I wonder if a more powerful and compelling response is just to worship—to be the church in worship and let the Spirit do what only the Spirit can do in the heart of the seeker. We do not need to force the issue; we can be patient, hospitable, and generous. Those who seek can walk with us for as long as it takes, letting God do God's work in their lives in God's time.

But it does mean that we practice a fundamental and radical hospitality. We do not "dumb down" the liturgy; that gains nothing. We remain the church in worship, however foreign that may be to the seeker. But we avoid the arcane, and we make it as accessible as possible. In our preaching, we do not assume that everyone present is an insider, and at the Lord's Table, we welcome, with a radical generosity, those who might be inquirers—with simple explanations of how the rite is observed so that awkwardness can be avoided—and so that, in time, they can also come to a knowledge of the love of God in Christ.

We invite one and all, visitor, inquirer, and regular attendee, to be part of the great journey of worship and mission—giving praise and adoration to the living and ascended Christ, seeking the grace of God through worship that will sustain the church, each one of us actually, in mission in the world.

---

[1] Simone Weil, *Waiting for God* (New York: G. P. Putnam's Sons, 1951).

10

Missional Spirituality *and* Justice

Mae Elise Cannon

FOR CENTURIES, IF NOT MILLENNIA, Christians have identified the mission of the gospel: to preach the good news of Jesus Christ and to make disciples of all nations. Matthew 28 clearly professes the authority given to Christ who then commanded his disciples: "Therefore go and make disciples of all nations, baptizing them in the name of the Father and of the Son and of the Holy Spirit, and teaching them to obey everything I have commanded you. And surely I am with you always, to the very end of the age" (Mt 28:19-20). Few Christians contest this understanding of a Christian call to mission. Christ clearly commanded for the good news of the gospel to be spread throughout the world. He unmistakably instructed his disciples to call the lost to conversion and to set the captives free by offering a message of salvation through the person of Jesus Christ. This evangelistic missional understanding of Matthew 28 is completely true! And yet, it is also incomplete.

What is a holistic understanding of the gospel of Christ? And what does the New Testament, and even the

Hebrew Scriptures, teach us about the call to discipleship and evangelism? We must not ignore Jesus' words: followers are called not only to make disciples through conversion, but also to "[teach] them to obey everything I have commanded you." What are the commandments of Christ? For committed evangelicals, a review of the Scriptures and the teachings of Jesus must be inclusive of his directives about justice, his call to respond to the needs of the poor, and his example of prophetic witness which commands a merciful response to the "least of these" (Mt 25:40).

Defining Justice

This past year, I was a guest lecturer for a doctor of ministry class on justice at a prestigious evangelical seminary. In talking with the students, I asked them how they would define justice, particularly in light of its necessity in Christian mission. They responded by quoting Timothy Keller and his writing in *Generous Justice*. Keller is the founding pastor of Redeemer Presbyterian Church in New York City. He writes that justice's most basic meaning is to "treat people equitably."[1] He continues by identifying an Old Testament understanding of justice as "acquitting or punishing every person on the merits of the case, regardless of race or social status. Anyone who does the same wrong should be given the same penalty."[2] I believe these definitions of justice are helpful, but also somewhat limited. Too often, our understandings of justice are limited to a legal understanding of actions and consequences. More broadly, justice is about doing the right thing.[3]

Tim Keller describes justice as caring for the vulnerable, giving people their rights, taking up the care and causes of the widows and the orphans, immigrants, and the poor.[4] When I asked the doctoral students where

---

[1] Timothy Keller, *Generous Justice: How God's Grace Makes Us Just* (New York: Penguin, 2010), 3.
[2] Ibid.
[3] I wrote extensively about what the Bible teaches about justice in my book *Social Justice Handbook: Small Steps for a Better World*. My goal was to better understand a more holistic definition of justice as described through the Scriptures: "Justice is the manifestation of God's righteous character in the world—the execution of God's righteousness. Justice is the expression of God's righteousness through right action. When justice completely exists on this earth, everything will be the way God intended it to be. The righteous actions of Christ followers is the execution of faith. As believers practice good works, they become agents of justice." Mae Elise Cannon, *Social Justice Handbook: Small Steps for a Better World* (Downers Grove, IL: InterVarsity Press, 2009), 20.
[4] Keller, *Generous Justice*, 4.

Keller garnered his definition, where these ideas could be found in the Scriptures, they were unable to come up with a response. Further evidence that we as evangelicals often overlook scriptural teachings about God's heart for justice.

In our discussion, I suggested that we can find teaching on justice in the book of Leviticus. In defense of the doctoral students, not many people would claim the book of Leviticus, the laws given to the priestly tribes of the Levites, to be one of their favorites in the canon of Scripture. The detailed and descriptive verses describing the methodology for slaughtering sacrifices and making offerings to God may not seem the most relevant for many Christians today. Nonetheless, Leviticus paints a picture for the people of God about the way God intends the world to be. This picture, one could argue, is a glimpse of attributes of the kingdom of God if it were ever to be manifested on the earth. This picture is fleshed out in Leviticus 25, where the Scriptures teach about the sabbath law and the Year of Jubilee. After forty-nine years, a year was consecrated as a year of freedom, the year of the Lord's favor. Jubilee was the year following seven sabbath years. It was the year that proclaimed freedom for the captives, the restoration of land to its original owners, the forgiveness of debt. The Jubilee year was holy, set aside to honor God. The Year of Jubilee celebrated holistic renewal for the entire community.[5]

In ancient times, during the normal course of events, people who experienced hardship often went into great debt and some sold themselves to servitude to their family members or others, and some sold their land. In fifty years' time, these types of transactions would have led to a terrible disparity between the rich and the poor. But Jubilee rectified this problem. The debt of the people was to be completely wiped away. A relative state of equality was brought back to society. Israel was dependent on the land, which was not to be used as a possession to exploit but to be shared equitably.[6] These sabbath principles taught the people of Israel that the land and everything in it belonged to God. Jubilee "is God's comprehensive unilateral restructuring of the community's assets" that

---

[5]Descriptions of the Year of Jubilee come from Cannon, *Social Justice Handbook*, 27.
[6]Ched Myers, "God Speed the Year of Jubilee!," *Sojourners* 27, no. 3 (1998): 24-28.

reminded the people "that they were an exodus people who must never return to a system of slavery" (Lev 25:42).[7] The people of Israel were freed from captivity and were called by God to extend to others around them the same kind of deliverance and compassion he showed them.

Think of these concepts from Leviticus in light of Jesus' life and ministry. Christ began his ministry with a declaration pointing to the Year of Jubilee from the prophet Isaiah:

> The Spirit of the Lord is upon me,
>> because he has anointed me
>> to proclaim good news to the poor.
> He has sent me to proclaim freedom for the prisoners
>> and recovery of sight for the blind,
> to set the oppressed free,
>> to proclaim the year of the Lord's favor. (Lk 4:18-19)

Jesus was declaring himself to be the manifestation of the Year of Jubilee. He, as Savior and Redeemer, was coming to right the wrongs of human sin and destruction and to provide restoration of not only lost souls, but of all creation, to God the Father. Jesus' sermon in Luke 4 is a declaration of God's heart for justice where good news would be preached to the poor and the oppressed would be set free.

Lest this brief survey of Leviticus 25 and Luke 4 is unconvincing about God's heart for justice, it is helpful to look more deeply at the ways justice is so deeply integrated throughout the Hebrew Scriptures. Throughout the Old Testament there are two concepts that go hand in hand; righteousness and justice. Justice is right action—doing the right thing. Righteousness speaks to the condition of our hearts and is the attribute of being pure (or "right") before God.[8]

In the Old Testament, the Hebrew word often used for justice is *mishpat*.[9] This Hebrew word occurs over four hundred times throughout

---

[7]Shane Claiborne, *Irresistible Revolution: Living as an Ordinary Radical* (Grand Rapids: Zondervan, 2006), 171.

[8]Cannon, *Social Justice Handbook*, 19-21.

[9]There is substantial scholarship around the meaning of *mishpat* in the Old Testament. Consider reading the perspectives voiced in Sylvia Huberman Scholnick, "The Meaning of *Mišpat* in the Book of Job," *The Journal of Biblical Literature* 101, no. 4 (December 1982): 521-29.

the Old Testament—over sixty times in the Psalms, thirty-six times in Deuteronomy. *Mishpat*, or divine justice, refers to the execution of God's righteous standards. The Hebrew word for righteousness is *tsedeq*, the quality or state of mind of being justice, morally upright, or without sin.

These two ideas—God's justice and his righteousness—are inextricably linked throughout the Scriptures. Throughout history followers of God have wrestled with what it means to maintain both. In the Old Testament, God expressed his frustration when the Israelites were obedient but seemed to be missing the whole point (Is 58). In the New Testament, Jesus criticized the Pharisees for focusing on outward actions while missing the inward transformation toward righteousness (Mt 23). It is helpful to study the degree to which these two words are used in parallel throughout the Old Testament. Consider the following verses:

> Righteousness [*tsedeq*] and justice [*mishpat*] are the foundation of your throne;
>> love and faithfulness go before you. (Ps 89:14)

> Praise be to the LORD your God, who has delighted in you and placed you on his throne as king to rule for the LORD your God. Because of the love of your God for Israel and his desire to uphold them forever, he has made you king over them, to maintain justice [*mishpat*] and righteousness [*sedaqa*]. (2 Chron 9:8)

> The LORD loves righteousness [*sedaqa*] and justice [*mishpat*];
>> the earth is full of his unfailing love. (Ps 33:5)

> This is what the LORD says:
> "Maintain justice [*mishpat*]
>> and do what is right,
> for my salvation is close at hand
>> and my righteousness [*sedaqa*] will soon be revealed." (Is 56:1)

It is clear from these passages, and the many others throughout the Hebrew Scriptures, that justice and righteousness go hand in hand. Justice is the manifestation of God's righteous character in the world—the execution of God's righteousness. Justice is the expression of God's righteousness through right action. When justice completely exists on this earth, everything will be the way that God intended it to be. The righteous actions of Christ-followers are the execution of faith. As believers practice good works, they become agents of God's justice in the world.[10]

Here is where things get really exciting. I have the privilege of speaking all over the country and this past year gave a talk on spirituality and justice at the Apprentice Institute in Wichita, Kansas. Often when I get to this part of my talk, I am fearful that the audience will become completely disengaged because it contains an elaborate exegetical study in Greek and Hebrew. Yet, when we look more closely at the implications of the Koine Greek translations of justice and righteousness in the New Testament, I really believe the result expands our understanding of what the Scriptures have to say about God's heart for justice, and how it is central to the gospel and mission of Jesus Christ.

In the New Testament the Greek word for righteousness, *dikaios*, appears over two hundred times. *Dikaios* has many meanings and connotations, including the observation of right laws, keeping the commandments of God, being virtuous, and righteousness or justice. Sound familiar? In the New Testament Greek, *dikaios* refers to both Old Testament ideas—justice and righteousness. The King James Version translates the word *dikaios* thirty-three times as being "just" and forty-one times as "righteous." A lot has been lost in the translations of the Scriptures from their original languages to English. Consider the following verses where *dikaios* appears—use the idea of both justice and righteousness in your translation:

> Jesus replied, "Let it be so now; it is proper for us to do this to fulfill all righteousness [and justice]." Then John consented. (Mt 3:15)

> Blessed are those who hunger and thirst for righteousness [and justice], for they will be filled. (Mt 5:6)

> For in the gospel the righteousness [and justice] of God is revealed—a righteousness that is by faith from first to last, just as it is written: "The righteous [and just] will live by faith." (Rom 1:17)

---

[10]Cannon, *Social Justice Handbook*, 20.

As it is written:

"They have freely scattered abroad their gifts to the poor;
    their righteousness [and justice] endures forever." (2 Cor 9:9)

Of the two hundred times that *dikaios* is used in the Scripture, most versions only use the translation "justice" once (Col 4:1), in regard to slavery.

Contemporary evangelicalism has emphasized personal righteousness and piety and has missed much of the intended meaning bursting through the Scriptures about justice. It is critical to understand that righteousness and justice are interconnected in both Testaments. In the Old Testament, righteousness was obedience to the laws of Moses. New Testament righteousness is received through faith in Christ. The demonstration of righteousness in our lives is *just* living—living out the justice of God motivated by love for God and love for his people.

The popularity of justice-oriented activism has been growing among evangelicals in the twenty-first century with an organized antitrafficking movement led by nonprofits such as the International Justice Mission (IJM) and scores of books about the topic, including the following: Shane Claiborne's *The Irresistible Revolution* (2006); *Just Courage* by Gary Haugen of IJM (2008); *Journey Toward Justice* by Nicholas Wolterstorff (2013); and *The Hole in Our Gospel* by World Vision's Richard Stearns (2014), to name a few.[11] On one hand, this trend is deeply encouraging. The formerly bridgeless divide between adherents of the social gospel and an emphasis on justice-oriented societal engagement on the one hand, and evangelicals who believe in the inerrancy of Scripture and the necessity of evangelistic efforts, on the other, seems to be lessening significantly. Increasingly students, young people, pastors, and Christian leaders are mobilizing toward both domestic and international missions with an

---

[11]Claiborne, *The Irresistible Revolution*; Gary Haugen, *Just Courage: God's Great Expedition for the Restless Christian* (Downers Grove, IL: InterVarsity Press, 2008); Nicholas Wolterstorff, *Journey Toward Justice: Personal Encounters in the Global South* (Grand Rapids: Baker Academic, 2013); Richard Stearns, *The Hole in Our Gospel: The Answer That Changed My Life and Might Just Change the World*, rev. ed. (Nashville: Thomas Nelson, 2014).

emphasis on sharing the good news of salvation in Christ while also offering material responses and humanitarian assistance to those who are hurting and suffering around the world. This is a beautiful thing! It would seem the Holy Spirit has been encouraging the church toward greater engagement in holistic mission, committed to both conversion and justice-oriented activism.

Need for More Justice Than Acts of Service

As the conservative church reengages with ministries of justice, it is important to differentiate between acts of service, compassion, mercy, and charity. *Compassion* means to suffer with or to walk alongside someone by empathizing with his or her needs and experience. The church is clearly called to be compassionate to those around us. Christ was the greatest example of compassion as he took our pain and the consequences of our sin completely on himself. We know that God showed us comfort and compassion "so that we can comfort those in any trouble with the comfort we ourselves receive from God" (2 Cor 1:4).[12]

The contemporary church actively seeks to respond to people's immediate needs. There are compassion ministries (also called mercy ministries) for people suffering from the loss of a loved one, for those going through divorce and for people going through other personal crises. There are also compassion ministries that extend benevolence to those who are in need by distributing food and clothing, providing homeless shelters, and other acts of charity. These are all wonderful things! However, these ministries often are only responding to the consequences of injustice rather than working to fix the source of the problem.

The church must learn to move beyond acts of compassion and ask, Why are so many people homeless? Why are so many people getting divorced? Why are so many African American boys and young men incarcerated? Compassion responds to the effects of these problems. Social justice seeks to address their systemic causes. When we work to solve the

---

[12]Cannon, *Social Justice Handbook*, 32.

roots of these problems, a Band-Aid is no longer being put over the wound. Instead, the emphasis is on getting rid of the disease that caused the wound in the first place. When the disease is eradicated, social justice is being lived out. My friend, Dan Schmitz, a pastor in Oakland, California, puts it this way: "Compassion is about effects. Justice is about causes."[13] The church must learn to address systemic issues of injustice and to address root causes of problems in our communities, society, and around the world.

Shane Claiborne is a friend and mentor when it comes to living out Christian social justice in the world. He models transformative justice in his daily life, as he lives in an intentional community called *The Simple Way*, doing life beside people who are homeless and often discouraged mentally and materially by challenges in life. When I first began participating in justice-oriented ministry in downtown Chicago, I began to write and identify numerous "issues of social justice," often related to race, poverty, and gender. The entire second half of *Social Justice Handbook* is committed to facts, resources, and steps that can be taken to address hundreds of justice issues, from AIDS to sex trafficking to poverty in the developing world. I will never forget one of the first conversations Shane and I had about global justice issues. While encouraging my work and ministry, he also graciously reminded me that justice is about people, not issues. While on one hand his exhortation stung, it was a meaningful reminder that fighting against injustice is not simply about addressing core ills related to racial disparities, poverty, disease, natural disasters, violence, and oppression; fighting injustice means learning and being in intimate relationship with the men, women, and children whose lives are broken and daily affected by unjust systems. As Christ-followers and the church live more fully into our missional calling, we will certainly come face to face with issues of injustice. However, the powerful transformational relationships we have with mothers, fathers, brothers, sisters, boys, and girls will forever change and transform the ways we both respond to injustices and the ways in which we encounter God.

---

[13]Ibid., 33.

Prayer for a Broken Heart

After about a decade of ministering alongside the homeless and working with courageous men and women toward racial and economic justice in Chicago, I began to feel like my spiritual life could not sustain the brokenness I was witnessing in the lives of members of the community around me. During my years on staff with World Vision, we would often pray the prayer of the organization's founder, Bob Pierce: "Break my heart for the things that break the heart of God." And yet, I increasingly felt like my heart could not handle being any more broken. In 2015, when I was asked to speak at the Apprentice Institute, the title of my talk was supposed to be the "Joy of a Social Justice Life." At various times over the past couple of decades, I have thought to myself, "What joy is that?" Social justice is hard. And when one has intimate relationships with people who are hurting, it sometimes feels like your heart is breaking into a thousand pieces. How can our hearts sustain the brokenness of the painful things we witness around us when it often seems like there is more injustice than righteousness in the world? I believe these questions are at the heart of the mission of the gospel. We must not forget that pursuing biblical justice is a spiritually transformative experience.

As a result of this struggle, I wrote a book that sought to integrate questions of spiritual formation and justice. How did heroes of the faith maintain intimate relationships with God and stay motivated, inspired, energetic, and healthy while fighting against the ills of the world? The book *Just Spirituality: How Faith Practices Fuel Social Action* wrestled with some of the struggles in my own soul. I cried out to God,

> As a Christian leader and activist, I resonate with the social justice tradition. I live a fast-paced life. I am more productive when I am busy, but I wrestle with what it means to operate from a sense of peace rather than one of frenzy. Spiritual rhythms challenge me. . . . My work focuses on responding to global poverty and injustice. I travel several days every month. I work long hours. I am passionate about my job and consider it a privilege to pour myself into my passion and calling. As deeply meaningful as I find my life and ministry, I struggle with what it means to

be spiritually centered. I want my life to be fueled by the power of God and intimate connection to the person of Jesus. I wrestle with the connection between my justice oriented activism and my desire for intimacy with the Creator.[14]

Do you resonate with any of these struggles? Where does the intersection of these struggles meet? I have become increasingly convinced that the cultivation of the soul through spiritual disciplines is one of the primary ways that God transforms us to better understand missional spirituality as it relates to both evangelism and justice. Transformational growth necessitates that Christians create the space for intentional opportunities to meet with God through spiritual practices such as silence, prayer, studying the Scriptures, worship, meaningful engagement in community, observation of the sabbath, and entering into sabbath rest; and ultimately the spiritual discipline of submission.

You can read in greater detail in *Just Spirituality* about the things I learned as I studied certain justice-oriented heroes of the faith, including Mother Teresa, Dietrich Bonhoeffer, Watchman Nee, Martin Luther King Jr., Fairuz, Desmond Tutu, and Oscar Romero. These world changers were deeply influenced by their spiritual practices and the various ways they sought intimacy with God. They each, in their own way, faced their individual "dark nights of the soul" and emerged not without doubts or struggle, but with an unyielding conviction to live out God's unique call on each of their lives.

Here is a little taste of some of their lessons about missional spirituality. Mother Teresa wrote regularly that it was "in the silence" that God speaks. She believed silence was a core practice that creates space for one to listen and commune with God. She wrote, "Silence is at the root of our union with God and with one another."[15] One was empowered and compelled to engage and love their neighbor by the nourishment and love communicated by God in silence and solitude. The example of Mother Teresa's service and compassion at the hands of the poor in

---

[14]Mae Elise Cannon, *Just Spirituality: How Faith Practices Fuel Social Action* (Downers Grove, IL: InterVarsity Press, 2013), 10.
[15]Ibid., 17.

Calcutta is the greatest witness to the power she experienced in her communion with God in the midst of silence.

The German theologian Dietrich Bonhoeffer is known and esteemed by many because of his works such as *Discipleship* and *Life Together*. Not only did Bonhoeffer's life and teaching embody devotion to Christ, but he stood firm in his convictions about God's heart for justice. Bonhoeffer's theology formed his faith, which in turn compelled him to act in direct response to injustices he observed. He expressed his personal piety in his reading of Scripture, daily meditation, and prayer. Bonhoeffer believed prayer was the primary mechanism by which a Christian could esteem God and diminish the self. Prayer served as a spiritual resource for Bonhoeffer and equipped him to carry out the work he felt the Lord most laid on his heart.[16]

Absolute submission requires the complete denial of self for the sake of Christ. This spiritual practice was exemplified in the life of Oscar Romero, a Latin American priest who served as a bishop of the Roman Catholic Church in El Salvador. Bishop Romero, who was deeply committed to the faith and regularly engaged in contemplative practices, reminded the church of the need for submission to the cross of Christ. His leadership directly challenged people in El Salvador by criticizing injustice, oppression, assassinations, and torture. Ultimately, he was martyred for his advocacy on behalf of the poor and the oppressed. His last act before being murdered on March 24, 1980, was officiating over communion, when he shared these words:

> This holy mass, this Eucharist, is an act of faith. With Christian faith we know that at this moment the wheaten host is changed into the body of the Lord, who offered himself for the world's redemption, and in this chalice the wine is transformed into the blood that was the price of salvation. May this body immolated and this blood sacrificed for humans nourish us also, so that we may give our body and blood to suffering and to pain—like Christ, not for self, but to teach justice and peace to our people.[17]

[16]Ibid., 39-47.
[17]James R. Brockman, *Romero: A Life* (Maryknoll, NY: Orbis Books, 2005), 60.

Oscar Romero's example and willingness to devote his life to ending injustice is a profound example of the spiritual discipline of submission.

My hope is that the example of such heroes of the faith such as Mother Teresa, Bonhoeffer, and Bishop Romero will inspire us to stay in the fight against injustice for the sake of the gospel. I believe each of their lives are a witness of the whole gospel in Christ—his saving grace and his commandments to address injustices in the world by responding to the needs of the least of these.

Can the Pursuit of Justice and Joy Go Together?

I would be remiss to not address the question of whether or not a justice-oriented life is joyful. At first glance it might seem not. What kind of life could be filled with joy when that emphasis is overwhelmed by the daily realities of poverty, brokenness, abuse, and neglect? And yet, "joy" is clearly identified as one of the fruits of the Holy Spirit and one of the attributes of a Christ-centered life (Gal 5:22). How might there be joy in a spirituality of justice?

The Bob Pierce prayer of "break my heart for the things that break the heart of God" is profound in that it reminds us of God's closeness to people who are broken and hurting. I believe one of the ways Christians experience joy in brokenness is because we experience God in the midst of the "least of these." The idea that God is present with those who are suffering is rife throughout the Scriptures, from Abraham, David, and the prophets in the Old Testament, to Jesus, the disciples, and Paul in the New. Several Scriptures remind us of this truth.

> The Lord said, "I have indeed seen the misery of my people in Egypt. I have heard them crying out because of their slave drivers, and I am concerned about their suffering." (Ex 3:7)

> But those who suffer he delivers in their suffering;
> he speaks to them in their affliction. (Job 36:15)

> For he has not despised or scorned
> the suffering of the afflicted one;

he has not hidden his face from him
> but has listened to his cry for help. (Ps 22:24)

Learn to do right; seek justice.
> Defend the oppressed.
Take up the cause of the fatherless;
> plead the case of the widow. (Is 1:17)

Immediately her bleeding stopped and she felt in her body that she was freed from her suffering. . . . He [Jesus] said to her, "Daughter, your faith has healed you. Go in peace and be freed from your suffering." (Mk 5:29, 34)

"Never again will they hunger;
> never again will they thirst.
The sun will not beat down on them,"
> nor any scorched heat.
For the Lamb at the center of the throne
> will be their shepherd;
"he will lead them to springs of living water."
> "And God will wipe away every tear from their eyes." (Rev 7:16-17)

Over and over again the Scriptures highlight evidence of God's concern for those who suffer. The final picture of Christ being worshiped at the center of the throne in Revelation includes language from the prophet Isaiah and a reminder of the promises of God to respond to those who are poor and oppressed. In a powerful image of the kingdom, the writer of Revelation reminds his readers that hunger and thirst will dissipate and God himself will wipe away every tear from the eyes of those who have experienced injustice and brokenness.

Spiritual Life Through Loss

I sometimes have felt closest to God when I have had the privilege of spending time with people who are in the final stages of life. Somehow approaching death sheds a bright light on the history of one's life—both the triumphant memories and the tragic ones. Over the years, I have spent a fair amount of time developing relationships and ministering alongside of the men who are serving time in the Louisiana State Penitentiary at Angola, which for many years was known as the "bloodiest prison in America." More than five thousand inmates reside in this prison in Southern Louisiana. Most have committed crimes that resulted in a life sentence. In Louisiana, a life sentence means life without parole. Many have been prisoners for decades. Over the years, many of these men have also committed their lives to Christ. I consider many of these inmates my teachers, as they often exemplify a freedom in Christ that is far more profound than any "free people" I know living outside of the walls of prison.

One of the inmates who particularly captured my heart was a man named Pete. I got to know Pete over the years. He had been an avid smoker prior to serving his prison sentence. When I met Pete, he was dying from lung cancer. Pete grew up in poverty. He spent most of his life at Angola. And yet Pete, even on his deathbed in a hospital ward in the middle of a prison, possessed a peace that seemed to transcend human understanding. The littlest of things seemed to be the greatest gift to Pete. When we met together, we would often tell stories about where we had come from, our families, and other social niceties. I sometimes believe the ministry of presence is the greatest gift we can give to one another. We would talk about Jesus and about God's saving grace. But one of the Christian teachings to which Pete held the most dear were the words from Jesus' sermon in Luke 4, a passage that talks about Christ "setting the captives free." Pete seemed ready to die. He seemed ready to be rid of the mantle of imprisonment that marked decades of his human life. On his deathbed, his body was overcome by the cancer that had riddled its way throughout his entire body. And yet, in his profound state of physical suffering and at the end of his life, he radiated a hope and profound sense of longing for intimacy with God. He held on deeply to the teachings that God would one day set the captives free. Only a few weeks after my last visit with Pete, he took his last breaths on this earth. I believe he is one of the "least of these" who is seated at God's right hand. Fully forgiven. Fully healed. Fully redeemed. Is this not the hope that we profess as followers of Jesus? Regardless of the wrongs we have done, regardless of the injustices that we witness and seek to overcome, regardless of the brokenness in this world, we rest in the promise that Christ has overcome the world (Jn 16:33)!

In 2014, I had a more personal encounter with death. About two years before, my father was diagnosed with terminal lung cancer. He had never been a smoker and in fact was a marathon runner for most of his life. Healthy and young, it seemed he should have decades more of life to spend with his family and loved ones.

When I think of a spirituality of justice, I often think that my dad was one of the best living examples of a Christ-follower living out a just spirituality. He possessed courage of faith that is difficult to describe. As a young man, he had a rough time making sense of life. He made poor choices, stole things, and was continually getting into trouble. Embittered at the world, at the age of eighteen he volunteered to go to Vietnam to serve his country. After two decorated tours, he returned to the United States and fell in love with my mother. Determined to finish college, he attended classes at Towson State in Baltimore. In a philosophy class, he was introduced to the person of Jesus and had a profound conversion experience. He frequently tells the story about how his introduction to Christ put his entire life on a different course. He began to live differently. He often went back to people he had stolen from and paid them what he owed. He was determined to be faithful to this new call on his life by expressing the love of God toward people.

Eventually, Dad had the opportunity to go to work for my grandfather, who owned a lumber construction company. Over the course of several years, he worked his way up from menial labor in the lumberyard to the manager of the truss plant. Eventually he became the president of the company and bought my grandfather's business. In addition to working hard, he was determined to care for the people who worked for him. Continually he put their needs ahead of his own. Over the course of several years running the family business, my dad provided work for people who seemed to have no other opportunities. He gave work to people struggling with alcoholism, depression, and other life challenges. He often would hire felons and men who had been previously incarcerated, but who seemed to have no other options for meaningful work because of their records. In years of recession, he went without a salary while being sure to pay the rest of the employees first. As I watched my dad's leadership, I have been continually humbled by his commitment to do the right thing—regardless of the cost—and to put others ahead of himself.

As I think of what it means to have courage in the face of life's challenges, my dad's selfless leadership continues to be an example. When my father was diagnosed with stage 3 lung cancer in August 2012, the doctors connected the illness to his tours in Vietnam. He had been exposed excessively to the carcinogenic herbicide Agent Orange, which doctors say caused his deterioration in health. As my dad began the course of treatment for cancer—daily radiation for a period of seven or eight weeks and two different types of chemotherapy once a month—he did not express fear. Instead, he got his life in order and began to establish a plan in case he did not live through the treatment. As we talked about his health and his approaching death, he told me that when the time came he was ready to go and to be with Jesus. He loved his family, but was not afraid. Rather he desired to be faithful with the many blessings God had given him and to approach his journey to the next life with both courage and peace.

My father died on June 24, 2014. At his funeral a few days later, the funeral home was full of bouquet after bouquet of beautiful flowers. The attendant told us she had never seen such an overwhelming response of affection and appreciation at someone's death. During the service we gave the opportunity for people to share words of remembrance as a testimony to the life my father lived. Not only did several of his thirteen brothers and sisters share stories about his life, several of the men who worked for him at the company talked about how he was the most generous person they knew. My father was an advocate of justice. He sought to address injustices in society by providing work and jobs for people who are often considered "unemployable." And when employees made mistakes, time and time again he sought to respond with an overwhelming kindness and grace that was often undeserved. His generosity was compelled by his love for Christ. We began this chapter reflecting on Tim Keller's definition of justice as care for the vulnerable, giving people their rights, and taking up the cause of the oppressed, the immigrants, and the poor.[18] My father's life was a living witness of a missional spirituality committed to both righteousness and justice because of his love for Christ. May each of our lives be so inspired.

---

[18]Keller, *Generous Justice*, 4.

11

Journey *in the* Spirit

George R. Hunsberger

Spirit of the living God, fall afresh on me.
Spirit of the living God, fall afresh on me.
Break me, melt me, mold me, fill me,
Spirit of the living God, fall afresh on me.[1]

I GREW UP SINGING THIS PRAYER chorus every Sunday following the benediction. The congregation sang it every week without fail, but not merely because it had been composed by its founding pastor (Dan Iverson). Rather, it was because the chorus expressed his and our most basic aspiration. This was our spirituality, put to music.

It was, in the words of this book's title, a spirituality for the *sent*. With God's blessing echoing in our ears, we sang our plea to the Spirit of the living God as we left the gathering and went on our way to the nooks and crannies of life where we would be bearing the witness of the Spirit in the Miami of mid-twentieth century.

This, no doubt, begins to explain why I view missional spirituality as a "journey in the Spirit," and why I believe

---

[1]Daniel Iverson, "Spirit of the Living God," 1926. The third line of the chorus preserves the original text. Some subsequent versions have dropped "break me" from the beginning of the line and added "use me" at the end of it.

spirituality and mission are so closely bound together that separating them does violence to both. Think, for example, of the theme of this book of essays: "spirituality for the sent." To some that might suggest naming those aspects of spirituality that apply to mission activities and relationships. But if, as I and others have argued in the book *Missional Church* and elsewhere, the adjective *missional* intends to say that the church is by its very nature "sent," then "spirituality for the sent" is not a subset. It is simply "Christian spirituality," a fitting spirituality for the church, the whole church, as God's sent people.

The link I am suggesting was present in a pregnant way as the post-Easter, postascension journey commenced. At the beginning of Acts, the sequel to Luke's account of the gospel, the apostles are still not clear about what Jesus had been saying to them about "the kingdom of God." They asked, "Lord, are you at this time going to restore the kingdom to Israel?" Jesus said that it was not for them to know "the times or dates the Father has set." What Jesus *did* make clear, however, was this: "But you will receive power when the Holy Spirit comes on you; and you will be my witnesses in Jerusalem, and in all Judea and Samaria, and to the ends of the earth" (Acts 1:6-8).

You will receive power. You will be my witnesses. Be ready. When the Holy Spirit comes on you, both will be true! Whatever we mean by spirituality, and whatever we mean by mission, they are bound together by the Spirit of the living God.

Having affirmed this to be so, I wish to describe some of the implications by looking closely at three ways of speaking in the biblical writings, especially in the New Testament. I will consider the adjective *spiritual*, the verb (!) *disciple* used by Jesus in his commissioning, and the God-likeness to which both themes point as a "spirituality for the sent."

SPIRITuality

When a noun is made into an adjective (by adding *-ual*, meaning "of, or pertaining to" what that noun designates), and when the adjective is then made into a noun (by adding *-ity*, signifying the "state of being" what the adjective describes), we have been taken some distance away from the original noun. With respect to the noun *spirituality*, and the adjective from which it is derived, *spiritual*, it makes a difference what the reference point is. To what *spirit* does *spirituality* refer? Whether it is stated clearly or is simply assumed, some reference point is at work in defining the territory. It may be vague or specific; it may have a singular point of reference or several points of reference. But it makes a difference. Which "spirit" is primarily in view when we talk about spirituality?

The dominant answer in our day is that the "spirit" in view is the human spirit. It begins with the recognition that the human person has a spiritual (nonmaterial) side. Attention is given to practices of mind and will that develop that spiritual side, releasing its potential and enhancing the quality of a person's life. As an example, the Theosophical Society in America envisions the goal of "spiritual practice" to be "the practical application of spiritual principles geared towards promoting a balanced and holistic unfoldment of our emotional, mental, and spiritual lives."[2]

It is about the human person, the self. Spiritual means "of, or relating to" the side of a person's life that is called "spirit." Spirituality, then, is conceived to be the pattern of attention given to the cultivation of that spiritual side of a person. Within such a reference point, there are certainly varieties of spirituality. *Psychology Today* reviews the territory and concludes, "Spirituality means something different to everyone. For some, it's about participating in organized religion: going to church, synagogue, a mosque, and so on. For others, it's more personal: Some people get in touch with their spiritual side through private prayer, yoga, meditation, quiet reflection, or even long walks."[3] To be sure, even when the accent is on the "spirit side of a human person," there are hints that some impression of what is transcendent, what is above and beyond the person, is at play. The human person's recognition of a transcendent arena, power, or even deity, and their relatedness to it, is part of the spirituality quest. But the focus is on how the spiritual side of the person is to be properly attuned to the transcendent and is transformed by it.

---

[2]"Spiritual Practice," the Theosophical Society in America, accessed March 1, 2016, www.theosophical.org/teachings/spiritual-practice.
[3]"Spirituality Basics," *Psychology Today*, accessed March 1, 2016, www.psychologytoday.com/basics/spirituality.

The widening divide involved in being "spiritual" (personal, private practices) "but not religious" (organized religion becoming its form or substitute) emerges quite naturally. But the accent by either route tends to remain the same. The reference point for spirituality is the human spirit. Particularly in Western society, it has come to be true that "in modern times the emphasis is on subjective experience. [Spirituality] may denote almost any kind of meaningful activity or blissful experience."[4]

For those of us who seek a more distinctly Christian understanding of spirituality, it has been difficult not to echo the trend. In a great deal of the literature on the subject, it is not apparent that the core reference point is different from that of the secular society. We speak of the nature of the Christian life that the human person and community is called and enabled to live because of the gospel of Jesus Christ. And we emphasize practices that give us divine nourishment to be transformed to live that way. Yet, it would seem that in too many cases the focus of attention, the *spirit* in terms of which we consider *spirituality*, is the same: the human spirit. It has to be asked whether this conception is too easily assumed, and not adequately enough tested.

I am not saying that spirituality does not touch the human spirit, nor that it is improper for the human person to attend to one's spiritual dimension. But in the process, I believe we may have overlooked the obvious, and by doing so have missed the most dynamic of visions for a robust spirituality. This is my thesis: the *spirit* in terms of which *spiritual* and *spirituality* are understood must be the Spirit of God, the Holy Spirit. In other words, we are speaking about "Spirit-ual-ity." Any relationship the terms may have to the human spirit is derived from their primary reference to the Holy Spirit. While this is too rarely recognized in the literature, on occasion it is stated directly. Christopher Cocksworth, an Anglican bishop in the UK, says it well:

> The Holy Spirit is fundamental to a Christian understanding of spirituality. Indeed, formally and properly, spirituality does not in the first place concern the experience of the human spirit itself, or even the expression

---

4 "Spirituality," *Wikipedia*, accessed March 1, 2016, https://en.wikipedia.org/wiki/Spirituality.

of religious belief in piety and practice, but rather the effect of the divine Spirit on individual and corporate life. When Paul referred to the *pneumatikos*, the "spiritual," his mind was on the activity and presence of the Holy Spirit in and among God's people.[5]

With Cocksworth, I take Paul's use of *pneuma* ("spirit") and *pneumatikos* ("spiritual") to be the most instructive. Paul uses the noun *pneuma* mostly in reference to the Holy Spirit. At times he uses it in reference to the human spirit—his own, or that of others. He also uses the word a few times to refer to other spirits alien to God's purposes (e.g., "the spirit of the world," 1 Cor 2:12; "the ruler of the kingdom of the air, the spirit who is now at work in those who are disobedient," Eph 2:2). And at times, he uses it not to speak of a spiritual being but of the qualities or characteristics someone's spirit manifests (e.g., "a gentle spirit," 1 Cor 4:21). When it comes to the adjective based on the noun, *pneumatikos*, most of its use by Paul is found in 1 Corinthians (sixteen of twenty-four occurrences). It is there, in chapter two, that he engages in a deliberate conversation that makes clear that when he speaks about people or things as "spiritual," he means they are "of, or related to" the divine Spirit.

But, as it is written,

> "What no eye has seen, nor ear heard,
>   nor the human heart conceived,
> what God has prepared for those who love him"—

these things God has revealed to us through the Spirit; for the Spirit searches everything, even the depths of God. For what human being knows what is truly human except the human spirit that is within? So also no one comprehends what is truly God's except the Spirit of God. Now we have received not the spirit of the world, but the Spirit that is from God, so that we may understand the gifts bestowed on us by God. And we speak of these things in words not taught by human wisdom but taught by the Spirit, interpreting spiritual things to those who are spiritual.

---

[5]Christopher Cocksworth, "Spirit, Holy," in *The New Westminster Dictionary of Christian Spirituality*, ed. Philip Sheldrake (Louisville, KY: Westminster John Knox Press, 2005), 594.

Those who are unspiritual do not receive the gifts of God's Spirit, for they are foolishness to them, and they are unable to understand them because they are spiritually discerned. Those who are spiritual discern all things, and they are themselves subject to no one else's scrutiny.

"For who has known the mind of the Lord
   so as to instruct him?"
But we have the mind of Christ. (1 Cor 2:9-16 NRSV)

There are two important things to be learned here. First, it is very clear that for Paul, the term *spiritual* means people or things that are *related to the Spirit of God.* The human spirit comes into his argument only as an analogy. He asks, "For what human being knows what is truly human except the human spirit that is within?" Like that, "the Spirit searches everything, even the depths of God. . . . So also no one comprehends what is truly God's except the Spirit of God." That is why we must be taught by the Spirit rather than by human wisdom, because it is the Spirit alone who can interpret Spirit-related things, to Spirit-related people.

Second, the Holy Spirit is not called the "Spirit" of God accidentally. The Holy Spirit is the presence of the triune God in all the ways that God simply *is.* The Holy Spirit's presence in us and among us is the presence of the spirit with which God thinks, feels, behaves, chooses, and acts. That is, just as we can speak about the spirit with which a human person completes a task (whether happily, grudgingly, spitefully), or the spirit with which one relates to people (with gentleness, meanness, kindness, aloofness, showing mercy or not), we can speak that way about God's spirit (lower case). The Spirit, Paul tells us, "searches everything, even the depths of God" and "comprehends what is truly God's." The Spirit manifests all that God is like, the spirit in which God lives and acts. By the Spirit, we come to know God's inclinations and impulses, we understand the purposes that move God to action, and we experience God's character and dispositions.

Not only does the Spirit manifest God's spirit, but the Spirit has come on us to infuse, to inculcate the same spirit in us. The Spirit knows and communicates the "mind of the Lord," and therefore we are made to have the "mind of Christ" (1 Cor 2:16). The Spirit bears fruit within us that corresponds with God's character: "love, joy, peace, forbearance, kindness, goodness, faithfulness, gentleness and self-control. Against such things there is no law. Those who belong to Christ Jesus have crucified the flesh with its passions and desires. Since we live by the Spirit, let us keep in step with the Spirit" (Gal 5:22-25).

This means that the Holy Spirit is not merely the *divine agent* who energizes the dynamics of Christian life and transforms us into the image of Christ. Many who see little more than a spirituality of the human spirit will acknowledge that. The Holy Spirit not only transforms us, but as a manifestation of the life and spirit of God *defines* the very form to which we are being transformed. We are being made like God.

This opens up a fresh path for the journey of spirituality. Follow the narrative of God. Live in sync with the logic of God. Imbibe God's longings, react with God's disappointments and joys, be predisposed to value those things in the world that bring gladness to God's heart, and share in God's biases toward justice and mercy and faithfulness (cf. Mt 23:23). Strive for those things God is most determined to bring about in and for this world, its full and flourishing *shalom*, its peace. Imbibe God's instincts about what or who in any situation is important and contend for the fair treatment of all. Enter every social arena disposed, as is God, toward mercy, truth, justice, forgiveness, and the reconciling of enemies.

Jesus shows this form of life. Coming to his home synagogue in Galilee, he opened the scroll of Isaiah's prophecy and read, "The Spirit of the Lord is on me." He took it to be speaking about himself. If the Spirit of the Lord is also upon us, we should expect the same inclinations and impulses that the prophet anticipated and Jesus owned as the trajectory of his calling:

> because he has anointed me
>> to proclaim good news to the poor.
> He has sent me to proclaim freedom for the prisoners
>> and recovery of sight for the blind,
> to set the oppressed free,
>> to proclaim the year of the Lord's favor. (Lk 4:18-19)

Can you hear the echoes of what is happening even as you follow along the path of Jesus? "As the Father sent me, so I am sending you. The Spirit of the Lord is upon me, the Spirit will come upon you." Whenever *you* take up the scroll, and open to Isaiah (or elsewhere), recognize that what is happening is the same as when the Spirit came upon Jesus and comes upon us: we are enveloped by the Spirit in such a way that God's purposes and priorities become ours. As did Jesus, lean into those priorities, biases, and dispositions that are God's. Bend yourself to them till you are so saturated by them that your choices correspond to God's, the manner of your life approximates God's manner, and the atmosphere of your presence exudes the character of God's presence. That is what "being Spirit-ual" is all about!

DISCIPLEship

> Then the eleven disciples went to Galilee, to the mountain where Jesus had told them to go. When they saw him, they worshiped him; but some doubted. Then Jesus came to them and said, "All authority in heaven and on earth has been given to me. Therefore go and make disciples of all nations, baptizing them in the name of the Father and of the Son and of the Holy Spirit, and teaching them to obey everything I have commanded you. And surely I am with you always, to the very end of the age." (Mt 28:16-20)

Not long ago, I had occasion to address the PC(USA) Presbytery, of which I am a member, about that Presbytery's stated purpose: "To challenge, encourage and equip worshiping communities of faith to make disciples of Jesus Christ with the gifts God gives them." I observed what the statement clearly marks as the end game, "to make disciples." I noted that we were not alone these days in reckoning that this lies at the heart of our calling. Jesus gives us a clear warrant to focus on it, setting us on this path, and taking us along with him on it—our mixed worship and doubt notwithstanding! But as well, our context calls us to it. The present North American social climate is disinclined to see in the Christian faith anything more than the personal religious preference of a like-minded few, and we churches have been muted at best, seemingly unable to represent in life, word, and deed the good news of a Christ who has been given all authority in heaven and on earth. It is time, on all accounts, for a funda-mental rerooting of discipleship at the core of our communal and personal life and witness.

Now the hard work begins. What does it mean to be a disciple, and what does it mean to make disciples? What is the substance that makes this purpose tangible and compelling? Does it mean setting up a particular curriculum of basic Christian teachings? Will there be somewhat for-malized ways that some of us longer in the faith will coach those newer in it? Will it involve helping people outside our circles discover the good news and make their journey into the faith?

Some of each, I expect. But something more is needed, something deeper down than the strategies themselves. And I wonder if we do not find a clue to that precisely where there is a serious dilemma in the English translation of the text. Our translations have found it difficult to put into smooth English the main verb in the commission of Jesus: *dis-ciple*. Disciple all peoples (including Gentiles!). The verb says something about what we do with regard to other people we meet along the way. In translation, however, its verb character is lost—even contradicted! The best the translators seem able to do is change the verb idea into a noun, and add a different verb, *to make*. The result produces a subtle but detri-mental shift. It leads us to believe that we are sent to *make* people into something—but that shifts the meaning and imports a very different focus of action.

The Greek word here (sorry, but we have to get at this) is *mathēteuo*, a verb meaning "to learn" someone. Its cousin noun, *mathētēs*, is the word we translate "disciple"—literally, "a learner." Another related verb speaks of someone doing the learning (e.g., Jesus said, "Take my yoke upon you and learn from me." In that case, we are invited to do the learning.). But the particular verb in the word group that we encounter in Matthew 28 speaks of "learning someone else to something." In this case, it is not the subjects of the verb who are told to do the learning. Rather they are told to bring about the learning of someone else.

This is where it gets tricky. How can this be expressed in smooth English? It's bound to feel awkward: "As you go, learn all the peoples, baptizing them . . . and teaching them." Awkward, surely. But perhaps there are some precedents in more colloquial English expressions. Imagine with me the scene: a woman is walking along and comes on a young boy from a family she knows well. He's involved in some unacceptable mischief, and she says to him, "Your momma didn't learn you like that!" Yes. Is that not what mommas do? They learn you. At times that might involve teaching you a thing or two, but in a wider view it is bigger than that. They learn you into being all grown up and living in a particular way.

It is probably very intentional that Matthew has tucked into his Gospel a few additional clues about what to make of this strange way of putting the commission of Jesus. Matthew uses this same verb, in a similarly awkward way, in two other places in his Gospel. And in those instances, we are shown the trajectory of the learning, the substance of what discipleship *is*.

The first clue is in Matthew 27:57: "As evening approached, there came a rich man from Arimathea, named Joseph, who had himself become a disciple of Jesus." Again, as in chapter 28, what is rendered in most translations as a noun ("a disciple") is in fact a verb! This time it is in the passive voice, so literally it should read, "Joseph, *who had also been learned to Jesus.*"

Recently, Gregory Vall has given fresh attention to the theology of the early church father Ignatius of Antioch. In his book *Learning Christ,* he identifies as the centerpiece of Ignatius's theology his sense that Christianity is fundamentally *Xristomathia* (Christ-learning). By that he meant "not merely learning *from* Christ or *about* Christ but learning the very person of Christ," affirming that "Jesus is not only our teacher but is also the truth that we are attempting to learn."[6] That captures what Matthew is saying about Joseph, and that is what discipleship is—learning Jesus, being learned to Jesus.

The second clue is found in Matthew 13:52. In the NRSV translation, it reads, "And he said to them, 'Therefore every scribe who has been trained for the kingdom of heaven is like the master of a household who

---

[6]Gregory Vall, *Learning Christ: Ignatius of Antioch and the Mystery of Redemption* (Washington, DC: The Catholic University of America Press, 2013), 256-57.

brings out of his treasure what is new and what is old.'" As we found in the previous clue, behind the translation here is the same passive verb, captured here a little better with the word *trained*. More literally, it is describing such an honorable scribe as one *"who has been learned to the kingdom of heaven."*

Taken together, these two examples offer some reorienting imagination for our sense of discipleship. A disciple is a learner; but more to the heart of it, a disciple is one who has "been learned to Jesus," one who has "been learned to the kingdom of heaven."

Last year, I was reviewing the final project dissertation for a doctor of ministry student I had been supervising. As I read, I stumbled on an expression that has a lot of resonance with this cumbersome "being learned to" way of speaking. In the opening chapters he described his learning journey toward completing his project. He noted the important role that curiosity has played in his learning, particularly with respect to understanding people's motivations. He expressed that curiosity in this way: "The *student* is always ready to be schooled." Ah, I thought. There is a helpful way to render the "being learned" idea. He went on to illustrate "being schooled to something" by reflecting on the three-decades-long career that had preceded his entry into pastoral ministry.

> Out of thirty-plus years in theatre curiosity developed into habit, it became imprinted. It has become deeply ingrained in the personhood of this writer. Over the three decades in theater and out of sixty-five plus roles learned, the need to understand the meanings of what the actor must accomplish has intensified. The need to comprehend *motivation*—why people do what they do—has always existed. Motivation . . . is never simple, nor obvious, nor immediate. One needs to know far more than the words of the dialogue to comprehend motivation in the character of a player in a play.[7]

"The student is always ready to be schooled." The disciple is always ready to be learned to Jesus, to the kingdom of heaven. This notion, which Matthew locates at the heart of discipleship, has a lot to say about what it

---

[7]James Croom, *Intervention Manual for Episcopal Congregations Separated from Clergy out of Conflict* (DMin diss., Western Theological Seminary, Holland, MI, 2015), 62-63.

means to disciple another (which it is our commission to do!). It tells us a lot about how each of us who is now a disciple came to be one—we were learned to it, schooled to it by others.

Some time ago, after I had shared these perspectives on the verb *disciple* in one of my classes, one of the students, remembering his previous work experience in the construction trades, said, "Well, isn't this describing apprenticeship?" Precisely.

Stanley Hauerwas, the Duke Divinity School ethicist, grew up as a bricklayer, and the son of a bricklayer. The memory of that never failed to kick in, whether he was talking about how theology, or virtue, or discipleship is formed. One is apprenticed to it, one is learned into the art and craft of it, one is apprenticed to a master of its tradition, and is "learned into it" by a community that inhabits it.

> It's a little like this analogy: I used to be a bricklayer. My father was a bricklayer. When I was eight, I was taken out on the job, put up on scaffolds, and taught to catch brick. The next summer I learned to stir the mud after it hardened. Eventually I learned how to pitch brick, build scaffolds, and chop mud. I mastered all the necessary skills. I didn't actually lay a brick until I was eighteen.[8]

Bricklayers, he says, have to be "initiated into the craft. And that's how one needs to think about the virtues."[9] So also, about discipleship.

> To learn to lay brick, it is not sufficient for you to be told how to do it, but you must learn a multitude of skills that are coordinated into the activity of laying brick—that is why before you lay brick you must learn to mix the mortar, build scaffolds, joint, and so on. Moreover, it is not enough to be told how to hold a trowel, how to spread mortar, or how to frog the mortar, but in order to lay brick you must hour after hour, day after day, lay brick.[10]

To this, Hauerwas adds, "Of course, learning to lay brick involves not only learning myriad skills, but also a language that forms and is formed

---

[8]Stanley Hauerwas, *The Hauerwas Reader*, ed. John Berkman and Michael Cartwright (Durham, NC: Duke University Press, 2001), 528.
[9]Ibid.
[10]Stanley Hauerwas, *After Christendom? How the Church Is to Behave If Freedom, Justice, and a Christian Nation Are Bad Ideas* (Nashville: Abingdon Press, 1991), 101.

by those skills. . . . To lay brick you must be initiated into the craft of bricklaying by a master craftsman."[11]

That brings us back to the way Jesus launches us. To "learn others" to Jesus, to the kingdom of heaven, consider first how you have "been learned" to Jesus, to the kingdom of heaven. By whom were you learned to him and the reign of God he proclaimed? Through what sort of relationships, and surrounded and propelled by what community of Christ-followers, did you come to learn Jesus? Do certain people, times, or places come to mind? They do for me.

I think of one particular woman who introduced me and my friends as second-graders to the message of God's grace in Jesus the Christ and the biblical world created by this very grace. She learned me into the faith. I also think of the community of faith that surrounded my family and at times financially supported the six of us as we were being learned to the faith. In my early days of university campus ministry, my staff supervisor learned me into much, much more than what he taught me in the official supervisor capacity. He learned me into ways the gospel is communicated in ordinary language and attentive relationships. Over many years, a great number of African and Asian and Latin American friends have learned me into the realities of a world beyond my own and widened my horizons to see the peoples, cultures, and communities where Christ has been learned in ways that now enrich my own learning.

But now, put yourself on the other side of the equation. Already, I expect, you have been learning many others to Jesus, to the kingdom of heaven—not just teaching them, though that plays a role. Rather, in all the ways of apprenticeship, we are learning others to the One who invites and welcomes all to the kingdom of heaven.

GODlikeness

There is an important convergence here. As those who have been "learned" to Jesus and the reign of God, we have been sent to "learn others" to the same. Such a way of seeing our mission converges with a spirituality that

---

[11]Ibid., 101-2.

recognizes "we are enveloped by the Spirit in such a way that God's purposes and priorities become ours." Whether in the language of spirituality, or in the language of commission, what is fundamental to one is fundamental to the other. We are being made to have the mind of God, the mind of Christ, the mind of the Spirit. We are being made like God in the inner and outer dimensions of our life.

To catalog all that is entailed in such a "spirituality for the sent" is beyond the scope of this essay. But a few critical markers may prove helpful to chart the kind of "journey in the Spirit" on which we have been called to embark.

A spirituality for the sent is attuned to the biblical narration of the dispositions and purposes of God. It makes a difference *how* we read the Bible. And *how* we read it is governed by *what* we think it is. I am again and again drawn to Lesslie Newbigin's critique of approaches to the Bible that have arisen in modernity under the influence of the Enlightenment. As a way forward, he testifies to a way of understanding and receiving the Bible that he believes to be the liberating way of the Spirit and of the *missio Dei*. Acknowledging his indebtedness to the narrative theologians of the Yale school, Newbigin affirms, "I would want to speak of the Bible as that body of literature which—primarily but not only in narrative form—renders accessible to us the character and actions and purposes of God."[12] What he says the Bible renders accessible are the very things the Spirit knows deeply and manifests in the world. Such are the things in which the Spirit wraps us, and to which the Spirit conforms us—the character and dispositions evidenced in God's actions, and the purposes and priorities toward which God's actions are directed. For Newbigin, this leads to a way of approaching the Bible that brings together the presence and work of the Holy Spirit and the fulfillment of the calling to "learn others" to Jesus, to the kingdom of heaven.

> In this view, the Bible, taken as a whole, fitly renders God, who is not merely the correlate or referent of universal natural religious experience but is the author and sustainer of all things. But this fitness can only be understood as

---

[12]Lesslie Newbigin, *Foolishness to the Greeks: The Gospel and Western Culture* (Grand Rapids: Eerdmans, 1986), 59.

we ourselves are engaged in the same struggle that we see in Scripture, the struggle to understand and deal with the events of our time in the faith that the God revealed in Scripture is in fact the agent whose purpose created and sustained all that is, and will bring it to its proper end.[13]

A spirituality for the sent exhibits sympathy with the pathos of God. Readers of the Jewish theologian Abraham Joshua Heschel will recognize this idea immediately. In his classic work of a half-century ago, *The Prophets,* Heschel searches among the writings of the prophets of Israel to discern how best to grasp their experience of God and the impact that had on them. His basic conclusion adds vivid depth to a spirituality that is oriented to the Spirit and to the witness the Spirit empowers.

> An analysis of prophetic utterances shows that the fundamental experience of the prophet is a fellowship with the feelings of God, a *sympathy with the divine pathos,* a communion with the divine consciousness which comes about through the prophet's reflection of, or participation in, the divine pathos. The typical prophetic state of mind is one of being taken up into the heart of the divine pathos. Sympathy is the prophet's answer to inspiration, the correlative to revelation.[14]

It is the style of the prophet that he "dwells upon God's inner motives, not only upon His historical decisions. He discloses a *divine pathos,* not just a divine judgment. The pages of the prophetic writings are filled with echoes of divine love and disappointment, mercy and indignation. The God of Israel is never impersonal."[15] Fundamental to the notion of God's pathos is the recognition that the God of Israel "does not reveal himself in an abstract absoluteness, but in a personal and intimate relation to the world. He does not simply command and expect obedience; He is also moved and affected by what happens in the world, and reacts accordingly. Events and human actions arouse in Him joy or sorrow, pleasure or wrath."[16] Sympathy with God's pathos is the hallmark of the prophets; it is "a response to

---

[13]Ibid., 59-60.
[14]Abraham J. Heschel, *The Prophets* (New York: The Jewish Publication Society of America, 1962), 26. Emphasis in the original.
[15]Ibid., 24.
[16]Ibid., 223-24.

transcendent sensibility . . . the assimilation of the prophet's emotional life to the divine."[17]

What Heschel represents here is a form of prophetic "participation" that lends a more profound meaning to the oft-quoted mantra among many who seek to be missionally faithful: that we are called "to *participate in the mission of God.*" In many of its casual uses this seems to mean little more than pitching in to help achieve God's projects. But what if we followed the path of the prophets? This is how Heschel describes Jeremiah's experience: "The overwhelming impact of the divine pathos upon his mind and heart, completely involving and gripping his personality in its depths, and the unrelieved distress which sprang from his intimate involvement."[18] Thus conceived, "participating in the *missio Dei*" cannot be about a project, a joint effort to get something done. It must be about prophetic sympathy with the pathos of God, about sharing the life and spirit of God.

A spirituality for the sent follows a cruciform logic. The accent in this essay has been on the Holy Spirit as revealer of God's spirit, transforming Christ-learners to have that same mind and spirit. In fact, all that we have said has affinity with the admonition of Paul to the Christian community in Philippi.

> If then there is any encouragement in Christ, any consolation from love, any sharing in the Spirit, any compassion and sympathy, make my joy complete: be of the same mind, having the same love, being in full accord and of one mind. Do nothing from selfish ambition or conceit, but in humility regard others as better than yourselves. Let each of you look not to your own interests, but to the interests of others. Let the same mind be in you that was in Christ Jesus. (Phil 2:1-5 NRSV)

The call to the church is to be one in spirit and of one mind, in light of what has been given to it in Christ and in the Spirit. The route toward the church's unity together is the common pursuit to have the "same mind . . . that was in Christ Jesus." In what follows, Paul puts on display a virtual hymn tracing the "mind" of Christ!

---

[17]Ibid., 26.
[18]Ibid.

Who, being in very nature God,
    did not consider equality with God something to be used to his own
        advantage;
rather, he made himself nothing
    by taking the very nature of a servant,
    being made in human likeness.
And being found in appearance as a man,
    he humbled himself
    by becoming obedient to death—
        even death on a cross!
Therefore God exalted him to the highest place
    and gave him the name that is above every name,
that at the name of Jesus every knee should bow,
    in heaven and on earth and under the earth,
and every tongue acknowledge that Jesus Christ is Lord,
    to the glory of God the Father. (Phil 2:6-11)

The way the grammar goes here, the opening clause, often translated "though he was in the form of God," is built around a participle of the verb "to be," which in its basic form means, simply, "being." So here, literally, it is "being in very nature God." Greek participles, however, by their nature may function in a variety of ways depending on other factors in the context. So "though" or "although" would be technically possible here. And it might seem at first blush that it *should* be taken that way, because that would square with the common understanding we tend to bring to the text, that being God is quite the opposite of emptying oneself and "taking the very nature of a servant, being made in human likeness"—let alone ending in "death on a cross." But New Testament scholar Michael Gorman, in a meticulous exegetical treatment of the hymn, argues for understanding the initial participle in another sense that it could bear: "because." He argues that Christ's humility and self-giving and incarnate humanity and death on a cross do not represent a move in a direction alien to what God is like. In fact, Christ's "downward mobility" corresponds directly with what God is like!

    Christ, "*because* he was in very nature God, did not consider equality with God something to be used to his own advantage; rather, he made himself nothing by taking the very nature of a servant."[19] If Gorman's argument is correct, and I believe it is, then our response after reading the hymn should be, "How very like God Christ is!" And if we had thought God was otherwise, we should say, "So, this is what God is like!" In other words, we dare not divorce the pattern of Christ Jesus from the nature of the God whose incarnation he is.

Based on this text and extensive study in all of Paul's writings, Gorman concludes that "*cruci*formity [being cross-shaped] is really *theo*formity or, as the Christian tradition (especially in the East) has sometimes called it, deification, divinization, or theosis."[20] For the purposes of this essay, Gorman is suggesting that the path by which Jesus came finally to be put to death on a cross is a guide to our spirituality and the manner of our mission. Jesus' death and resurrection are the narrative model, and in that model we see the kind of God—a cruciform God—to whose likeness we are being conformed by the Spirit. The mind of Christ *is* the mind of God *is* the mind of the Spirit. And it is to be our mind as well. Paul puts what Gorman calls his "narrative spirituality"[21] in personal terms: "I want to know Christ—yes, to know the power of his resurrection and participation in his sufferings, becoming like him in his death, and so, somehow, attaining to the resurrection from the dead" (Phil 3:10-11).

A spirituality for the sent grows amid daily avenues of witness. The convergence of spirituality and witness for which I have been arguing may be illustrated best in the opening chapters of Acts. We have noted Jesus' promise (prediction!) to the earliest company of disciples: the Spirit will come upon you, and you will be my witnesses. On Pentecost day, ten days later, it happened in remarkable ways. Aside from the sounds (like the rush of a violent wind) and sights (divided tongues, as of fire, resting on each of them), and the fact that they began to speak in other languages, more miraculous still may have been how clearly the disciples knew and told the significance of what was happening. Peter, well

---

[19]Michael J. Gorman, *Inhabiting the Cruciform God: Kenosis, Justification, and Theosis in Paul's Narrative Soteriology* (Grand Rapids: Eerdmans, 2009), 9-39.

[20]Ibid., 1-2.

[21]See Michael J. Gorman, *Cruciformity: Paul's Narrative Spirituality of the Cross* (Grand Rapids: Eerdmans, 2001).

known for not getting it right, gets it right! He understands that this is what Joel prophesied: God declares, "I will pour out my Spirit on all flesh." This is the new day God promised. The Spirit is upon us and fills us.

Not only on that day, but in the days that followed, the disciples are notable in two respects. First, they kept testifying to what they had witnessed: Jesus is the long-awaited Messiah of Israel. It is about Jesus that the Scriptures speak. The Jesus who had been killed by the powers that be has been raised from the dead by the power of God. The Spirit has been poured out on all flesh, as promised. People are being healed of their infirmities in the power of the name of Jesus.

Second, there is a parallel set of observations to make: The community lived in the way of a Godly hospitality, holding goods in common and providing especially for the most poor among them. These unschooled people had wisdom and courage and boldness beyond all expectations. They were filled with the Spirit, which filled them with a discernment of the spirits of all. Especially notable in this regard are the comments Luke adds along the way describing the kind of spirit exhibited by many of them. This stands out in chapter six. When complaints arose regarding the unfair distribution of food for the widows, the Twelve called the community together and asked them to select "seven men from among you who are known to be full of the Spirit and wisdom" (Acts 6:3). Among the seven chosen was Stephen, about whom Luke adds the comment that he was "a man full of faith and of the Holy Spirit" (Acts 6:5). A little later, Luke notes that he was "full of God's grace and power" and that he "performed great wonders and signs among the people" (Acts 6:8). In the midst of Stephen's witness to Christ in the "Synagogue of the Freedmen," arguments and controversy arose. All the more consternating to his opponents was the fact that "they could not withstand the wisdom and the Spirit with which he spoke" (Acts 6:10 NRSV).

This way of cataloging traits that were being exhibited seems to be Luke's parallel accounting. Along with the disciples' witness, which the Spirit had come to empower, the Spirit's fruit in the character and spirit of the disciples was increasingly evident as well. A spirituality of Godlikeness was being formed, just as the mission of witness was unfolding.

A spirituality for the sent thirsts for God's Spirit to inhabit ours. Perhaps there is no more basic—nor a more fitting—word on which to conclude than King David's expression of his deepest thirst, found in Psalm 51. The prophet Nathan has just confronted him regarding his affair with Bathsheba. The psalm begins with confession of sin:

> Have mercy on me, O God,
>> according to your steadfast love;
> according to your abundant mercy
>> blot out my transgressions.
> Wash me thoroughly from my iniquity,
>> and cleanse me from my sin. (Ps 51:1-2 NRSV)

He knows that God "desire[s] truth in the inward being" (Ps 51:6 NRSV), and David tells the truth about himself and his sin in the best way he knows how, pleading for the mercy of God to purge him and wash him (Ps 51:7). And in the end, his heart surges toward God and pleads for his spirit and God's Spirit to be held together in transforming power. His song and ours are a perpetual postlude attending our steps:

Postlude: A Psalm of David

> Create in me a clean heart, O God,
>> and put a new and right spirit within me.
> Do not cast me away from your presence,
>> and do not take your holy spirit from me.
> Restore to me the joy of your salvation,
>> and sustain in me a willing spirit. (Ps 51:10-12 NRSV)

General Index

Scripture Index

Finding the Textbook You Need

The IVP Academic Textbook Selector
is an online tool for instantly finding the IVP books
suitable for over 250 courses across 24 disciplines.

ivpacademic.com